Ireland in the World Order

IRELAND IN THE WORLD ORDER
A History of Uneven Development

Maurice Coakley

PLUTO PRESS

First published 2012 by Pluto Press
345 Archway Road, London N6 5AA

www.plutobooks.com

Distributed in the Republic of Ireland and Northern Ireland by
Gill & Macmillan Distribution, Hume Avenue, Park West, Dublin 12, Ireland.
Phone +353 1 500 9500. Fax +353 1 500 9599. E-Mail: sales@gillmacmillan.ie

British Library Cataloguing in Publication Data
A catalogue record for this book is available from the British Library

ISBN   978 0 7453 3126 3   Hardback
ISBN   978 0 7453 3125 6   Paperback
ISBN   978 1 84964 731 1   PDF
ISBN   978 1 84964 733 5   Kindle
ISBN   978 1 84964 732 8   ePub

Library of Congress Cataloging in Publication Data applied for

This book is printed on paper suitable for recycling and made from fully
managed and sustained forest sources. Logging, pulping and manufacturing
processes are expected to conform to the environmental standards of the
country of origin.

10   9   8   7   6   5   4   3   2   1

Designed and produced for Pluto Press by Chase Publishing Services Ltd
Typeset from disk by Stanford DTP Services, Northampton, England

Contents

Acknowledgements

I owe a huge number of debts to those who shared time and ideas and who bore with me over the course of writing this. Peter Hannon and his colleagues in the Education Department of the University of Sheffield were always open minded and engaging. I am grateful to Roger van Zwanenberg for persuading me to update the earlier work to address contemporary developments and to all the staff at Pluto. My colleagues in the Journalism and Media faculty of Griffith College have been supportive and I am particularly grateful to the staff in the College library and printroom for their patience and assistance. Brian McCarthy very kindly permitted me to use the 'Sword of Justice' image for the book cover. Andy Storey, Margaret Kelleher and Paddy O'Brien read earlier drafts and commented helpfully on them. My greatest debts are to Petra Schurenhofer without whose assistance and encouragement I would most likely never have completed it.

Preface

In November 2010, when the Irish government was negotiating with the European Union (EU) and other transnational bodies on schemes to resolve Ireland's financial problems, the International Monetary Fund (IMF) came up with a proposal that would have involved the major bondholders taking a significant 'haircut', in the process reducing the Irish debt to a potentially manageable level. The European Central Bank (ECB) strongly opposed any 'haircut' for the bondholders, insisting that the Irish state pay all the debts incurred by the privately owned Irish banks, even though this would most likely bankrupt Ireland. In this dispute, the Irish government officials sided with the ECB, leading one IMF staff member to describe the Irish government negotiators as displaying elements of the 'Stockholm syndrome', a situation whereby hostages sometimes come to identify with their captors (Kelly, 2011).

Why were Irish government officials suffering from 'Stockholm syndrome'? Or to put the question differently, how was it that Irish government officials had come to identify with transnational institutions that were seeking to impose severe penalties on the Irish population, rather than with their own people?

The answer to this question is related to the story of this book. It began from a sense of dissatisfaction with the dominant interpretation of Irish history and with an attempt to present an alternative approach that might make sense of that history. The events surrounding the collapse of the Celtic Tiger make it clear that these issues are not just of academic import, but are of contemporary relevance. This water is still flowing.

The dominant currents within Irish historical studies avoided any exploration of the structural relationship between Ireland and Britain as a matter of methodological principle. Notions of colonialism were considered redundant. Irish historians, for the most part, tended to minimise the significance of the Conquest, and to interpret it as the unfortunate consequence of misunderstandings and policy mistakes. More than that: the work of many Irish historians carried a sub-text whereby British governance of Ireland was perceived as civilised, rational and cosmopolitan, while Irish resistance was seen as narrow, primitive and atavistic.

This attitude was compounded by a consistent downplaying of the close association between the quest for democracy and national independence.

How far this understanding of history has contributed to the development of a 'Stockholm syndrome' mentality among Irish intellectual and political elites is certainly open to debate, but it has undoubtedly played a role. It helped legitimate the British state in the Northern Ireland conflict and has acted as a deterrent to critical debate about Irish development and European integration.

This book is not intended as a comprehensive history of Ireland. It is rather a study of a particular aspect of Irish history, an exploration of how Ireland fitted into the formation of the modern world order, and specifically why it developed so differently from England, Scotland and Wales. The final section of the book explores the relationship between Ireland's earlier historical experience and its current predicament. A world order or world system only came into existence in the Renaissance era, in the sixteenth century. I begin my analysis earlier, in the twelfth century at the point where Ireland first came under the sway – albeit only partially – of the English state, in order to understand why it was that Ireland came to occupy such a radically different position within the emerging world order.

Glossary

Aisling	Gaelic allegorical poems in post-conquest Ireland. Ireland (or Gaelic society) is usually represented as a woman awaiting a saviour.
Aosdana	Gaelic term for learned strata, including poets, lawyers etc.
Bailie	Scottish Gaelic term for townlands, similar in Ireland.
Betagh	Term used in Anglo-French areas for serfs.
Brehon	Anglicised term for Gaelic lawyer/judge.
Clan	Gaelic term for larger family-linked groups, theoretically lineage based.
Clan na Gael	American Fenian organisation.
Cyfarwydyd	Welsh cultural heritage, equivalent to Gaelic *seanchas*.
Duthchas	The notion that being part of the clan network involved a set of responsibilities and duties, and that the clan leadership had a duty of care for clan members in periods of distress.
Eraic	Gaelic term used for payment of compensation in lieu of punishment for crime.
Érennaigh	Late medieval Gaelic term for people born in Ireland, that included both those of Gaelic and Anglo-French extraction.
Feu farming	Commercial usage of land in late medieval Scotland.
File(s) Filí(p)	Irish for poet/poets. Used also to refer to the literate caste as a whole.
Fíne	Medieval Gaelic term used for 'inner' lineage group, later replaced by *slíoght*.
Foirm na n-Urruidheadh	Scottish Gaelic translation of the *Book of Common Order*.
Gaedhil	Late medieval Gaelic for indigenous Irish.
Gaidhealtachd	Scottish Gaelic speaking region(s).
Gaill	Gaelic term originally used for foreigners in general, but by the late Middle Ages, came to

	be used exclusively for the Anglo-French (or Anglo-Gaelic).
Galloglaigh	'Mercenaries' from Gaelic Scotland. Anglicised as 'gallowglass'.
Kerne	Gaelic 'mercenaries' originally used by Anglo-French lords and later by Gaelic chiefs.
Leabhar Galldha	*Book of Invasions.*
Plaid	Welsh for armed retinue.
Pride	Welsh legal practice of collective inheritance.
Sasanaigh	Gaelic term used in the fifteenth and sixteenth centuries to designate the English government and recent English settlers, as distinct from earlier settlers.
Sasine	Legal instrument for transferring land in Scotland.
Seanchas	The Gaelic cultural tradition.
Sept	English term used for Gaelic clans.
Slíoght	Late medieval Gaelic term for 'inner' lineage group, similar to *fíne*. The *slíoght* was the 'inner' family grouping, part of the wider *clan* network.
Tacksmen	Tenants of the chief who not only collected rent from sub-tenants, but also acted as political overseers of their areas.
Táiniste	Gaelic term for second-in-command to chief. The anglicised term 'tanistry' derived from this and was used to designate the political structure of Gaelic clans.
Tuath	Basic political unit of territory in Gaelic Ireland, roughly corresponding to the later English baronies.
Villein	Term used in medieval England for serfs.

Historical Timeline

5th century Christianity arrives in Ireland.
6th–7th centuries Flowering of monastic literate culture in Ireland.
11th century Norman-French knights conquer England and most of Wales.
1169 Anglo-French knights arrive in Ireland.
12th–13th centuries Spread of Anglo-French power in Ireland.
14th century General crisis of European feudalism.
1366 Statutes of Kilkenny prohibit use of Gaelic language and customs by settler community.
1541–3 Irish Parliament recognises Henry VIII as head of Church and introduces 'surrender and re-grant' programme.
1590s Revolt by Ulster Gaelic clan leaders turns into island-wide 'Nine Years War'.
1603 Defeat of Gaelic rebellion; Death of Elizabeth I; England and Scotland united under Stuart monarchy.
1640s–1650s Revolt in Ireland; Civil War in England and Scotland; Cromwellian conquest of Ireland.
1695 Introduction of Penal Laws against Catholics.
1760s–1770s Industrial Revolution in England; growing commercialisation of agriculture in Ireland and Scotland.
1778 Catholic Relief Acts allow property and inheritance rights.
1791 United Irish movement formed.
1798 United Irish rebellion suppressed.
1845–9 Great Famine in Ireland.
1850s Irish Republican Brotherhood (Fenians) formed.
1879 Land League formed in alliance with Home Rule movement.
1880s Land War.
1912 Home Rule Bill.
1913 Formation of Ulster Volunteers and Irish Volunteers; Dublin Lockout.
1914–8 First World War.
1916 Easter Rising in Dublin.
1918 Sinn Féin win most Irish seats in elections.
1919–21 War of Independence.
1920 Partition; Northern Ireland Parliament established.
1921 Treaty signed.

1922 Irish Civil War.
1932 Fianna Fáil wins elections.
1957 Ireland joins World Bank and International Monetary Fund (IMF).
1968 Civil Rights protests in Northern Ireland.
1971 Republican insurgency begins.
1972 Bloody Sunday; Northern Ireland parliament suspended. Direct Rule by Westminster.
1973 Ireland joins the European Economic Community.
1994 IRA ceasefire.
1998 Belfast Agreement.
2008 Financial Crash.
2010 European Union/IMF impose structural adjustment program.

Introduction

Why do societies develop unevenly? Why have some societies advanced, while others seem to have stalled or regressed? The question itself is a thoroughly modern one. The idea that some societies were more advanced than others would have made little sense to earlier thinkers. Pre-modern peoples were conscious of differences, but these were understood as peculiarities of character, not as indices of development. The Romans, the Greeks and the Chinese distinguished between civilised societies and barbarians, but they did not imagine them on a timeline, nor did they develop social theories to explain their differences. While ancient historians were quick enough to impute various character defects to foreigners, it never occurred to them that these others might be more 'advanced' or 'backward'.

The theorists of the Scottish Enlightenment were the first to develop the idea of history as progress. The Scottish Enlightenment thinkers were in a singular position to observe the great changes arising in the eighteenth century. To their south, an industrial revolution was underway in England, to their north, the Scottish Highlands still retained elements of a clannic-pastoralist social order. In order to make sense of these changes and to ensure that Scotland followed the English model, the Scottish theorists developed the notion of a universal history divided into stages of development. History came to be perceived as progress, both in terms of the accumulation of knowledge and productive capacity as well as increased emancipation (Callinicos, 1999).

While Marx wrote about the origins of capitalism, his main objective was to understand capitalism as a *historical* phenomenon, to grasp its distinctiveness from other societies. Unlike many of his contemporaries in the German democratic movement he became conscious early on that the new modern order taking shape was not merely a force for human progress, but also had a darker side. He was convinced nonetheless that capitalism would sweep away all other social forms. In the *Communist Manifesto,* coauthored with Engels during the 1848 revolutions, it is the cheapness of capitalist products that forms 'the heavy artillery with which it batters down *Chinese walls*'. Writing a few decades later in the first volume of *Capital* he had come to recognise that, at least in the case of China, it was British artillery which forced the way for 'free trade'. Despite this he still held the view that 'the country that is more developed industrially only shows, to the less developed, the image of its own future' (Marx, 1976, p. 91). It was Marx's study of Ireland as much as anything else, which led him to doubt his earlier optimism about the spread of capitalist production. After all, Ireland had experienced the 'benefits' of free markets at least since 1800 but instead of industrialising, it regressed economically and socially, becoming not England's industrial partner but its dependent agricultural province (Arrighi, 2008; Anderson, 2010).

The classic social theorists of the *fin de siècle,* Emile Durkheim and Max Weber, shared Marx's fascination with the character of the modern social order, albeit seeing it from a very different perspective. Durkheim focused on the contrast between this new 'industrial' order and pre-modern society, while Weber was particularly concerned with the genesis of capitalism. In contrast to Marx's stress on technological development and class struggle, Weber emphasised the role of culture in furthering historical change, giving particular weight to the role of the literate strata and religious belief. His most famous work *The Protestant Ethic and the Spirit of Capitalism* contrasts Catholic and Protestant regions of Europe. It seemed clear enough at the time that the Protestant regions of Europe were the most industrialised, while the Catholic regions were the most backward.

Weber sought an explanation for the uneven development of capitalism in the realm of religious belief itself. Both Luther and Calvin preached the doctrine of 'predestination'; if God was omniscient and omnipotent then He knew already who was saved and who was damned. The sacrament of penance saved nobody. Protestant believers found themselves in a position of ontological insecurity: they could never be sure whether they were saved or damned. Only by living a saintly life could Protestants find reassurance. Protestants tended to be more God fearing and law abiding than Catholics, who could always have their sins pardoned by penance. As a consequence, Protestants sought to avoid excess in their daily lives, preferring to save money rather than spend, to invest rather than consume, and over an extended period of time laid the foundations for a capitalist order (Weber, 1958; 1991).

Weber's theory could have been tailormade for Ireland. Not only was 'Catholic Ireland' more backward than 'Protestant England', but the only part of Ireland to industrialise was the predominantly

Protestant northeast. It seems likely that the Irish case played a role in his thinking. Explanations of socioeconomic differences in terms of cultural values or religious beliefs were commonplace in nineteenth-century Europe. Bismarck famously quipped that if the Dutch lived in Ireland they would feed half the world, if the Irish lived in the Netherlands they would drown. Not every part of Europe fitted Weber's theory so well. Catholic Belgium was the second most industrialised part of Europe in the nineteenth century. By the time Weber was writing, industrialisation had developed in northern Spain and in northern Italy, and was also spreading to parts of the Habsburg and Tsarist empires.

Nowhere was the issue of the *unevenness* of capitalism discussed more intensely than in Russia. Throughout the nineteenth century, Russian thinkers were bitterly divided about the impact of 'Western' influences and the slow spread of capitalist social relations. Some viewed Westernisation as an advance against the tyranny and superstition of Russian tradition, others looked to Russian culture as a bastion against the crass utilitarianism of modern commerce. For the Russian Social Democrats, Bolsheviks and Mensheviks alike, the development of capitalism was a positive element in Russian life, or at least an inevitable one, and it offered the prospect of creating a modern democracy from within which a labour movement could begin to create a different kind of social order. Only with the outbreak of the First World War did the majority of Russian Social Democrats begin to question this view.

From Europe's southern margins came one of the most original takes on the issue of uneven development. Antonio Gramsci, a founder of Italian Communism, grew up in Sardinia, though he spent most of his adult life in Turin, and later in Mussolini's prisons. His thinking reflects not only on the huge divide between the north and south of Italy, but also the gap between Italy and northern Europe (and North America). Much of Gramsci's writing was an attempt to explain why Italy had 'fallen behind' other parts of Europe. Gramsci stressed that the roots of uneven development needed to be located not just in technological barriers, but in the structures of class power, which he understood as the totality of social relations, including culture. He shared Weber's interest in the Reformation, though for Gramsci the crucial significance of the Reformation was not its theological innovations, but its educational role. Likewise, while Gramsci wrote at length about the role of intellectuals, and of their importance in historical situations, this was always seen in the context of their relationship to the 'fundamental' classes: aristocracy and peasantry, bourgeoisie and proletariat (Gramsci, 1967; 1971).

In the decades after the Second World War North American social theorists, drawing on the work of Durkheim and Weber, developed their own approach: modernisation theory. This sought not only to outline the shape of human history, but also to provide a programme for the de-colonising world to achieve modernisation by following the path of the American founders. As well as emphasising the importance of private property, they also stressed the significant role played by education and literacy, as well as endorsing a role for the state in building infrastructure (Rostow, 1962).

Another writer who stressed the central importance of writing and literacy in human development was Jack Goody, though coming from a very different perspective to the modernisation theorists. Goody wrote from within the historical materialist tradition, arguing that writing should be seen as a productive force, and that in explaining long-term historical change, the development of the productive forces needed to be given (at least) equal weight to social relations. With the introduction of writing, people were no longer so reliant on memory; this enabled the accumulation of knowledge. Writing also permitted more complex organisational systems to evolve. While recognising that literate groups often played a conservative role, Goody argued that on the whole literacy had been a force for development and emancipation (Goody, 1968; 1977; 1986).

In the 1960s and 1970s, modernisation theory was sharply criticised by many scholars, not least because it was seen to legitimate US imperial policies. One of the criticisms made against modernisation theory was that while it explored aspects of the transition to modernity, it failed to distinguish between pre-modern societies, treating them as undifferentiated 'traditional' worlds. In fact, pre-modern or pre-capitalist worlds differed enormously and these differences were hugely important in determining their transition to modernity (Bernstein, 1971).

By 1974, when Immanuel Wallerstein published the first volume of his *Modern World System*, the picture of the world looked very different to that proposed by modernisation theory. The most striking feature was not the advances in global development but the persistence of global disparities of income and wealth; if anything it seemed that the world was becoming more unequal. For Wallerstein, the huge inequalities of the contemporary world had their roots in Western domination of global trade. By monopolising the global circuits of trade from the Renaissance era, the Western powers were able to establish an international division of labour which favoured their own economies, and to siphon off surplus profits from elsewhere. Uneven industrialisation and uneven prosperity were not so much the source of Western power as a product of that power. Geopolitics and trade shaped history. This approach has been developed by a number of scholars, most notably by Giovanni Arrighi. For Arrighi the driving force responsible for the 'rise of the West', and uneven development, has been a combination of the military competition between states and the endless accumulation of capital and territorial expansion, with military competition between states having primacy (Arrighi, 1994; Wallerstein, 1974).

For Robert Brenner, this focus on exchange and trade missed the crucial point about what determines social change: the way societies organise the production of goods. It was changes in this arena, and not control of trading routes, which were really crucial for long-term development. Why was it England, he asked, and not France or Spain, which pioneered industrialisation? Brenner's answer was that England had already established a capitalist system of agriculture and this in turn fostered the conditions for Industrial Revolution. Agriculture was crucial because it produced the most important goods for human survival: food. The great majority of mankind up until recent times worked in agriculture. Advances in agricultural production increased food output and 'freed up' labour for producing all kinds of other goods. This created the essential preconditions for the Industrial Revolution in England, which would in turn come to transform the world (Brenner, 1985).

Ireland's proximity to the heartland of the emerging modern world order makes it an interesting case study because instead of emulating the English pattern of growth in the nineteenth century, Ireland came to display all the classic features of underdevelopment: immiseration, 'overpopulation', famine, revolt. Not only was Ireland geographically close to England, it shared a government. More than that: Ireland was inextricably bound with England from the Middle Ages. Why did they develop so differently and what does this tell us about the development process? This work attempts to address these questions by exploring the relationship between socioeconomic, political and cultural forms in Ireland from the medieval era to the present.

1
Passages from the Medieval

Ireland in the late medieval period can be roughly divided into two different entities: the Gaelic territories, under the control of Gaelic chiefs, and the Anglo-French regions, under the control of the Anglo-French aristocracy. While there were no clear demarcation lines, and a good deal of interaction between the two, Gaelic Ireland and Anglo-French Ireland possessed different social structures and developed along different lines.

In the twelfth century Anglo-French knights colonised substantial parts of Ireland, especially in the south and east. They established a social organisation and an administrative system along mainstream western European lines and owed loyalty to the English monarchy. Yet over the next few centuries, Anglo-French Ireland came to diverge sharply from England in its politics, culture and social organisation.

The Impact of the Anglo-French

Superficially at least, the socio-political evolution of England and the southern and eastern regions of Ireland in the eleventh and twelfth centuries seem fairly similar. Both were conquered by French-speaking knights who established a seigniorial social order under the authority of the English monarch. In both territories a manorial economy was developed along with castles, trade and urban centres. The Latin Church played a crucial role in their cultural life; most of those who could read and write were clerics, and the Latin language played a central role in their culture.

A few centuries later, certainly by 1500, literacy was becoming diffused throughout England, not only among the nobility, but more widely. Among the elite, French had been superseded by English as a spoken language. Latin retained a position of importance, but it was in decline. Alongside the development of a vernacular English literacy in the second half of the sixteenth century, English itself came to acquire a standard written form (Clanchy, 1993; Fisher, 1986).

Across most of the south and east of Ireland, the descendants of the French-speaking warrior elite retained control and for the most part remained loyal, at least nominally, to the King of England. But while a good deal of administrative writing survives, there appears to have been little general diffusion of literacy. The same period saw the initial rise of English as a spoken language followed by a sharp decline until it was hardly spoken at all outside the cities, and even within the cities, English would seem not to have been the language of the urban poor. What accounts for these linguistic changes and why did literacy in eastern Ireland not undergo the same diffusion that occurred in England?

Before examining these issues it is worth pointing out the very real achievements of the Anglo-French elite in medieval Ireland.

Political supremacy: Within a few decades the Anglo-French aristocracy had established military supremacy across most of the island. Gaelic power was confined to the western regions or mountainous and marshy areas of the south and east, and even there, the Gaelic communities were usually subordinate to the local Anglo-French feudal lord.

Government and law: While the Anglo-French knights' involvement in Ireland began as something of a freelance adventure, it was quickly brought under the control of the English monarchy, with the imprimatur of the Papacy. The institutions of royal government and law were developed in subsequent decades.

Manorial organisation: Throughout most of the south and east of Ireland, the Anglo-French lords established a vibrant manorial economy, based upon intensive arable agriculture and involving a significant movement away from pastoral husbandry.

Urban growth and commerce: Alongside a manorial economy, an extensive trade network and urban development occurred. The Vikings had already established towns along the Irish coastline; these were occupied and consolidated by the Anglo-French forces, and new cities were established.

Religious organisation: The conquest was accompanied by the introduction of 'orthodox' religious structures and monastic organisation; from the twelfth century onwards, the Christian Church in Ireland was systematically reorganised in line with orthodox Roman practices.

These social, political and cultural developments, which transformed Ireland in the twelfth and thirteenth centuries, were part and parcel of a wider European dynamic that would lay the foundation for the early modern state with its extensive pattern of literacy. Yet despite their achievements, the Anglo-French elite in Ireland did not bring about a more general diffusion of vernacular literacy, neither in English, French or Gaelic, nor – as occurred in England – did a new linguistic synthesis emerge.

The Language Question in Anglo-French Ireland

The Anglo-French colonisers of the twelfth century brought with them to Ireland a regime founded upon literate practices, similar to that operating in England. The English system of law and government was transferred to Ireland virtually unchanged. As in England, writing was focused upon religion, law and government and was carried out in two languages: Latin and French. Latin was the primary language of religion; Latin and French were the only languages of law and government.

Record keeping was at the heart of the system of law and government. All landholdings derived ultimately from royal bequest and all such holdings had to be recorded. The functioning of government depended upon its ability to tax, and any taxes raised, in whatever form, had to be carefully documented.

The warrior and clerical elite who conquered the south and east of Ireland spoke a dialect of French as their first language, though this began to decline over the course of the thirteenth century. French continued to be used (alongside Latin) for government documents and legal records up until the end of the fifteenth century, and was also used as the *lingua franca* of trade and commerce (Picard, 2003).

Apart from the French-speaking elite, the twelfth century witnessed a substantial popular migration of English – and to a lesser extent Welsh and Flemish – speakers into Ireland. For a period the three languages – English, French and Irish – appear to have vied with each other for supremacy. However, by the late thirteenth century English had clearly become the dominant language of the towns and large parts of eastern Ireland developed its own dialect characteristics, known to historians as Hiberno-English (not to be confused with modern Irish dialects of English).

English was not widely used in official documents in Ireland until the later part of the fifteenth century. After 1500 English was widely used in writing, though by the middle of the century no longer displayed features of the Hiberno-English dialect. This increased use of written English in the later part of the fifteenth century is somewhat paradoxical: it came *after* English had declined as a *spoken* language in Ireland, to be replaced by (Gaelic) Irish (Bliss, 1976).

From the mid-fourteenth century onwards English, from having been widely spoken across eastern Ireland, declined significantly to a point where by the early sixteenth century it was not spoken at all outside of the towns and a couple of small rural areas (the Forth and Bargy area south of Wexford town, and Fingal in north county Dublin). In the towns the poorer population seem to have spoken Irish as a first language and it would seem that most English speakers were bilingual. The clearest evidence for the decline of English in medieval Ireland comes from the acts passed by an Irish parliament in 1366 – the Statutes of Kilkenny – which prohibited the use of the Irish language, on pain of losing one's lands. The statutes make clear that the English colony in Ireland had undergone a profound transformation in the fourteenth century, of which linguistic change was only one element (Bliss & Long, 1987).

Law and Social Structure in the English Colony

There is no way of calculating the exact size of the English community in medieval Ireland though it seems clear that there was a mass English settlement in Ireland in the twelfth century. Historians cannot quantify quite how dense the settlement was, though there is little doubt that there was a substantial merchant, artisan and peasant English community in the south and east of Ireland in the twelfth and thirteenth centuries. This mass migration clearly differentiates the thirteenth century conquest of Ireland from that of England a century earlier, where the settlement was confined to an aristocratic – warrior and clerical – stratum (Empey, 1986; O'Brien, 1993).

From the broader perspective, this migration can be seen as part of the wider expansion of the feudal social order across the European continent. The knights were able to use their superior military power to seize large stretches of territory but these territories were of no use to them without peasants to work them. This same period saw a demographic boom which ensured that there were large numbers of peasants looking for new land to farm. In order to make it worth their while to travel long distances to a new home, the lords granted them favourable conditions, including freedom from servile status (Bartlett, 1993; Brenner, 1996).

The conquest of England occurred before the major demographic expansion of the twelfth and thirteenth centuries. Perhaps more importantly, England had been manorialised long before the coming of the Norman-French and it was more densely populated than Ireland. While arable agriculture did exist in Ireland before the Anglo-French conquest, it had always played a subordinate role to pastoralism. To develop demesne agriculture and take advantage of trade, the Anglo-French lords needed to encourage settlers. As well as building castles and dividing up their new lands, the lords established towns, or at least burgage tenure appropriate for urban growth (Empey, 1986).

By the mid-thirteenth century the Anglo-French colony was at the height of its power. Most of Leinster, Munster and eastern Ulster had been subdued, and Anglo-French knights had even established military supremacy in Connaught. Throughout most of the conquered region, a manorial economy had been established which produced a surplus large enough to permit a substantial export of grain and other produce. The existence of a large agricultural surplus encouraged the formation of an extensive urban settlement and helped finance many of the English wars against Scotland and France (Down, 1987; O'Brien, 1993).

The peasant population was divided into two main groups: a small stratum of free peasants who were predominantly of English extraction, and the unfree *betagh* population, the original Irish inhabitants or *hibernici*. In the documents of the time the terms *hibernici* and *servi* (in this context meaning serf) tend to be used interchangeably. It seems that the *betagh* continued to farm in their traditional manner, in kindred groups, while at the same time contributing labour services to their Anglo-French lords. This servile Irish population, like the unfree *villein* class in England, was excluded from royal law. They were also prohibited from making wills and testaments. The killing of an Irishman was not a felony, while, correspondingly, to accuse someone of being Irish was considered defamatory. A petition by leading clerics to have English law extended to the Irish population of the colony in the 1270s was rejected by the Crown (Bartlett, 1993; Hand, 1966a).

The exclusion of the Irish population – like the exclusion of *villeins* in England – from royal law had the effect of increasing the power of the lords; the unfree peasants had no legal protection from their arbitrary demands.

> The essential point is that the services were uncertain. The only restriction on the lord's power to set the number of days to be worked on his domain was the custom of the manor. If any dispute arose it could only be litigated in the lord's court. Villeins

had no right to bring an action in the king's court. The villein's unfree status meant that he had no rights against the lord: the relationship was one of power, the power of the lord over the tenant, rather than a relationship of law in which the parties had rights and duties in relationship to each other. (Lyall, 1994, p. 57)

Such a situation would hardly have seemed propitious for the Gaelicisation of the English population in Ireland, yet over the next century, much of the English colony did indeed become gaelicised. While the formal legal framework persisted, the actual social context of the Anglo-French colony was transformed. Historians have traditionally explained the Gaelicisation of the fourteenth century in narrowly military or political terms, but neither Edward Bruce's military engagement in Ireland in the course of the English/ Scottish wars, nor the increased military capacity of the Gaelic septs can convincingly explain this transformation.

The records of the 1297 parliament, long before the Bruce campaign (1315–18) make it clear that the colony was in a deep crisis, while the military weakness of the Dublin administration in the fourteenth century is directly related to their declining revenues. The breakdown of the Anglo-French order in the fourteenth century becomes less mysterious if it is borne in mind that all the evidence points to a generalised crisis of European feudal society in these years (Connolly, 1984).

The Statutes of Kilkenny in 1366 were not directed solely, or perhaps even primarily, against the indigenous Irish community. They clearly targeted people of English descent (defined by law as 'English') who were unable to speak the English language. Any 'English' person holding a benefice who did not speak English was given six months to learn it, or they would forfeit their benefice. These prohibitions were not confined to language issues; they were directed against a whole range of social customs, including the use of Irish dress, names, music and sport. They testify to the gradual Gaelicisation of the 'English' population in the colony. This process of Gaelicisation involved more than simple cultural absorption; it seems clear that the colony was experiencing a deeper social crisis. Many of the statutes were of a more direct socioeconomic import. The price of merchandise was to be fixed by officials, as were the wages of labourers. Labourers were forbidden to emigrate and any caught doing so were to be sentenced to a year's imprisonment (Hand, 1966b).

Such measures were not confined to Ireland. The European feudal social order as a whole was rocked by a deep social crisis throughout the fourteenth century. One of the symptoms of this crisis was widespread revolt against servile conditions and status. While interpretations of the fourteenth-century crisis differ, some of its key features are beyond dispute. The productive capacity of medieval agriculture had reached its limits. Feudal lords found themselves facing increased costs and reduced income, and attempted to deal with this by making new impositions upon the peasantry. The peasants responded with resistance or flight. It would seem that the relative ease of flight in the Irish context made full-scale resistance unnecessary.

Many of the measures proclaimed by the Kilkenny parliament in 1366 were repeated across the Latin Christian world with varying degrees of success. The attempt to restrict the rights of labourers replicated the Statutes of Labourers passed by the English parliament in 1349–51 (Hilton, 1985). What is not clear is how these attempts to restrict the freedom of labourers related to the laws against the use of Irish language and customs. What was the connection between the attempted imposition of serfdom and the assault on Gaelicisation?

The Crisis of the Feudal Order

The fortunes of Anglo-French Ireland in this era mirrored those of European feudalism as a whole. The amount of land under arable cultivation increased considerably, with a corresponding decline in pasturage and meadowland; as a result manure was less available to fertilise the land. Despite the large surpluses of grain exported or sold on the home market, yields were low. Population had increased and seems to have reached a point of overpopulation in settled areas by the end of the thirteenth century (Down, 1987; Nicholls, 1982).

Given the low yields and large surpluses extracted, the living conditions of most of the peasant population must have been precarious. Throughout the High Middle Ages, there was little real technical advance in Europe's agricultural production. Increases in agricultural output were achieved not by greater productivity of the land, but by greater productivity of labour: the peasants worked longer. In this respect feudal Ireland was hardly unique (Brenner, 1996).

Overpopulation and ecological depletion set the stage for conflict between lords and peasants. The earlier privileges enjoyed by the free peasants began to be eroded. Rents appear to have risen considerably and many lords increased the size of their demesne holdings at the expense of small tenures, a practice that reduced the position of free tenants to labourers (Down, 1987).

By the beginning of the fourteenth century, many of the formerly free peasants were little better off than serfs, and perhaps worse. In north county Dublin, in the heart of the colony, English tenants, technically free, were subject to servile labour harsher than that imposed on the *betagh* peasants. The laws passed against the flight of labourers do not specify whether these labourers were of English or Irish extraction but, given that many were fleeing to England, it seems reasonable to conclude that a substantial number were indeed of English origins (Lyons, 1984; Mills, 1890/1891).

These social antagonisms seem likely to have undermined any latent sense of solidarity between the lords and the immigrant peasants against the native population. The colony's earlier cohesion against Gaelic raiding parties depended upon such solidarity, but already by the end of the thirteenth century the Irish parliament was complaining that 'felons frequently escape with their plunder because the people of the district do not rise together' and some of them were even 'rejoicing in his neighbour's damage and ruin, whereas rightly they should grieve, feign and hide themselves, allowing such felons to pass unscathed with their plunder' (quoted in Connolly, 1984, p. 153).

Even the legal advantages which the English peasant community had earlier enjoyed appear to have been eroded by the fourteenth century. The *betagh* communities, while excluded from English common law, maintained a customary tradition of law by which they were bound. In theory, Irish felons could have been punished by English (royal) law. In practice, lords found it expedient to maintain a relationship with their Irish tenants *as communities*, and the best way of doing so was to operate by customary law, which was probably a mixture of Gaelic law and French baronial law. By 1316, the English king was petitioned with a complaint that Irish felons were getting off with fines, even for the homicide of an Englishman (Hand, 1966a; Nicholls, 1982).

By the fourteenth century the flight of English tenants – free or otherwise – had reached such proportions as to undermine much of the manorial economy. Faced with a population flight of English tenants and labourers, the lords were compelled to offer better tenure conditions to their *betagh* communities. Unlike the English tenants, the Gaelic peasants would have been in a better position to depart, with their animals, to autonomous Gaelic areas, and would no doubt have felt less vulnerable to Gaelic raiders. By the early fourteenth century, labour services in Ireland were significantly lighter than in England (Otway-Ruthven, 1951).

The Black Death, the great plague that cut a swathe through Europe in the fourteenth century, reached Ireland in 1348. It appears to have affected the country unevenly, impacting most on the anglicised areas, especially the towns, with the Gaelic areas suffering much less (Lydon, 1998). It seems likely that in Ireland, as elsewhere, poverty 'brought about an enfeeblement of the population's resistance to disease' (Hilton, 1985, p. 244). Recurrent plague and famine certainly deepened the crisis of the feudal order in Ireland, resulting in serious population loss. The state papers of the time give reports of abandoned villages and depopulated lands. The collapse of population strengthened the position of the peasantry against the lords. The institution of serfdom – in Ireland known as *betaghry* – declined throughout the late fourteenth and fifteenth centuries and had virtually died out by 1500 (Down, 1987).

Fourteenth century Ireland saw a substantial shift back to pasture, and with it a different form of social organisation. 'The classical kindred organisation of Irish society was particularly suitable for pastoral husbandry, but arable farming worked better with either servile or wage labour' (O'Brien, 1993, p. 86). In much of the colonised region a hybrid system seems to have emerged, combining features of Gaelic pastoralism and 'feudal' village organisation, with much of the formerly 'English' population becoming assimilated to the surrounding Gaelic communities. The disappearance of serfdom forced lords to adopt alternative strategies for acquiring income. Rather than manage their own demesne lands, they increasingly found it expedient to let the land instead. By the fifteenth century the peasantry was renting land, for the most part, and was consequently in a stronger position vis-à-vis the lords because they now had direct control over their own productive resources.

The Changing Role of Towns

The Anglo-French lords – keenly aware of the economic importance of towns – consolidated their hold on the earlier Viking-built urban settlements and also organised the building of new urban centres across the southern and eastern regions of Ireland. The prosperity of the towns was dependent on trade – on the surplus produced by the agrarian economy. They flourished during the agricultural expansion of the twelfth and thirteenth centuries, and were hit hard by the fourteenth-century crisis.

The decay of the manorial economy in fourteenth-century Ireland was accompanied by a dramatic decline in the urban population. Urban decline was common enough across Europe in the fourteenth century, but it seems to have been particularly marked in Ireland. Exact population figures are unavailable, but it has been calculated that the population of Dublin was in the region of between 20,000 and 30,000 inhabitants in the mid-thirteenth century; it fell heavily in the fourteenth century and by as late as 1476 it was still below 6,000. A similar situation is apparent in the other urban centres. Some towns disappeared altogether while others saw their agricultural hinterland severely shrunken. Even in the capital, Dublin, defence became a serious problem: the frontier began a few miles south of the city walls (Down, 1987).

This new vulnerability appears to have increased the towns' reliance upon the crown. There were frequent appeals to London for military and financial aid, or at least for the abrogation of taxes due. Not only did the towns maintain close relations with the English government, they also battled to maintain their English identity. Fifteenth-century ordinances in Dublin sought to exclude people of 'Irish blood' from becoming citizens or living within the town walls. Similar statutes were introduced in Waterford and other towns. Despite these rulings, many Irish people did become citizens, though few held high office (O'Brien, 1993).

For much of the fourteenth century the English monarchy was itself in a poor position to help the Irish towns. The English kings had their own problems at home and on the continent, while Ireland no longer produced a substantial surplus of grain that might have attracted their interest. Over the course of the century the towns became more distant from the crown and developed closer links with the regional magnates: Dublin with Kildare, Waterford and the southeastern ports with Ormond, Cork and the southern ports with Desmond.

The changing political direction of the towns in the late fifteenth and early sixteenth centuries corresponded to a shifting economic orientation. Despite their efforts to maintain an English exclusiveness, they had no option but to trade with the Gaelic – and gaelicised – countryside. Though such trade was illegal, the crown had little choice but to tolerate it; besides, they had little power to prevent it. The new commerce reflected the altered social character of the Irish countryside – it was no longer grain which was being exported but hides, wool and fish, while the main imports were luxury goods, especially wine. The trading partners also changed.

Irish ports, especially the southern ones, came to trade in the main with France and Spain, England's major rivals (Down, 1987; O'Brien, 1993).

Christianity in Anglo-French Ireland

These social trends in mid-to-late medieval Ireland have interesting parallels with developments in the religious sphere. For medieval people, religion was not really a separate domain at all, but an integral part of life. The natural and the social worlds were part of a greater cosmic order, shot through by forces of good and evil. Developments within, or against, the Christian Church had ramifications across society.

The Christian Church was not only an integral part of the Anglo-French colonisation, but in many ways it spearheaded the process. In the decades before the arrival of warriors in 1169, dozens of Cistercian and Augustinian houses were established in Ireland. Their arrival in Ireland occurred at a time when the Latin Church across western Europe had itself been transformed and had come to play a pivotal role in the whole social order. The new visitors were clearly welcomed, but before long deep tensions developed which set the Christian churchmen against Gaelic tradition (Southern, 1953; Watt, 1998).

The conflict between the clerics and Gaelic tradition was not, at this stage, motivated by ethnic prejudice, rather the whole evolution of the Latin Church in the eleventh and twelfth centuries set them strongly against central features of Gaelic society. The 'evangelical awakening' of this era was strongly directed against social chaos and the violence of the warrior elite across western Europe. The Church response was not to advocate pacifism, but rather to advocate obedience towards legitimate authority (Chenu, 1998). The failure of Ireland to establish a stable monarchy no doubt discredited the Gaelic polity in their eyes. As for Gaelic literary culture, it is difficult to imagine a 'structure of feeling' more at variance with the mood of twelfth-century churchmen than that expressed in the heroic sagas of the Gaelic tradition. If the first Christian missionaries came to Ireland when the Latin Church was at its lowest point, and showed exceptional tolerance towards Gaelic tradition, the twelfth-century visitors came when the Papacy was at the summit of its power and they displayed a corresponding intolerance towards the 'pagan' legacy of the Gael. In the words of St. Bernard of Clairvaux: 'Never before had he known the like, in whatever depth of barbarism: never had he found men so shameless in their morals, so wild in their rites, so impious in their faith, so barbarous in their laws, so stubborn in discipline, so unclean in their life. They were Christian in name only, in fact they were pagans' (quoted in Watt, 1998, p. 17). Clerical fire was likewise directed against the loose marriage practices of Gaelic society; this too, was part of a broader campaign to consolidate the marriage institution and, in the process, to institute clerical celibacy (Goody, 1983).

The monastic houses were initially founded as cooperative type ventures, aiming at self-sufficiency and worked by lay brothers; the monks themselves focused on prayer. By the mid-thirteenth century they had greatly increased their holdings and changed their character. No longer concerned with self-sufficiency, and with seemingly fewer lay brothers, they no longer farmed for themselves, but behaved like any other landowner. Lands were either rented out to peasants or else worked by labourers, dependent or otherwise (Graham, 1993).

The Church in Anglo-French Ireland was a massive landholder. By the end of the Middle Ages, they owned something like half of all the land in county Dublin alone (Down, 1987). The picture here is consistent with the general European pattern by the late Middle Ages, with much of the clergy having become a virtually indistinguishable part of the feudal ruling class: rich, venal and little loved by the laity.

Alongside tensions between land-owning clerics and their peasantry, the late medieval church in Ireland was riven by divisions between Gaelic and Anglo-French clerics. In the thirteenth century, in the powerful Cistercian order, conflict between Gaelic and Anglo-French monks led to violent confrontations, and resulted in the suppression of houses and the expulsion of monks. New rules were instituted insisting that only someone who spoke French or Latin could be admitted as a monk, and Irish monks were prohibited from being appointed to the position of abbot. In some dioceses a formal administrative division occurred between an *Ecclesia inter Hibernos* and an *Ecclesia inter Anglos* (Watt, 1998).

The ethnic polarisation of the Church in Ireland in this period was not an absolute. The arrival of the mendicant orders in the thirteenth century added a novel element to the religious picture in Ireland. The mendicant movement emerged on the Continent in response to the spiritual crisis that flowed from clerical decadence and the absence of pastoral leadership within the new urban communities. The mendicants looked back to the early forms of Christian monasticism and appear to have been close in spirit to the early Gaelic monastic tradition. They rejected the comfortable life of the wealthy monasteries and subsisted by begging for alms. Initially in Ireland, as elsewhere, they were urban based but within a short period they opened up friaries across the country, especially in Gaelic areas where Church institutions had decayed. Both in terms of their own orders, and in terms of their audience, they appear to have played an important role in bringing together the popular Gaelic and Hiberno-English communities (Mooney, 1969; Rosenwein & Little, 1974; Walsh, 1988; Watt, 1998).

The Gaelicisation of the Anglo-French

It was not only among the peasant communities that a trend towards Gaelicisation emerged in the fourteenth century. A similar tendency was apparent among the aristocracy, at least in the 'frontier' regions. At the boundaries of Anglo-French territory, life was never quite the same as in the settled areas. A study of the manorial economy in medieval Ireland shows that the closer a manor was to autonomous Gaelic areas the less the labour services, the smaller the demesne area and the lower the rents. English settlers were harder to attract, and if attracted, harder to keep, while Irish tenants would no doubt have demanded the continuation of their own customary arrangements (Lyons, 1984).

If the income from these frontier lands was lower, the price of maintaining them was a good deal higher. To compensate, land grants in frontier regions tended to be larger. For the aristocracy, keeping a grip on frontier lands was inseparable from military engagement. The construction of the network of castles, large and small, that dotted the frontier between Anglo-French and Gaelic zones obviously contributed to their defence. But castles themselves do not produce an income. Without tenants to work their lands, the land was of no value. The English tenants fled the danger zones, while the Irish tenants had little inclination to engage in the heavy labouring that went with arable agriculture. If the frontier lords permitted Gaelic tenants to engage in pastoral farming, they left themselves open to the cattle raids familiar to Gaelic Ireland. Faced with empty lands or Gaelic pastoral farmers, they chose the latter. In many regions Anglo-French lords invited Gaelic septs to farm their lands in return for rent, and often required their military services in the event of conflict. Elsewhere Gaelic clansmen simply seized land conquered in the twelfth or thirteenth centuries or declared their autonomy from the feudal lordships.

Over time the Anglo-French elite learnt that the most effective way
to limit, if not prevent, cattle raiding was to establish agreements
with local Gaelic chiefs. They also learnt the value of 'brehon law'
and its subtleties, much of it designed for these very purposes.
Sometimes the agreements with the Gaelic septs were secured by
exchanging hostages and sometimes through developing friendships
and alliances, not least through inter-marriage. The priorities of
defence and self-reliance militated against heirs dividing up their
possessions and many families of Anglo-French descent found it
useful to elect a head capable of providing political and military
leadership, rather than risk the vagaries of primogeniture. A strict
adherence to English law could have had disastrous consequences
for a ruling lineage that produced no direct heir: absentee
landowners could hardly protect a frontier lordship (Cosgrove,
1981; Frame, 1998).

The ubiquity of inter-marriage between natives and settlers
ensured that much of the population of Anglo-French or English
background – patrician or plebeian – would have spoken Irish
fluently. This in turn facilitated the assimilation of other aspects
of Gaelic custom and *mentalité*. By the sixteenth century the old
Anglo-French elite had begun to adapt many of the literate practices
of the Gaelic order. Many lords began to cultivate Gaelic bards, who
in turn composed extravagant praise poems in their honour. Their
social function here would seem to have been essentially the same
as in Gaelic areas: 'to confer an aura of legitimacy on the authority
of the reigning chief' (Simms, 1989, p. 181). They likewise drew on
the services of Gaelic brehons for legal proceedings.

To speak of the 'Gaelicisation' of the Anglo-French elite is not
to suggest that this was a completed process. On the contrary,
there appears to have developed a hybrid social formation – which
one could describe as 'Anglo-Gaelic Ireland' – which combined
Gaelic and English (or Latin-feudal) elements in a somewhat
unstable mixture.

Across much of the colonised region of Munster and Leinster,
the old village pattern of settlement appears to have survived into
the early modern era. The 'Anglo-Gaelic' lords in these regions
appear to have had considerably greater power over their peasant
populations than did Gaelic rulers over their subordinates. However,
this did not involve a simple return to servile conditions (Curtis,
1932). The major losers from the development of this variant of
'bastard feudalism' in late medieval Ireland may have been the
lower sectors of the aristocracy. Whereas in England the crown

ensured – through the recognition of their land titles – that there would be a substantial lower aristocratic layer to check the power of the larger feudal magnates, in Ireland no such check operated. The major feudal lords developed substantial armed retinues of their own, and the only real protection that the lesser lords had was through developing close ties with their more powerful neighbours.

If many 'Anglo-Gaelic' lords abandoned all pretence of loyalty to the English crown, many others, including the most powerful (the Butlers and the Geraldines) continued to give formal allegiance to London, and indeed sought to control the English government administration in Dublin. Maintaining formal, albeit tenuous, loyalty to the Crown carried with it a practical obligation to keep in touch with the workings of English law. Legal practice in 'Anglo-Gaelic' areas combined features of 'brehon' law, English common law, and probably French manorial law. They also maintained close links with the predominantly English-speaking towns. The export of grain, however, gave way to the export of products associated with a pastoral economy (Lennon, 1994; Nicholls, 1982).

If the 'Anglo-Gaelic' world was distinctive, it was not a unitary formation; some sectors were almost wholly gaelicised, others barely. Its unity was derived less from within than from without. Thirteenth century English government documents distinguish between the King's Irish enemies and his English enemies; by 1500 they are referring to the 'degenerate English' in Ireland, while later they refer to them simply as the 'English-Irish'. In Gaelic parlance, the 'Anglo-Gael' were referred to as *Gaill*, a term which originally meant 'stranger' or 'foreigner', but by 1500 had come to refer exclusively to the Irish descendants of the 'high' medieval migration/ invasion (in contrast to the later English arrivals who were referred to as *Sasanaigh*). From as early as 1418, the Gaelic annals refer to the *Gaill* alongside *Gaedhil* (Gaelic Irish) as *Érennaigh* (people of Ireland) (Nicholls, 1982).

Historians have their own problems trying to tie them down. Some have spoken of a 'Middle-Nation'; others refer to them as 'Hiberno-norman' and others again as 'Anglo-Irish'. This last characterisation can be confusing because it does not take into account their historical distinctiveness and conflates them with those descended from later (Tudor, Stuart and Cromwellian) settlements. 'Hiberno-Norman' preserves the myth that the feudal conquerors of England and Ireland in the eleventh and twelfth centuries were not really French, while neglecting the significance of the English connection. Using the term 'Anglo-Gaelic' runs the risk, as does

'Middle-Nation', of implying that this stratum possessed a stable ethnic identity, but it does have the merit of stressing the political and cultural coordinates within which they functioned.

The Pale

Only in the 'Pale', the lowland region around Dublin, does a substantial English-style gentry appear to have emerged. Only here was the English government strong enough to guarantee the operation of royal law. But even the Pale gentry felt themselves threatened by the power of the Earl of Kildare. In terms of its social structure the Pale also diverged from the English model. In the late Middle Ages there does not appear to have been any equivalent of the English yeomanry – a prosperous peasant stratum – in the Pale, acting as a social buffer between the landowners and the rest of the peasantry. It was, however, the only region in Ireland where arable farming was dominant throughout the late Middle Ages. The intensive labour that arable farming demanded, led to the Pale peasantry being contemptuously referred to as *coloni* by their neighbours (Canny, 1975).

Ethnic divisions within the peasantry would certainly have made it more difficult for the English peasants to consolidate their social position, while the exclusion of the Gaelic peasants from English law would have prevented them acquiring legal security of tenure. Without the protection of the law, the Gaelic peasants' strongest card would surely have been to maintain durable kinship networks and attempt to retain whatever customary practices most benefited them. Failing this, they could always flee to Gaelic areas. The persistence of strong kinship ties and customary practice would together have inhibited social differentiation within the peasantry.

By 1500 what contemporaries called the 'English Pale' had shrunk to the relatively small region to the north of Dublin city, where tillage continued to predominate. The local landowners were English-speaking and saw themselves as upholders of a civilised order, resisting both the 'barbarous Irish' and the 'degenerate English'. Most of them, however, were bilingual; a knowledge of Irish was essential for communicating with their peasants (Canny, 1975).

The position of the Pale by the beginning of the sixteenth century was paradoxical. The upper echelons modelled themselves on English society and upheld English law; the lower orders operated by different rules. The written codes, and the codes of writing, did not flow downwards.

Summary

While the Irish colony adopted a very similar system of law, politics and social organisation to that prevalent in England, it did so in a very different environment. Once the general crisis of the fourteenth century struck, these differences became magnified. In the Irish colony, the general crisis resulted in the effective disintegration of the manorial economy. Neither the lords nor the state possessed the capacity to prevent peasant flight and uphold serfdom. The medieval colony in Ireland was always something of a frontier region. Even the capital city of Dublin was only a short distance from the Wicklow Mountains, a Gaelic citadel, where a distinctive social order persisted.

The collapse of the manorial economy undermined commerce and the urban settlements and led to a substantial decline in the revenues available for the central state. Public administration persisted but in a decayed state in the fourteenth and fifteenth centuries. Its geographical scope was greatly reduced, and its operations were less intensive. The weakness of the royal government forced the colonial aristocracy to rely on its own resources, and to retain its own military capacity. This survival of the land/military nexus diminished the significance of written title in an environment where the sword was mightier than the pen.

The continued exclusion of the Irish from English law further reduced the significance of written law while encouraging the survival of oral-based custom. The absence of legal security would have done little to encourage the peasantry to develop a market orientation. Rather than promoting the Anglicisation of the Gaelic population, this situation encouraged the Gaelicisation of the colony.

The language issue was clearly of importance in these developments. Four languages were present in the Anglo-French colony: English, French, Latin and Gaelic. As in the Gaelic territories, Latin was used solely for writing and religious ritual. However, the other three languages were spoken: English by the plebeian elements among the colonial settlers; French by the aristocratic and clerical elites; and Gaelic by the native peasantry and many of the urban poor. French was the first to decline as a spoken language, being replaced by English as the colony's vernacular in the thirteenth century, though it continued to be used as a written language until the late fifteenth century. In the fourteenth century the use of spoken English declined across the colony to a point where, by 1500, it was only spoken in the towns and a few small rural areas. Elsewhere the colonial settlers, both plebeian and aristocratic, came to speak Irish. A standardised form of written English emerged via the royal bureaucracy at the very time that the English State in Ireland was at its weakest and the English language had virtually disappeared *as a spoken language* from the Irish countryside. Latin, accessible to the learned laity and clergy alike, remained the lingua franca of educated Ireland, linking the 'pure' Gaelic, the Anglo-Gaelic and anglicised areas.

POLITICS AND SOCIAL ORGANISATION IN LATE GAELIC IRELAND

The previous chapter examined the Anglo-French region in the late medieval era, arguing that the specific social developments in the region encouraged a different political evolution to other parts of the Latin Christian world. In particular, the Anglo-French region did not see the emergence of a more centralised state organisation premised upon an expanded legal system and a vernacular literacy.

In the case of Gaelic Ireland the picture is different again. While Gaelic Ireland was in close touch with Anglo-French Ireland and was heavily influenced by it, it never developed a manorial system. Neither did it produce an administrative or legal system typical of western Europe, despite the fact that it maintained a tradition of vernacular literacy. The distinctive features of Gaelic politics and social organisation are clearly evident if viewed through the prism of how writing functioned in Gaelic Ireland.

Writing and Writers in Gaelic Ireland

A wide variety of texts from mid-to-late medieval Ireland survive, mostly from the period after 1350. These include poetry, annals, genealogies, sagas, romances and religious writings as well as legal and medical texts; they are written in both Latin and Gaelic. Aside from the work of religious scribes, these texts were composed by members of the traditional learned stratum, the *aosdana*. There seems little doubt that they were, in general, highly conservative, determined to preserve the traditions – real or imagined – of the Gaelic order. In particular, they were understandably anxious to preserve their own privileged position within that order. The archaic character of Gaelic literacy is clear from the structure of the literate stratum – dominated by learned families – and from the range of genres they produced (Nicholls, 1972).

The Gaelic literate stratum enjoyed a high status, but the poets, or at least the chief poets, were held in particularly high regard. Not only were the poets respected, they were feared. Legend had it that a satirical attack in a poem could have fatal consequences; more prosaically, it could seriously damage a reputation. Members of the literate stratum could and did travel throughout Gaelic Ireland – and Gaelic Scotland – and could expect to receive a hospitable welcome (Nicholls, 1972; Simms, 1987).

The component branches of the *aosdana* – the poets, lawyers and medics – each ran their own schools where initiates received their training. These schools survived until the early seventeenth century. While the main schools of law, medicine and poetry were conducted through Irish, there were also schools of Latin in Gaelic Ireland. Some Irish scholars received higher education abroad, especially the mendicant bishops, but there were also many instances of Gaelic law and medical students studying abroad, the former particularly in Oxford, the latter in Montpellier (Caball & Hollo, 2006; Nicholls, 1972; Simms, 1998).

The relationship between the clergy and the secular literate strata seems to have been complex: close at times, and at other times antagonistic. In the twelfth and thirteenth centuries there is evidence of mutual antipathy between the clergy and the poets. It seems likely that a secular literate stratum emerged at least in part as a response to twelfth-century reforms within the church that resulted in a sharper distinction between the religious and secular functions of the clergy. In the second half of the fourteenth century a rapprochement between the churchmen and the *aosdana* seems to have occurred. While literacy was important for all of the learned groups, in practice they operated within an oral environment. The poets composed their work in darkened rooms, only later putting it into writing. The poems themselves were for public performance, often accompanied by music. While the brehons (lawyers) might draw on a written tradition of legal principles, in practice they operated without case files, giving judgements at public assemblies (Fitzpatrick, 2004; Fletcher, 2000; Flower, 1994; Patterson, 1989).

The Influence of Anglo-French Feudalism

On the wider European stage the late Middle Ages saw an increase in administrative, legal and commercial activities, which greatly encouraged the spread of literacy beyond the specialised fraternity of scribes. Each field was characterised by particular genres, though these were not necessarily exclusive: administrative files, legal documents (such as contracts and property titles) and commercial records. While all these genres were well represented in Anglo-French Ireland, they were virtually absent in Gaelic Ireland (Clanchy, 1993).

The conventional assumption is that the administrative, legal and commercial sectors remained underdeveloped in Gaelic Ireland because it was poor and backward, but this explanation seems insufficient. Feudal kings, princes and lords elsewhere did not develop efficient administrative systems because they were wealthy; they developed them in order to acquire wealth. Perhaps the most striking evidence pointing to the weakness of such explanations was the change in political fortunes of the two Irelands. From the beginning of the fourteenth century, it was not the Gaelic world which found itself on the defensive, rather the reverse. Not only did the Gaelic clans reclaim substantial territory, but their language and customs, and even law, also came to be adapted by much of the Anglo-French community. By the sixteenth century, Gaelic had become the dominant language throughout most of Ireland. French had long since disappeared and English was spoken only in the towns and in a few small rural areas, to the north of Dublin and south of Wexford. It seems that most of the lords of Anglo-French extraction who attended the 1534 Parliament in Dublin – where Henry VIII was declared King of Ireland and head of the Church – did not understand English (Quinn, 1966; Quinn & Nicholls, 1976).

In explaining the reverses suffered by the Anglo-French order in late medieval Ireland, historians have tended to concentrate on military and constitutional factors, and to under-emphasise the broader socioeconomic context within which this reversal occurred. It is certainly the case that from the late thirteenth century the feudal colony had serious difficulties defending itself from Gaelic attacks, yet it seems clear that these military difficulties were linked to the colonial administration's inability to raise the material resources necessary for their defence. Moreover, the changed military balance in Ireland was indicative that the Gael were learning from their enemies. Military reverses and cultural assimilation were organically bound (Frame, 1998).

From a broader perspective it is evident that the difficulties experienced by the English colony formed part of a more general political and social disorder – the fourteenth-century crisis – that tore apart the medieval world. The old feudal order could no longer function in the way it had in the preceding centuries and new social, political and cultural forms emerged. These new forms, the outcome of the crisis, varied greatly in different parts of Europe and would have immense long-term consequences (Anderson, 1974a; Brenner,

1996). In the case of Ireland, the fourteenth-century crisis resulted in a resurgent Gaelic power. Gaelic resurgence though, led to greater, not less, contact between the English and the Gaelic worlds, which came to be interconnected in a myriad of ways.

The Evolution of the Gaelic Polity

From the thirteenth century onwards, Gaelic chiefs began building castle-type fortifications, first of wood and later of stone. They also began to recruit warriors from outside their own kin groups. These changes in the physical and social structures of military power suggest that the chiefs significantly increased their power in the late medieval period, which might justify the claims by Elizabethan administrators and propagandists that they operated as despotic rulers within their own territories. There are grounds, however, for doubting whether the power of the Gaelic chiefs really was as great as it appears in the writings of the Elizabethan commentators (Quinn, 1966; Spenser, 1970).

The annals of the fifteenth and sixteenth centuries document a seemingly endless succession of cattle-raids and feuds – the two went hand in hand – between and within septs, which makes the picture of the Gaelic chiefs exercising a monopoly of force within their territories difficult to credit (Annals of the Four Masters; Annals of Ulster). Right throughout the late Middle Ages one finds the English administration trying to pressurise the Gaelic chiefs to control their own followers, and while the chiefs were willing enough to give such guarantees they appear to have been unable to implement them. One historian has described political life in late medieval Ireland as 'very much an endless competition for power between chiefs and would-be chiefs. In such a struggle the decisive factor was the possession of the wealth likely to attract support' (Frame, 1998, p. 253).

As well as controlling their followers, despotic chiefs might have been expected to ensure a peaceful succession. In fact, uncontested successions of chieftainship seem to have been rare in late Gaelic Ireland; uncontested cases of primogeniture rarer still. The survival of the institution of 'tanistry' – whereby a deputy chief had his own power base – certainly militated against the passing of power from a chief to one of his sons (Nicholls, 1972). The very fact that such an institution as tanistry survived into the late sixteenth century, despite the best efforts of the Tudor government, suggests the operation of power in Gaelic Ireland was a good deal more complex than the Elizabethan writers imagined. If chiefs were so powerful within their own territories, why would they permit a rival centre of power to exist?

The increased use of warriors from outside their own sept in the late medieval period would certainly have changed the balance of forces within a given territory, as well as making late Gaelic Ireland a more militarised society. It was not only the major chiefs who began hiring outside fighters; it would appear that most of the sub-chiefs did so too. Historians normally refer to these warriors as mercenaries, which implies that they worked for a wage, but money played only a limited role in the Gaelic economy. As late as the 1590s, Gaelic clansmen were bartering cattle to acquire weapons from the towns (Calendar of State Papers, 1860–1912).

The first 'mercenary' grouping were the *Galloglaigh* (literally foreign warriors) recruited from the Norse-Gaelic communities of the Scottish islands who served Gaelic chiefs of the north and west from the fourteenth century. Significantly these groups of warriors were themselves organised on a kinship basis and were compensated for their services by grants of land. The Anglo-French lords were the first to use *kerne*, foot-soldiers of Gaelic extraction, once again organised in kin-groups, but by the sixteenth century their use was widespread throughout Gaelic Ireland. In the sixteenth century, these *kerne* were being compensated for their services with cattle (though valued in money terms) (Nicholls, 1972; Simms, 1987).

Mercenaries, especially outsiders, have always been useful to rulers because they are not part of networks of local loyalty. The great danger with using mercenaries is that they become too powerful and attempt to usurp power themselves, as happened on occasion in Renaissance Italy. There are no examples of this happening in Gaelic controlled regions, though it did happen in Leinster, where Gaelic warriors employed by Anglo-French lords seized territory in their own name claiming it as their ancestral lands. This suggests that while mercenaries were important in Gaelic regions in late-medieval Ireland, they never acquired too much power.

For any ruler seeking to centralise power, be it locally or regionally, it would have been clearly necessary to significantly increase the resources available to them, or to increase their share of those resources. If the Gaelic chiefs had acquired a monopoly of power in their territories, it would surely have involved a considerable increase in the level of exactions, to use the Elizabethan term, that they were able to impose. The evidence here is interesting, because a document from the sixteenth century makes it clear that in the O'Neill country – the most powerful Gaelic chiefdom – no such increase had occurred. It is only at the beginning of the seventeenth century that there is evidence of a significant increase in the level of surplus extraction (Dillon, 1966; Simms, 1987). This would seem to point to the late sixteenth century as the crucial era of transformation of power *within* Gaelic Ireland.

The failure of Gaelic chiefs to develop a bureaucratic administration based on writing becomes less puzzling if it is accepted that throughout the late medieval period they actually possessed fairly limited power within their own territories. Only in the Renaissance era, especially towards its end in the late sixteenth century, were there really dramatic changes in the structures of power in Gaelic Ireland.

Law in Gaelic Society

Alongside the failure of the Gaelic chiefs to develop an administrative system based on writing, the legal system in late Gaelic Ireland was atypical in a wider European context.

The role of law in late Gaelic society seems puzzling: there are numerous texts on or about Gaelic or brehon law but no case files. This has led some scholars to doubt whether brehon law functioned at all in the late medieval period. It has been suggested that the brehons, whether acting as arbitrators or advisors, operated in a purely pragmatic way, while maintaining the fiction of adherence to ancient law (Binchy, 1975/1976).

There is ample evidence, not least from English sources, that central elements of brehon law continued in operation until the defeat of the Gaelic forces in the Nine Years War (1594–1603). A key facet of Gaelic law was the concept of collective responsibility for crime. Although this was strongly denounced by English commentators, the Dublin administration was willing to collude with it, when it suited its purposes, holding an entire sept responsible for the actions of some of its members (Frame, 1998; N. Patterson, 1989).

The principle of the ascendancy of the collective – the kin grouping or *slíoght* – ran through all aspects of Gaelic law. Despite the enormous changes that had occurred from the time Gaelic law was first written down to the close of the Gaelic order, a thousand years or so later, there are important elements of continuity in the basic features of law.

The primacy of the kin grouping was particularly important in the area where legality and the written word were at their most critical in late medieval society: land ownership. Individual land ownership did not exist in Gaelic society; control of land was vested in the corporate grouping, the *slíoght*. The whole notion of land ownership had little relevance to the Gaelic order: what mattered was *access to* and *rights over* land. Both were determined by membership of the *slíoght*. Documentary evidence of land ownership carried little weight here, and consequently there was no great requirement to be able to read such documents. All this would change of course once the Tudors began the process of incorporating Gaelic Ireland into their dominion, but it is precisely the radical character of these changes that needs to be underlined.

Social Production and Exchange in Gaelic Society

Another aspect in which late Gaelic Ireland differed from the 'typical' West European pattern, was the form of exchange and commercial activities. Throughout the high and late Middle Ages there was extensive trading between the Gaelic regions and the towns. Despite this, money remained on the margins of Gaelic life and (with one exception) Gaelic chiefs did not mint their own coins. This seeming resistance to monetisation needs some explanation (Dolley, 1987; Nicholls, 1972).

Historical anthropologists have distinguished three different forms of distribution of resources in societies: market exchange, redistribution and reciprocity (Polanyi, 1971). All three are to be found in late Gaelic Ireland, though not in equal measure. The major form of wealth was also the primary medium of exchange: cattle.

The major patterns of material production in Gaelic Ireland did not change very much from the early medieval to the late medieval period. Ireland was and remained a predominantly pastoral society. Cattle production was central, with the growing of oats a secondary element.

A distinctive feature of pastoral societies is the mobility of their major resources. Livestock circulate easily and increase rapidly, facilitating accumulation and inequality. They are also vulnerable to theft or seizure. As against this, cattle herders are well placed to avoid what they might consider to be excessive exactions placed on them by fleeing with their herds. Nor does pastoral production respond to strategies of labour intensification: cattle watched harder or longer do not increase more rapidly (Godelier, 1986; Runciman, 1989).

There was a close correlation between wealth and power in Gaelic Ireland. The possession of cattle attracted followers whose numbers were necessary to protect the cattle from seizure or theft. Without cattle – or the prospects of them – there was little chance of acquiring followers, and without followers or allies it might prove difficult to keep one's cattle. Substantial herds were certainly held by chiefs and other wealthy persons, yet it is in the very nature of cattle grazing that there are limits to the concentration of cattle. Aside from overgrazing, a significant degree of dispersal of cattle is important to prevent, or at least limit, the spread of disease (Patterson, 1994).

Pastoral societies display paradoxical features. The facility to accumulate cattle is accompanied by the need to disperse them, while the facility to seize the wealth of a more vulnerable party is matched by their ability to escape from domination. Because wealth and power were inseparable, these tensions went to the heart of power relations in Gaelic Ireland.

Strong kinship networks were common enough in medieval Europe; what distinguished them in the Gaelic world, even as late as the sixteenth century, were their durability and pervasiveness. These kinship forms persisted because they provided a framework for managing the basic tensions at the core of pastoral social organisation.

Gaelic Social Organisation

The key elements of power in Gaelic society centred on access to land and cattle. Access to land was, crucially, determined by relations of kinship: the notion of individual ownership of land was alien to the Gaelic order. Land was a collective inheritance, the legacy of the clan, and kinship gave one a share. Access to cattle was more complicated. Unlike land, cattle were individually owned. To prevent overgrazing, disease and seizure, cattle would be dispersed. This generally took the form of 'lending' cattle to poorer kinsmen or to other herders outside the sept. These 'clients' would look after the cattle, and provide the lender with calves and dairy products in return. Both parties could be seen to benefit from this arrangement. The lender had someone else look after his cattle, while still receiving meat and dairy products. The client had access to dairy produce and some meat (Nicholls, 1972, 1987; N. Patterson, 1994).

The early law tracts distinguished between two types of clientship: dependent and autonomous. While this distinction seems to have disappeared by the late Middle Ages, it captures something of the ambivalent character of the basic relationship of clientship. The receivers were clearly dependent on the 'generosity' of the donors, yet the fact that they were in actual possession of the cattle, which they could move if they felt they had to, gave them some real leverage in the situation. This leverage must have acted as a disincentive to the use of coercion in the event of dispute. While coercion might have worked in the immediate situation, in the long run it could be counter productive. What mattered most to the lender was the maintenance of an enduring association and this could best be achieved by mutual accord. Such an accord was more likely to be achieved where strong bonds of kinship existed (Kelly, 1988).

These barriers to extracting surplus produce at the micro level of the patron/client relationship were similar to those that operated at the broader level of the *tuath* (local territorial unit), or indeed at the national level. According to the old law texts, chiefs were chosen by the inner circle of the leading lineage, in consultation with other lineages of the *tuath*. In practice, by the late Middle Ages, the position of chief went to the person from the leading lineage that had the greatest number of followers. These followers would have included warriors, clients who were indebted to the would-be chief and allies, who could supply their own warriors as well as provisions. To create such a coalition of followers the prospective chief would have needed not only to be a charismatic figure, perhaps best measured in military prowess, but also to be bountiful. Without bounty, support would abate (Nicholls, 1976; Simms, 1987).

The office of chief entitled the holder to reserves of land across the *tuath*, as well as tribute. The same was true for the office of *táiniste* (second in command), who acquired a smaller reserve of land and tribute. Acquiring and maintaining these positions involved the use of force, but it also involved more than that. The distinction between subalterns and allies must have been a grey one.

The principle of reciprocity permeated every aspect of Gaelic society, from top to bottom. Land was shared among kinfolk. So too was agricultural labour, though the clan elite were of course exempt. 'Clientship', the most general form of social exchange, assumed the guise of reciprocity: the donor gave a gift of cattle to the client who reciprocated with calves and dairy produce. Aspiring leaders gave gifts of cattle to their followers. Every gift demanded a return. Generosity was the highest virtue; parsimony the most contemptible of vices (Nicholls, 1972; Watt, 1987).

This emphasis on gifts was most likely related to the weakness of centralised political power in Gaelic Ireland. Chris Wickham has noted what he describes as an essential tenet of comparative sociology:

the less hierarchy, and the less stable and inherited authority there is in a society, the more people one has to win with generosity, food or charisma to gain political support, and the longer one has to go on doing it. (Wickham, 1992, p. 241)

The principle of reciprocity here does not imply or assume an equality of power. Quite often it disguises a relationship which is not only unequal but exploitative, with the more powerful player extracting surplus produce. A major form of tribute in Gaelic society was 'guesting'. Chiefs and their retinues would tour their territories and expect lavish receptions wherever they stayed. While these occasions clearly stretched the resources of their hosts, they took place under the veil of customary hospitality (Patterson, 1994; Simms, 1978).

The major form of tribute to chiefs took the form of payment in cattle. There was small chance here of cloaking the asymmetrical character of the exchange. Nonetheless, the theme of reciprocity was maintained. In return for tribute, the chiefs guaranteed protection. Assurances of protection were of course the stock-in-trade of medieval lords across Europe. In a pastoralist economy, however, where communal resources were much more assailable, the issue of protection was more pressing and these pledges seem to have carried more weight than elsewhere. The emphasis on reciprocity remained.

The Social Function of Gaelic Writing

The above discussion on social power in the Gaelic order shows the social context within which Gaelic writing functioned. In the absence of a centralised authority, maintaining a sense of tradition was vital to upholding social order.

Most of the late Gaelic writings display a preoccupation with the past and an insistence on the importance of continuity, custom and tradition. One should not, however, assume that the *filí* were out of touch with what was happening in Renaissance-era Ireland. Given that they were the only grouping in Gaelic Ireland who really operated on a national basis, and who travelled throughout Ireland (and the Gaelic areas of Scotland), it seems most unlikely that they were either unaware of, or indifferent towards, the changes taking place around them (Caball, 1998; Dunne, 1980; Leerssen, 1996).

People living in medieval Europe had a very different sense of time from our modern conceptions (Gurevich, 1985). The Gaelic sense of time was not so different from the medieval norm, except that it persisted into the Renaissance era whereas elsewhere in Europe a new sense of time emerged. The term Renaissance is, of course,

notoriously difficult to define; the term itself was first used in the
nineteenth century. Yet certain elements do stand out.

> From the fourteenth to the sixteenth century and from one end of
> Europe to the other, the men of the Renaissance were convinced
> that the period in which they lived was a new age as sharply
> different from the medieval past as the medieval had been from
> classical antiquity and marked by a concerted effort to revive the
> culture of the latter. (Panofsky, 1960, p. 36)

This changed historical consciousness has been emphasised by other
scholars. It is precisely such a consciousness of living in a new age
that appears so strikingly absent in the Gaelic world, at least prior
to the Tudor expansion. Everywhere in Gaelic culture the emphasis
was on continuity with the past, not on any radical breach with it.
This emphasis of continuity does not mean that no changes occurred
or that there were no ruptures, even in the cultural sphere, but
that Gaelic writers, unlike most of their counterparts in Europe,
chose for their own reasons to emphasise continuity with the past.
Individuals and generations came and went of course, but the deeper
truth lay in the continuity of life.

All the major genres of Gaelic literate culture – the legal texts,
the bardic poetry, the genealogical texts, the lives of saints, the
heroic sagas – share this sense of time. It expresses, not so much a
preoccupation with the past as an insistence on continuity with the
past. This is clear even with the annals, the one genre which seemed
to be focused on the present. For anyone reading the annals the
message of time is clear enough: everything which happens merely
repeats what has happened in the past.

For the learned stratum of Gaelic Ireland, the alternative to
tradition was chaos. The perpetual spectre of chaos was a direct
counterpart to the weakness of any central power in the Gaelic
world. In this situation the normative power of tradition acted as
a vital contribution to the maintenance of order.

This is clearly evident with Gaelic law. Cattle raiding seems to
have been endemic in pastoral societies. A system of collective
responsibility for crime was probably the only form which was
likely to work in a society where powerful kinship networks were
crucially important and where state institutions were weak. Through
collective responsibility the Gaelic chiefs and their brehons could
prevent a crime turning into a full-scale feud; the payment of hefty
compensation, usually of cattle, helped ameliorate the feelings of

the injured group while encouraging the others to impose restraint on their own members.

A similar pattern is apparent with the poets. Their poetry legitimated contemporary chiefs by associating them with traditional heroism and generosity. The same association between tradition and social order can be observed in relation to all the genres in Gaelic literate culture. The *filí* then are not merely praising a particular leader within a poem, they are legitimating the traditional Gaelic social order. It is only when this social order is itself facing extinction that a rupture appears in the Gaelic literary tradition.

Summary

In the mid-to-late medieval period, Gaelic Ireland had a predominantly pastoralist economy. Tensions and antagonisms in this type of society could be best contained through the maintenance of strong networks of kinship. The primacy of the kin grouping was particularly important when it came to land ownership. Individual land ownership did not exist in Gaelic society and membership of a kinship network guaranteed access to, and rights over, land. Since land ownership was collective, there was no need to document individual possession of land and to keep written records.

The major patterns of material production in Gaelic Ireland did not change very much from the early medieval to the late medieval period. Pastoralist production was predominant and cattle remained the major form of wealth and the primary medium of exchange. Money operated on the margins of Gaelic life, and Gaelic chiefs did not mint their own coins. There was little evidence of markets in Gaelic regions and urban settlements were thin on the ground. The proliferation of money and of commerce in the high and late Middle Ages, which appears to have played a crucial role in the spread of literacy across western Europe, remained on the margins in Gaelic Ireland.

While the Gaelic chiefs significantly increased their power in the late medieval period, they never achieved a monopoly of force within their own territories. This limited power helps to explain their failure to develop a bureaucratic administration based on writing. While the development of administrative systems elsewhere in Europe encouraged the diffusion of literacy, this change did not occur in late Gaelic Ireland.

The literate stratum in other West European countries was drawn into administrative, legal and later commercial activities, and thus helped to spread literate practices. This, however, did not apply in

Gaelic Ireland. In the absence of administrative structures, it fell to the Gaelic literate caste to uphold a normative order, which was best achieved through the preservation of social and cultural tradition. Their role was to maintain the continuity of social order over time. The Gaelic literate caste was dominated by learned families who were anxious to preserve their own privileged position within that social order and thus, instead of helping the spread of literacy, they inhibited it.

REFORMATION AND STATE FORMATION IN THE ATLANTIC ISLES

Introduction

The sixteenth century is regarded by many scholars as being the crucial turning point in world history. It was the century when the European maritime empires gained control of the world's seas and began to colonise the Americas. It was also the century when the European states centralised their structures of social power, and laid the foundations for the modern nation state. This did not only involve political transformations, but also cultural ones, with the Reformation and Counter-Reformation playing a critical role. These changes were experienced in a particularly dramatic fashion in the Atlantic Isles, where political, social and cultural transformations converged, leading to deep structural ruptures. This chapter explores why Ireland diverged so radically from the rest of the Atlantic Isles.

Renaissance Politics and Culture

If the spread of firearms and the creation of professional armies was the most dramatic feature of state formation in the Renaissance era, it was part of a much wider process of social change. The expansion of a money economy enabled European states to develop military organisations (and military technology) that would not have been possible previously, and facilitated the emergence of state bureaucracies capable of tapping into the new monetary resources and expanding the internal cohesion of these states (Anderson, 1974b). These developments were accompanied by significant cultural shifts. In the sixteenth century the spirit of the Renaissance had migrated across the Alps, and over the course of the century enthusiasm for classical learning 'mutated' to encourage a new interest in vernacular literature. An appreciation of written culture was becoming a badge of social status.

The process of state centralisation heavily promoted literate forms. Being able to read, and to a lesser extent to write, became vital for anyone seeking to engage with the new institutions of power. The newly strengthened state institutions came to play a key role in standardising vernacular literacies. The growth of these bureaucracies also offered new opportunities for the children of the nobility, especially the lower nobility. The development of printing pushed this process further. Printing production was strongest in commercial – rather than university or ecclesiastical – towns. Books and pamphlets were becoming accessible to a wider segment of society, and enabled the written word to increasingly escape the clutches of ecclesiastical power. The translation of the Bible into the vernacular languages had a dramatic impact on literacy levels. Huge numbers of people across the European continent, especially in the north, learnt to read in order to have direct access to the divine word. This trend was greatly reinforced by the missionary drives of both the Reformation and Counter-Reformation, with their competing catechisms (Febvre & Martin, 1976; Houston, 1988; Nauert, 1995).

In the sixteenth century religious Reformation and political centralisation were closely associated throughout Europe. In Ireland the two developments failed spectacularly, culminating in catastrophic wars of conquest. This chapter will explore why religious Reformation and political centralisation did not take hold in either the Gaelic or anglicised regions of Ireland, and examine how Ireland came to diverge sharply from other parts of the Atlantic Isles.

Ireland

State centralisation and religious reform were not only concurrent, but were seen as part of the same process: the 'reform' of Ireland. At the heart of the Tudor reform programme was the attempted extension of English law to the whole Irish population. Tudor strategy was not simply a continuation of the original Anglo-French conquest; it was a significantly different project. It involved not only granting access to royal law – ending the earlier system of legal exclusion – to all the inhabitants of the colonised region, but also sought to bring the autonomous Gaelic communities into the English legal network. In part this was a pragmatic reaction to the actual social situation in sixteenth-century Ireland. Serfdom was finished in Ireland, as in England, and to continue to exclude the native Irish from royal law was merely to strengthen the hands of local magnates and urban monopoly groups. Likewise, the policy of seeking to assimilate the Gaelic elite, rather than simply dispossessing them, involved a recognition of political reality – that a policy of military conquest had hitherto failed (Bradshaw, 1979).

More than pragmatism was involved. The Tudor reformers in sixteenth-century Ireland were influenced by the humanist philosophy prevailing across Europe. The humanists believed that through cultural reform the 'civilised ethos' of ancient Greece and Rome could be recreated. The key to cultural reform and the advance of civility was the education of the elite. If difficulties were encountered bringing Ireland to civility, they were not likely to be qualitatively different to those experienced elsewhere (Bradshaw, 1979).

The programme for extending English law across Ireland was accompanied by a series of treaties between Irish chiefs and the Lord Deputy in the early 1540s. As part of the 'surrender and re-grant' policy, Gaelic chiefs surrendered their lands and had them 're-granted' by the King. They would henceforth agree to the operation of English law in their territories. They also agreed to accept Henry as head of the Irish church and to go along with the Henrican Reformation programme (Bradshaw, 1978).

Half a century later the country was convulsed in rebellion and war. Instead of being assimilated, the Gaelic social order would be extirpated, while the traditionally loyal cities and their hinterlands would end up committed to the Counter-Reformation cause.

Social Implications of Reform

The extension of the English centralised state system across Ireland had significant structural implications for Gaelic, and gaelicised, society. Reforming Ireland meant ensuring that wrongdoers appear before English courts and submit to English law. It involved not only supplanting Gaelic law but also bringing to heel the powerful Anglo-French feudal magnates. The formal adherence of Gaelic chiefs to English law was gained easily enough. Its implementation on the ground proved more difficult. For the English administration the core of the problem was the practice of *eraic*: the system whereby no real distinction was made between civil and criminal law. Members of a kinship group paid compensation – money or cattle – for any theft or injury (including killings) perpetrated by one of their own. For defenders of this custom it was the only sensible way to avoid bloody and protracted feuds, especially given that other members of the kinship group would be held responsible if compensation was not paid. For its detractors, *eraic* only encouraged theft and crime. Furthermore, it violated the emerging principle of individual responsibility for one's actions. Not least its continuance represented a challenge to the authority of the Crown (Ellis, 1985; Lennon, 1994).

Throughout the sixteenth century this differing approach to basic law would lead to bitter disputes between the government and various Gaelic communities. This confrontation between English common law and Gaelic tradition was not confined to the criminal sphere; differences in civil law were equally wide. Few areas of law were more contentious, and few more important, than the issue of land ownership. In Gaelic law, land was owned not by the individual but by the sept; the individual only had the use of it. In many areas land was periodically redistributed within the sept or kinship grouping. The sons of individual landholders had no automatic right of inheritance. What they did have, as members of a kinship grouping, was the right to a *share* of the collective inheritance (Nicholls, 1972; O'Dowd, 1986).

The introduction of individual ownership of land and of the practice of primogeniture in land inheritance was not only at variance with Gaelic customary law it was also threatening to those within the sept who were likely to lose out by the new arrangement. The codification of marriage laws accentuated the problem. Integral to the imposition of the Common Law was the regulation of marriage. Marriage records were not kept in the Gaelic system, nor was there much concern about marriage rules. Divorce was common, so too were extra-marital sexual unions. Illegitimacy was no disgrace; more specifically it was no bar to inheritance. Most pernicious of all, from the point of view of the Tudor reformers, was the practice of 'naming', whereby a mother could 'name' the father of her child, and the father, if he was in a position to do so, would accept the child as his own (Nicholls, 1972; Lennon, 1994).

The sexual laxity of the Gaelic order was linked to its general patterns of power and its landholding customs. Because land was not divided up but worked collectively, there was less pressure to limit the number of sons. A large number of close kinsmen was always an advantage in this society: the more sons the better. The use of written records to standardise marriage not only flew against custom, it also threatened those born outside these standards. The creation of a new form of land ownership transformed, or threatened to transform, the class structure of Gaelic society. It did not only affect 'younger sons' but the outer sectors of the clan whose support could be called on in internecine disputes, and for whom kinship connections were an important factor. For these outer kin layers, distant from the centre of power, kin still remained crucially important (Nicholls, 1976).

The expansion of the authority of the English state across the island necessitated the *reorganisation* of space. Not only was space to be transformed, so too was time, because the organisation of space and time were closely related. The Renaissance perception of time and space was very different from that of the Gaelic tradition. For the most part the Gaelic order had adapted itself to the natural environment. Defensive fortifications were located on hills or in lakes, rather than having man-made structures dominating the landscape. The patterns of landholding express this adaptation. Land units were not constructed from a map but from the seasonal rhythms of herding; each unit traditionally included winter and summer holdings, often at a considerable distance from each other. Following the military conquest, English administrators would find that the units of land division were literally incommensurable (Duffy, 2001; Nicholls, 1972, 1987; Palmer, 2001).

It is not that the Gaelic literate tradition was indifferent to space. The classical Gaelic sagas and the lives of the saints occurred in real space (though not in real time). Not only are real places mentioned in these stories, but in virtually every Gaelic locality there were places named after these narrative heroes, each with its own story. The effect of this was to localise tradition, as with the Greek legends, and create a spatial identity, but not to control space. In many respects the practice of writing in the Gaelic order was not so different from the older tradition of oral learning, rather it perpetuated and strengthened that tradition.

The Tudor reorganisation of the spatial also undermined the Gaelic sense of time. If Gaelic landholding and inheritance patterns were to be abolished, it would be difficult to maintain a sense of continuity with the past. In consequence the social and political transformations implicit in the Tudor reform programme represented a deep breach within Gaelic culture. Implicit in the establishment of a centralised state in Ireland was the overturning and abandonment of a wide range of social customs and perceptions. This is not to suggest that the reform programme was an impossible project. Similar transformations could and did occur across Europe, in different places and different times, though always involving considerable strains within these societies. In fact Gaelic society was already showing signs of wear and tear before 'surrender and re-grant'; the new Tudor order seems to have exacerbated these tensions, and created a deep social crisis which would have longterm consequences.

The close links between Gael and 'Gaill' (the gaelicised Anglo-French), especially in the fifteenth century, led the Gaelic elite to adopt many of the practices of the latter. Trade increased between the Gaelic areas and the coastal towns, who were also engaged in long-distance trade with French, Spanish and English ports. The clan elites began to develop a taste for wine and other luxury items unavailable in Ireland. They also began to build stone fortifications and stone houses, with some Gaelic chiefs attempting to impose labour services on communities for their construction. The building of stone fortifications seems to have increased significantly in the Elizabethan era. Alongside stone fortifications, Gaelic chiefs began to employ, following the Anglo-French pattern, professional soldiers, who were billeted on the population of their districts. These 'mercenaries' seem to have been paid in kind, rather than in money (Nicholls, 1976; Simms, 1987).

All of these changes had the effect of increasing the power of the chiefs in relation to the community they ruled over, and in relation to their own extended kin network – their own 'clan'. Gaelic society then was already changing *before* the Tudor state began to take charge. Quite how far these changes went is not clear. It is clear enough though, that despite the presence of stone fortifications and 'mercenaries' the Gaelic chiefs remained politically dependent upon the broader network of support from their own clans and auxiliary clans (O'Dowd, 1986).

Practical Impediments to Reform

The Tudor reform programme was not pre-determined to fail. A process of political centralisation and social differentiation was already occurring within Gaelic Ireland before Elizabeth ever came to power. The Tudor conquest of Ireland was not inevitable. But it did happen, and why it happened needs explanation.

While the idea of social engineering, introducing the Irish to 'civility', was attractive to the early reformers, there were certain practical obstacles along the way. First and foremost the English state did not have actual control of much of Ireland. To establish control they needed the cooperation of the local elite. Consolidating royal power in Ireland did not only involve anglicising the Gaelic elite. It also necessitated bringing the 'bastard feudal' magnates to book, chief among them the Earl of Kildare, head of the Geraldine lineage, who controlled two of the richest agricultural regions in

Ireland – the area east of Dublin and central Munster. The execution of the key members of the lineage on grounds of treason in 1536 captured the attention of the Irish political elite and convinced them of the seriousness of the Tudor project. In the years following, the crown made treaties with individual chiefs, and sought to establish garrisons to uphold English law (Ellis, 1985; Lennon, 1994).

This initiative brought its own problems. Chiefs used English support to buttress their position against other septs within the *tuath* (local region) and against rival contenders within their own sept. The effect of these changes was to disturb the traditional balance of power in Gaelic society, increasing the power of chiefs. The chiefs used their new power within the *tuath* to increase their military strength, relying ever more on mercenaries and building more castles (Edwards, 2001).

This development accentuated the problems of the Gaelic order. Chiefs laying claim to ownership of 'their land' breached customary conceptions of land rights. As owners they felt entitled to impose new 'exactions' on their territories. These demands were of course often resisted and the sixteenth century witnessed a significant rise in internecine conflict and the nomadic movement of septs, with their cattle, across Ireland. The Gaelic chiefs and the English government interpreted their new alliance in different ways. For the chiefs it provided an opportunity to increase their power within their territories, not to cede it to the English government (Edwards, 2001; Nicholls, 1976; Simms, 1986).

In order to counter the power of the chiefs, and to build a broader support for their programme of structural transformation, the Government later attempted, in Connaught and elsewhere, to secure property rights for sub-chiefs and other leading clan members (Lennon, 1994). This objective of consolidating a class of 'lower aristocracy', corresponding to the English gentry, encountered similar problems to the original 'surrender and re-grant' strategy. The social engineering envisaged by English government reformers was not easily implemented because there was no clear line of demarcation between elite and mass, or nobility and commoner. The Gaelic social order went all the way down. In Gaelic Ireland the number of people claiming noble origins was so great that they may well have outnumbered those without noble blood. A policy of extending land ownership to create a more substantial gentry simultaneously created a broader range of those who were 'excluded' and in the process deepened the social crisis of sixteenth-century Gaelic Ireland.

Government efforts to resolve these issues seem to have made matters worse. Confronted by the seemingly chaotic state of Gaelic Ireland, they attempted in the 1570s to impose, what was in effect, legal servitude. 'The inhabitants of each territory are to be summoned; the name of each one is to be recorded on a parchment roll, and every man is to acknowledge as his lord some chief who will take responsibility for him. Those without a chief to protect them are to be put to death summarily' (quoted in Breatnach, 1990, p. 28).

Whether or not a new 'more advanced' Gaelic sociopolitical organisation was in the process of coming into being is a moot point, but a hypothetical one. The actual consequence of the Tudor state enlargement was not to stabilise a new social order, but to unleash centrifugal forces within it. By the second half of the sixteenth century a Gaelic social 'disorder' had been created that would ultimately engulf the whole island.

The Crisis of the Gaelic Order

The structural impediments to the expansion of the English state in Ireland have already been spelt out, but there are grounds for doubting that these, on their own, would have provided an adequate basis for any sustained resistance to the process. Political fragmentation was endogenous to Gaelic society. Not only was there no central authority but Gaelic politics was based upon patterns of enmity and alliance with neighbouring septs, insofar as there was any coherence to it at all. The Arabic adage – 'my enemy's enemy is my friend, my enemy's friend is my enemy' – fitted the Irish context well.

Two key literate strata in Gaelic society appear to have played a central role in developing resistance, thus ensuring that the incorporation of Ireland into the English state would take the form of full-scale conquest, rather than piecemeal assimilation. The *filí* (poets) played a pivotal role in the Gaelic order. They were powerful because they could mobilise support for political leaders through their poetry and could equally well use satire to damage them. Because they were part of a broader, national network they were in a position of relative independence. This autonomy was limited though because they were dependent upon chiefs for patronage. The Renaissance-era changes in Gaelic society tended to weaken the position of the *filí* in relation to the chiefs. The increased power of the chiefs – their use of professional warriors and castles – would have had the effect of making the poets' traditional role of securing legitimacy and of mobilising support for chiefs less significant. The more military power one has, the less legitimacy one needs, or so the chiefs may have calculated (Nicholls, 1976; Watt, 1987).

The prestige of the *filí* would have been further weakened by the rise of literacy among the clan elite in the decades following surrender and re-grant. Their more general role of upholding the Gaelic cultural tradition, the *seanchas*, was becoming obsolete now that the chiefs were attempting to break with customary practice. The pattern of patronage changed too. Whereas in earlier centuries the position of chief's poet was a lifetime one, by the late sixteenth-century poets composed work for many patrons. The *filí* found themselves in a contradictory position, torn between their quest for patronage and their traditional role of upholding Gaelic custom upon which their power had ultimately rested. As the sixteenth century progressed, their hostility to Anglicisation became increasingly pronounced. The difficulties created by the *filí* were accentuated by the religious changes of the era (Caball, 1998).

Church Organisation in Late Medieval Ireland

In the late Middle Ages the organisation of the Church in Gaelic Ireland was in a state of serious decay. The priesthood had become a family affair, church lands had become clan lands, and the holders of clerical office were often related to the dominant family in a region. Many clerics became involved in inter clan warfare, and the traditional exemption from attack that the clergy and their property had once enjoyed was a thing of the past. Contemporary observers agreed that the only people preaching the Gospel in Ireland by the time of the Henrican Reformation were the mendicants (Mooney, 1969).

The mendicant orders, or poor friars as they were known – Franciscans, Dominicans and Augustinians – were a group of religious orders which emerged in response to the decadence of the high medieval church. Within these orders an 'observant' movement had developed in the sixteenth century which insisted upon 'observing' the rules of poverty and chastity. The observant branches of the order grew rapidly in Gaelic Ireland in the late fifteenth century and by the early sixteenth century had spread to the cities and anglicised areas. Part of the attraction may have been that the 'observant' branches of the orders, unlike their 'conventual' branches, were not under the authority of an English superior. All the evidence suggests that they came to occupy a highly influential position within Gaelic society (Bradshaw, 1998; Meigs, 1997).

This prestige appears, at first glance, to be somewhat paradoxical. They denounced the decadence of the regular clergy (parish priests, bishops, etc.) and indeed of society in general. By observing the strict rules of their orders they placed themselves at odds with Gaelic social custom, whereas the regular clergy were barely distinguishable from the society around them. Yet it was precisely because the observants distanced themselves from the kinship networks of the Gaelic order, through living out their vows of poverty and chastity, that they were able to operate so effectively. They were seen to be saintly. The Protestant goal of a saintly society was quite at odds with this notion of saintliness: the 'holy men' of Gaelic Ireland were esteemed because they were out of the ordinary. In a world of sinners, they stood apart. And because of their holiness they possessed great spiritual power. The friars were not, however, isolated 'holy men'; their orders were part of a broader literate community, extending across Europe and based on Latin. While elsewhere in Europe the friars were often in the vanguard of the Reformation – Martin Luther himself was an Augustinian – in Ireland they were resolute in resisting it (Bradshaw, 1998).

Gaelic Society and the Reformation

In 1542, two English Jesuits who visited Ireland in the hope of spreading the gospel of the Counter-Reformation concluded that their cause was lost. While the faith of the 'simple people' was strong enough, the leading Gaelic chiefs were committed to the Reformation and had refused to even meet them (Bradshaw, 1998; Meigs, 1997).

If the defeat of the Reformation in Gaelic Ireland was not a forgone conclusion, there were quite significant obstacles to its progress. Not the least important was the spiritual message of the Reformation itself. A common thread of Reformation thought from Luther to Calvin was the yearning for a more direct relationship to God, unmediated by ritual, image or intercession. Personal access to the Holy Word was crucial to this achievement and consequently the appearance of a vernacular Bible spurred on the demand for literacy. However, this need for a more 'personal God' was not a universal one. It seems likely that the success of the Protestant Reformation in early modern Europe was at least partially due to its ability to address a deep spiritual crisis of the era – a crisis that, arguably, was itself a response to the collapse of traditional kinship networks and customary values. These traditional networks not only provided medieval people with a very clear sense of identity, they also operated as systems of communal control. The decline of these external networks, especially – though not exclusively – in the cities, made the internalisation of order all the more necessary. It is certainly the case that order and discipline, as well as a renewed personal spirituality, were heavily promoted by the mainstream of the Protestant Reformation as later they would be by the Counter-Reformation (Bossy, 1985; Cameron, 1991; Gellner, 1981; MacCulloch, 2003; Scribner et al, 1994).

Such a spiritual message would seem to have had little appeal in Gaelic Ireland. Custom and kinship dominated people's lives, fashioning a very definite sense of identity and their own codes of control. Moreover the iconoclastic practices of Reformation zealots affronted their traditional religious custom. If the citizens of many North European towns needed a more direct relationship to God, the Gaelic population was happy enough to work through intermediaries. Saints were ubiquitous in Ireland, and devotion to them played a central role in people's spiritual lives. In the Gaelic regions most of the saints were local and tales of their lives and marvellous deeds were woven into the very landscape; they were remembered in both oral and written tradition. A major – perhaps *the* major – form of popular piety were visits to places associated with the saints: holy wells, sacred mountains and islands, saints' graves and old monastic sites. The saints did not only concern themselves with the afterlife and questions of high moral tone, but also with the more mundane issues of this life: illness, protection and crop failure. For the Protestant reformers such devotion to saints was anathema, but dealing with it raised serious problems. If they confronted the saints directly they risked alienating the lay population, but if they tolerated or overlooked these practices they diluted their whole message. In the event the message never got through: it was delivered in the wrong language (Meigs, 1997).

The Pale: Vanguard of Tudor Reform

The Tudor reform programme was strongly supported by the Pale gentry, some of whom played a prominent role in formulating the new approach. The elimination of Kildare magnate power caused few of them grief. A government commission into the state of the colony showed that most small-to-medium sized landowners regarded Kildare and the other magnates as tyrants and were pleased to see the back of them. The Pale gentry saw themselves as the vanguard of 'civility' in Ireland, a model for the rest of the country. They responded ardently to the new humanist culture, and encouraged the development of education and the building of schools. Some Pale gentry families went as far as offering to sponsor the children of Gaelic elite families, so that they could learn the English language, civilised values and good manners (Bradshaw, 1979; Canny, 1975).

The Pale gentry's enthusiasm for a conciliatory reform programme was based upon their own collective experience over an extended period. If they were used to conflict with Gaelic clansmen, they were also used to trading and negotiating with them. A significant section of the Pale peasantry, probably the majority, was Gaelic speaking and the Pale landlords tended to be bilingual themselves. Gaelic Ireland may have been very different from the Pale, but it was not entirely a foreign country (Canny, 1975).

The Pale gentry were also, for the most part, supportive of religious reform. The idea of having better trained English-speaking ministers made eminent sense. The monasteries in the anglicised regions of Ireland had long been corrupt and few shed tears at their closure by the government in 1537. Some of the Pale and English-Irish landed families resented the fact that the Crown monopolised too much of the seized land, but that hardly constituted a basis for serious resistance to the process. Under the leadership of St. Leger, an astute and liberal minded Lord Deputy, it seemed that the island of Ireland might be peacefully incorporated into an expanded English state, with the Pale gentry playing a central role in the proceedings (Bradshaw, 1979). Half a century later the Pale gentry had thrown their lot in with the forces of the Counter-Reformation. Something had clearly gone wrong.

The Social Position of the Pale Gentry

After removing the feudal magnates from their control of the Dublin administration, the Tudors were anxious to prevent it becoming too closely linked to local interests in Ireland and increasingly placed only English-born officials in senior government posts. Their gradual exclusion from high office rankled with the Pale English, but it was the policy implications of their exclusion that had the deeper effect. Beyond these specific areas of resentment, there seems to have been deeper sociocultural factors at work, which came to express themselves as religious difference, and which in turn came to justify the exclusion of the 'Old English' community – as they began to describe themselves – from government posts and initiatives.

As their programme for reforming Gaelic Ireland stalled, the administration came to rely increasingly on coercion, and began nourishing dreams of conquest. This coercive approach had a number of aspects: increased levels of militarisation, 'plantation' projects (i.e. establishing colonies of English settlers in Gaelic areas), and a more aggressive drive to implement the religious Reformation. The adoption of a coercive approach towards Gaelic (and gaelicised) Ireland could not help but have important implications for the more anglicised regions (Lennon, 1994).

There were in fact significant differences between the social structure of the Pale and a typical English region in the sixteenth century. One of the most striking differences was the very limited development of a 'yeoman' stratum among the peasantry of the Pale. The slow emergence of this prosperous yeoman stratum in England seems to have been associated with the development of market relations and the consolidation of peasant holdings through stable tenure, itself closely linked to the spread of written legal documentation. In the Irish colony, by contrast, the same level of social differentiation within the peasantry does not appear to have occurred, nor was land enclosure commonly practised (Canny, 1975).

The majority of the peasantry in the Pale was Irish speaking by the sixteenth century, with custom rather than written law regulating relations between the peasantry and the landowners. Among the peasants themselves, custom and kinship continued to play a significant role while fixed rents for plots of land gave way to share cropping, a system whereby the lords took a portion of the crop. With the effective collapse of serfdom in the fourteenth and fifteenth centuries, the gentry in the Pale and Anglo-Gaelic lords elsewhere seem to have increasingly resorted to a system of patronage to secure their social position. Unable to prevent peasant flight, securing adequate returns on land necessitated greater compromise (O'Brien, 1993).

The very insecurity of the Irish context would surely have instilled in the Pale gentry the necessity of social cohesion as a cardinal virtue. The Pale was not just a frontier zone: the Gael were inside the Pale. Surviving in this environment had induced in the Pale gentry a very different mindset from the gentry of the southern English shires. They had long experience of military conflicts with their Gaelic neighbours, but they had also learnt the need for negotiation and compromise. It was this very vantage point that put them increasingly at odds with the English government and the culture of the 'New English' elite who came to dominate the government in Ireland.

That the break with the government should come around the religious question was both symptomatic and paradoxical. It was paradoxical because initially the Pale gentry had little or no difficulties with the Henrican Reformation, and many were very supportive of it; religious reform being seen to parallel sociopolitical reform. The religious divide was, however, symptomatic of a deeper cultural disparity which reflected the differing sociocultural experiences of the two elites.

English historians speak about a reformation from both 'above' and 'below'; it was the congruence of the two movements that guaranteed its success. Neither in anglicised Ireland nor in Gaelic Ireland did a movement from below emerge. This was not because the institutions of the church were highly revered, but rather because popular religious practices had only a tangential relationship to the organised church. For a popular anti-clericalism to take a doctrinal form, a tradition of 'dissident literacy' would have needed to exist (Haigh, 2001).

The Reformation aimed to 'bring religion back to the people', and a common feature of the movement, or movements, across Europe was its strong emphasis on the use of the vernacular, both in prayer and through scriptures. This created difficulties for the 'Old English' elite. English was the main language of the Pale gentry and the urban patriciate, but it was not the language of the peasantry or, it would seem, of the urban poor. The elite wished to anglicise and civilise Ireland, but they had no desire to deepen the gap between themselves and the Gaelic speaking communities by excluding them from religious services, much less to engage in a full-scale confrontation with their traditional practices. Moreover, many clerics did not speak English so any attempt to impose English language services was doomed to failure (Bradshaw, 1998).

Some zealous reformers did seek to launch a missionary campaign using the Irish language to win over the population to the cause of the Reformation. Both the *Book of Common Prayer* and the New Testament were translated into Irish and printed in Dublin. Yet neither the 'Old English' elite nor the 'New English' elite showed much enthusiasm for the project. As Gaelic resistance to Anglicisation increased, the 'New English' elite came to view Gaelic society as incorrigible, and to identify Gaelic customs and language as fundamental obstacles to the civilisation of Ireland (Ford, 1985).

These issues became more clearly focused following Elizabeth's accession to the throne. The Act of Supremacy of 1560 directed that English be the language of church services, and that in the event of the minister not being an English speaker, Latin be used instead. The use of Latin seems to have appealed to the 'Old English' elite; from the 1540s onwards grammar schools teaching Latin began to flourish in the towns of Ireland. Latin was the language of European culture and of cultured Europeans, and a knowledge of it enabled educated members of the elite to communicate with others across Europe. It also crossed barriers within Ireland, establishing a common language between many, if not most, of the educated stratum of Gaelic Ireland and their counterparts in anglicised regions. Moreover, as the traditional language of religion it would have appealed to the instinctive caution of the English elite. It was of course incomprehensible to the great majority of the population of any part of Ireland, and as such anathema to the whole spirit of Reformation, but this itself was hardly a concern for the 'Old English' elite (Ford, 1985).

Anglicanism as a whole, of course, attempted to straddle the great religious divide of early modern Europe, combining elements of Catholicism and Protestantism within a single *national* church. In England itself the mixture proved to be difficult to sustain. In the Irish context, it had even less chance of enduring. While there were some Catholic and Protestant zealots within the 'Old English' community, the majority conformed to the Established Church while displaying no great interest in doctrinal change. By the late sixteenth century this position had become less and less tenable (Bradshaw, 1998).

If towns across Europe came to play a crucial role in the Reformation, in Ireland they played a corresponding role in ensuring adherence to the Counter-Reformation. For centuries the towns in Ireland had been loyal English enclaves, ever vigilant against Gaelic raids. In the second half of the fifteenth century they had increasingly to rely on their own resources, becoming in effect little 'city republics'. Economically they functioned as conduits between the Gaelic-speaking countryside and continental ports. Culturally, though still jealously guarding their autonomy, they became more flexible about permitting the Irish to live within their walls, and even to acquire burgher status. By the beginning of the seventeenth century they had very clearly come to identify with the Counter-Reformation (Bradshaw, 1998).

From Conciliation to Conquest

The path of English state policy over the course of the sixteenth century, from conciliation to conquest, was uneven but none the less cumulative. This unevenness reflected the fragmented character of the Irish polity. From the earliest period of the reform programme, conciliatory moves had been accompanied by force. Half a dozen members of the leading 'Old English' lineage, the Geraldines, had been executed in London, while a major Gaelic sept in the Midlands, the O'Moores, were wiped out and their lands settled by an English colony. Both were intended as exemplary moves, designed to encourage others to acquiesce with government policy. As resistance to the new social practices intensified within Gaelic (and Anglo-Gaelic) Ireland, the coercive side of state policy became more pronounced. More troops were called for, most of them stationed in the southeast of the island, where the burden for their upkeep fell upon the local population. Their presence seems to have increased the sense of distance between the government and the local population, while establishing closer bonds between the people and the 'Old English' elite. The peasantry had no-one else to rely on, while the elite itself suffered from the arbitrary actions of an unruly soldiery (Brady, 1986; Lennon, 1994).

The heart of the problem lay in the inability of the royal government to incorporate the Gaelic areas. The structural changes of the Renaissance era, coupled with the centralising effects of Tudor policy, had augmented the power of the chiefs without substantially altering the social relations of production in the Gaelic areas. However, despite their increased military power, the Gaelic chiefs never enjoyed absolute control over their own territories. If they were to attempt to impose a full-scale policy of Anglicisation on their territories, they ran the risk of being overthrown by a coalition of disgruntled clan members backed by the *filí* and the friars. Most chose instead to maintain some balance between tradition and loyalty to the government.

It seems likely that the frustration experienced by government officials (and the 'New English' elite who emerged around them) at the pace of reform encouraged them to seek alternative solutions to conciliation. More than that, in order to explain why there was so much resistance to the policies they proposed, they came to rely on a simple binary opposition – civility versus barbarity – to explain all their problems, an approach best exemplified by the work of Edmund Spenser. The insistence of the 'Old English' elite that the issues involved were a little more complex could be taken as further evidence that this elite had become so corrupted by their long stay in Ireland that they had become part of the problem (Bradshaw, 1998).

As this colonial mindset became more accentuated in the last decades of the sixteenth century, it came to influence the way in which the religious issue was perceived. If the Irish were barbarous so too was their language, and it would not only be futile but blasphemous to seek to spread the Holy Word through a barbaric tongue. The isolation of the 'New English' elite encouraged them to emphasise the distinctiveness of their religious beliefs and the Calvinist notion of a saved elect, surrounded by heathens, seemed an attractive doctrine. From the accession of Elizabeth the government began to pursue a policy of penalising dissenters and excluding them from public office. The strategy of coercion widened the scope of opposition, turning neutrality and indifference into enmity.

The international conflict between Protestant and Catholic Europe, and the hardening of 'New English' attitudes, placed the Gaelic chiefs in a precarious position. Their balancing act between upholding Gaelic custom and giving allegiance to English authority was becoming unsustainable. The rising power of Counter-Reformation Spain – their armies dwarfed Elizabethan England's – did however offer new opportunities and a way of escaping the trap they were in. The Nine Years War (1594–1603) was the culmination of decades of Gaelic resistance to Elizabethan policy. Triggered by a revolt of the leading northern chieftains, it rapidly became an island-wide insurrection against Tudor rule. The unification of the perennially fragmented Gaelic forces was only one index of the changed context. The scale of the confrontation was another. The northern chiefs mobilised the largest armies ever fielded by Gaelic insurgents, while the English forces which ultimately defeated them were also the largest of Elizabeth's reign (Anderson, 1974b; Lennon, 1994).

If the Nine Years War occurred against a background of a more general European conflict, it also showed the extent to which Ireland had itself become drawn into this wider European political theatre. Not only were continental (Spanish) troops involved in the Irish fighting, the themes of the European conflict fused with the native ones. One of the demands of the northern chiefs was for freedom of conscience, the same demand raised by the Dutch rebels against Spain (Morgan, 1993). These new motifs enabled the Gael to transcend their narrow clan perspectives. The two key purveyors of literacy in Gaelic Ireland – the poets and the friars – appear to have played a crucial role in the mobilisation of Gaelic Ireland against the new order.

One of the most striking features of the Nine Years War was the role played by the towns. Traditionally the English state's most loyal allies, during this period they sold arms to the Gaelic insurgents, and on news of Elizabeth's death in 1603, they rose in celebration. While this revolt was easily suppressed, the damage was done; the 'Old English' community would never again be the loyal ally of the English state.

It has been argued here that the persistence of a distinctive Gaelic order in Ireland represented a significant obstacle to Tudor attempts to incorporate the island into an extended English state system. Yet a similar type of social organisation also existed in other parts of the Atlantic Isles, specifically in Gaelic Scotland and Wales, but attempts to incorporate these regions in the Renaissance era did not produce anything like the same level of conflict as in Ireland. The rest of chapter will attempt to explain their divergent paths.

All parts of the Atlantic Isles were affected by the wave of expansion of the seigniorial feudal order that began in the second millennium, spearheaded by French-speaking knights and guided by the Latin Christian Church. However, the impact of this expansionary wave was uneven and the different regions developed in distinctive ways.

The contrast here is not a simple one, between the English 'core' and the Celtic 'periphery'. While elements of a core/periphery spatial dichotomy undoubtedly existed within the archipelago, such dichotomies also existed within the four countries. Even more crucially, there was no uniformity of experience binding Scotland, Wales and Ireland. Conflicts and contrasts certainly existed within each, but they shaped up very differently. Moreover, they shaped up in such a way that no alliance of sentiment or politics between the peripheral nations emerged in the early modern period. More often than not, they found themselves in opposite camps.

Wales

While Welsh and Gaelic are part of the same Celtic linguistic family, the differences between them were much too great to permit mutual comprehension. Indeed until modern linguists discovered their common roots, there was no collective memory of a shared heritage.

Despite the language gap, there were significant similarities between the two societies. In the words of one scholar, in both one finds:

> predominantly (though not exclusively) pastoral societies, a
> pattern of non-nucleated settlements, low populations, extensive

lordship (royal and/or seigniorial according to our designations), intensive kinship rights in land and in law, small scale and unstable patterns of political power and loyalties and very limited opportunities for the wealth accumulation, economic mobility and social differentiation already characteristic of lowland England. (Davies, 2001, p. 174)

The Welsh literate tradition, like the Irish, originated in the Christian Church. From the early Middle Ages there were close connections between the Churches in Ireland and western Britain. Alongside the Christian clerics, there was an educated lay stratum who upheld an indigenous tradition of learning – in the Gaelic world the *seanchas*, in Wales the *cyfarwydyd*. The poets and lawyers of Wales, like their Irish counterparts, enjoyed high social prestige. In both cultures, learning ran in families. There are far fewer texts in Welsh from the early medieval period than in Irish. Wales, unlike Ireland, had been part of the Roman Empire; perhaps because of this the vernacular may have been held in lower regard by the Christian scholars who introduced both societies to literacy (Pryce, 1998).

Wales, like Ireland, was subject to colonisation attempts by Anglo-French knights in the 'high' Middle Ages. Colonisation began earlier in Wales, from the end of the eleventh century. As in Ireland, colonisation was a piecemeal process, meeting considerable resistance and only being secured in the late thirteenth century by the armies of Edward I. The Edwardian conquest did not, however, eliminate the Welsh literate tradition. On the contrary, in the fourteenth century Wales experienced something of a cultural renaissance (Davies, 1987).

Law occupied a central role in the Welsh literate tradition, as it did in the Irish. The most comprehensive collections of Welsh law date from the fourteenth and fifteenth centuries. The persistence of a living Welsh legal tradition *after* the Edwardian conquest points to one of the most striking contrasts between late-medieval Wales and Ireland, and one which arguably had momentous consequences for both societies.

From the point of view of the English conquerors, Welsh law was every bit as objectionable as Irish law; indeed, their objections to both were very similar. Notions of kinship pervaded both Welsh and Gaelic legal systems. In both systems, the emphasis was on compensation for victims or their relatives, rather than on punishment for wrongdoers; the extended families of wrongdoers were obliged to compensate the injured parties. Arbitration between the conflicting parties rather than top-down judgements was the order of the day. From the point of view of the English administration such laws were a recipe for endless disorder because miscreants would never be properly punished, nor royal authority hold full sway (Davies, 1987).

In the Statute for Wales promulgated in 1284, shortly after the conquest, Edward I prohibited the use of compensatory payments for theft, robbery or violent crime. These were felonies and must be tried by English criminal law, with the appropriate punishment of death or mutilation being meted out to those convicted. However, the Statute for Wales did not proscribe the use of Welsh civil law. Traditional procedures could still be used in cases relating to land inheritance and pleas concerning movables. Land would be divided between all the legitimate sons, not passed on through primogeniture. Post-conquest Wales then came to have a composite legal system, with English criminal law and Welsh civil law functioning alongside one another. This hybrid legal order was replicated across other areas of post-conquest Welsh life (Davies, 1987).

The native Welsh, unlike the native Irish, were not excluded from royal law. Nor were they excluded from participating in government service, though the higher government posts in Wales were reserved for English officials. Within Wales, a wide gulf separated the Welsh and the English settler communities. They were often treated differently for administrative purposes, paid different forms of tribute or rent, and were treated separately for legal purposes, often in separate courts. The Welsh Church was brought under the control of Canterbury, and while Welsh churchmen were usually excluded from high office, there was no formal segregation of Welsh and Anglo-French clerics. The Edwardian conquest of Wales was not accompanied by any systematic programme of disinheritance. While the princely lineages and their allies had their properties seized, many Welsh noble families kept their land (Williams, 1989).

The fourteenth century has gone down in history, across Europe if not beyond, as a calamitous century characterised by plague, wars and insurrection. In Wales, peculiarly, it was a century of peace, during which a new social configuration emerged. Prior to the Act of Union in 1536 Wales, though ruled by the English monarch, was administered separately from England. Most of Wales was fragmented into forty or so 'Marcher' lordships. Within each of these lordships the power of the lord was unqualified, but that power did not extend beyond the boundary of the lordship. Wales had no common jurisdictional authority, no unified legal code, and no Parliament. Within the different lordships, different mixtures of English and Welsh law operated (Davies, 1987).

In the fourteenth and fifteenth centuries many, if not most, of these lords were absentee. Though profiting handsomely from their Welsh possessions, they were not present to exercise their power as lords. That role increasingly fell to Welsh intermediaries. This intermediary stratum, descended from old Welsh lineages, came to play a central role in the political and social life of post-conquest Wales. Each of these 'barons' or 'squires' had their own *plaid* (armed retinue) to impose their lord's authority upon their area (Davies, 1987).

This buffer role played by the Welsh elite was all the more important in the fourteenth century as the generalised demographic collapse that followed the Black Death weakened the bargaining power of the lords across the archipelago. Unable to prevent peasant flight, the manorial system in the South Wales lowlands fell apart and with it the institution of serfdom or villeinage. The Welsh from the hills began to reclaim the lowlands, bringing with them their cattle and their customs. With their understanding of Welsh traditions, the native elite was in a much better position to maintain social peace in the Welsh countryside (Davies, 1987).

The Welsh elite did not act merely as social and political intermediaries between English power and the Welsh community, but also as cultural intermediaries. These centuries saw a significant expansion in the use of writing and in basic literacy within Wales. To fulfil their function as managers of the English lordships – whether royal or seigniorial – the Welsh elite needed to acquire knowledge of reading and writing for legal and administrative purposes. The elite as a whole, rather than specialised sections of it, began to read and write. Titles, charters, privileges and agreements of all sorts came to be recorded in writing. These affected not only the upper layers of society, but also the population as a whole (Davies, 1987; Smith, 1998).

Though the old bardic order was silenced in the years directly following the Edwardian conquest, the fourteenth century saw a resurgence of Welsh writing. New rules of Welsh poetic practice were laid down, and a rich body of poetry produced, freed from the narrow concerns and regulations of the bardic schools. Among Welsh scholars, the fourteenth century is regarded as the great age of Welsh poetry. Important developments also occurred in Welsh prose. The old tradition of Welsh sagas was replaced by translations from Latin, French and English, not only of narrative but also of religious, legal and technical works (Davies, 1987).

Essential to the Welsh literary renaissance was the patronage of the new Welsh elite. They were in a position to give material support to the renascent intelligentsia, and in return won the praise of the poets for their generosity and for their commitment to the traditions of Welsh culture. However, even as they encouraged the writing down of Welsh legal and other traditions, the Welsh squirearchy was discovering the value of English law to the consolidation of their class position (Davies, 1993).

Over the course of the late Middle Ages there was increasing intermarriage between elite families of English and Welsh origins. Each began to borrow the others' customs and legal practice though 'it would appear that the Anglicisation of the Welsh was greater than the cymricisation of the English' (Davies, 1993, p. 209). English legal practice encouraged the consolidation of individual land holdings and facilitated the alienation and sale of land. Having acquired their estates by the Welsh practice of *pride* the Welsh elite then secured them by switching to English land tenure, backed up by charters and written records. What was happening was not merely the Anglicisation of the Welsh elite, but its 'gentrification', to use the word in its literal sense. Alongside the adoption of English legal practices of land holding, the Welsh gentry began to dwell in a new style of housing (Davies, 1987; Smith, 1998).

These developments greatly influenced their response to the Tudor reorganisation of government, and flowing from that, their response to the Reformation.

It is not difficult to understand the approval of the gentry. What they sought was the opportunity to build up their estates unhindered, to be free from the interference of English officials, to become masters of local government in Wales and to be assured that the Penal Code was a dead letter ... they were all achieved under the Tudors. When that dynasty came to an end in 1603, the Welsh gentry were firmly in place as the ruling class of Wales ... It was not a matter of the Tudors identifying themselves with the Welsh, but rather of the Welsh identifying themselves with the Tudors. (Davies, 1993, p. 219)

While the initial response to the Reformation was tepid – and fairly hostile during Edward's reign – over the course of the Elizabethan era Wales came to adopt the Reformation as its own. Welsh religious reformers stressed that the Reformation involved a reversion to the pristine Christian spirit which existed in Wales before the Anglo-French invasion. Roman domination represented a breach with this tradition, which could now be restored under the stewardship of a Welsh dynasty. The Welsh poets played a significant role in this 'cymricisation' of the Reformation. Welsh translations of the prayer books and the New Testament were produced in the 1560s, and a complete Welsh translation of the Bible was produced later in the century (Bradshaw, 1998; Davies, 1993; Williams, 1989).

The translation of the Bible into Welsh had a long-term significance for the survival of the Welsh language. While the gentry in Wales would become increasingly anglicised over the next two centuries, the central role of the Bible in Welsh culture would ensure that a tradition of Welsh literacy would develop which was significantly broader than that prevailing with either Irish or Scottish Gaelic. This tradition of popular literacy would in turn consolidate the position of the Welsh language down into the modern era (Davies, 2000).

Wales entered the modern era then, with two languages of mass literacy. In the Welsh language there existed a popular – largely poetic and religious – literate tradition, while English was the language of both official and elite literacy. In the centuries following the Union, two languages and two associated patterns of literacy would coexist in Wales: an 'official' one associated with commerce and power and a 'popular' one associated with religion, poetry and song. The former was of course dominant but it was delimited by the demotic tradition. Together they would define the manner of Wales' incorporation into the British polity: subaltern but forever recalcitrant.

Scotland

In the age of 'high' feudalism – the twelfth and thirteenth centuries – Ireland and Scotland showed some remarkable similarities. A mainly lowland region characterised by a manorial economy and a seigniorial social order coexisted somewhat uneasily with a mainly upland Gaelic-speaking region where a clannic social order and a pastoralist economy survived.

Literacy in both countries, and in both regions of the two countries, was very much a restricted affair. A few centuries later the contrast between Ireland and Scotland could hardly have been greater. In Scotland a wide level of literacy would provide a social and intellectual context within which the Reformation could flourish. Moreover, it would do so primarily through the medium of the English language. Whereas in Ireland resistance to both the Reformation and Anglicisation resulted in calamitous warfare, in

Scotland opposition was muted and the Gaelic region was largely absorbed into the new order.

The contrast between a seigniorial/manorial core and a clannic/pastoralist periphery was certainly a defining social characteristic of both Scotland and Ireland in the high Middle Ages. Crucially though, the relationship between core and periphery was very different in the two countries. Scotland had its own monarchy, based in the Lowland region, which could lay claim not merely to *kingship over* the Highlands and Islands, but to *kinship with* their Gaelic-speaking population (Barrow, 1981).

Scotland, like Ireland and Wales, was largely transformed by the arrival of the Anglo-French warrior aristocracy in the eleventh and twelfth centuries. In Scotland the Anglo-French knights were invited in by the Scottish king; they did not invade. Strictly speaking, the Anglo-French knights were also invited into Ireland by the king of Leinster to assist him in an inter-dynastic dispute. However, the power of the Anglo-French compared to the Leinster Gaelic forces was such that they quickly assumed control. In Scotland, powerful though the Anglo-French knights might have been, they were always subordinate to the Scottish king. The Scottish Gaelic rulers' prescience in seeking to assimilate the Anglo-French to their interests may have been due to their closer proximity to England. The first Scottish king to develop this alliance, David I, had been fostered in England and was able to see for himself the material benefits of the seigniorial system (Barrow, 1981; Whyte, 1995a).

Whatever the reasons for this difference, the Scottish kings were able to use the power of the Anglo-French knights to construct a monarchical state. As crucial as their arms were their organisational abilities. The arrival of feudal knights into Scotland was accompanied by a greatly increased use of 'pragmatic' documents – charters, diplomas and brieves – issuing instructions to the king's subjects and recording information on inheritance and disposal of property. By the middle of the twelfth century, the Scottish crown had come to use writing routinely for recording significant information and communications. Over the following century, the pragmatic use of writing had become commonplace among the higher Scottish nobility. By 1300 writing was found further down the social hierarchy, beginning with grants of land and followed later by 'bonds' – contracts between individuals and groups (Barrow, 1997).

The language of this new pragmatic literacy was, overwhelmingly, Latin. As the language of the Church, and all professional writers in this period were recruited from the ranks of the clergy, Latin was the obvious script. The use of Latin for official writing had another positive function here: it provided a *lingua franca* to overcome the linguistic fragmentation of medieval Scotland (Barrow, 1997).

Northern Scotland was part of the kingdom of Norway for much of the medieval era, and Norse continued to be spoken in the Shetland and Orkney Islands until the late Middle Ages. Gaelic was the language not only of the Highlands and western Isles but was also spoken across much of Lowland Scotland in the thirteenth century and later. Two other Celtic languages were also spoken in medieval Scotland, Pictish and, in the southwest of Scotland, a language akin to Welsh. In Lothian, in the east Lowlands of Scotland, a Germanic dialect similar to English was spoken. Added to this linguistic mixture was French, which by the twelfth century had become the principal vernacular among the Lowland aristocracy (Forsyth, 1998; Muirson, 1974; Price, 2000).

Two centuries later, the linguistic picture in Scotland had simplified itself. French, which had never been widely used as a written language, was also disappearing as a spoken one. A contemporary observer noted:

> The manners and customs of the Scots vary with the diversity of their speech, for two languages are spoken among them, the Scottish and the Teutonic, the later of which is the language of those who occupy the seaboard and the plains, while the race of Scottish speech inhabits the highlands and the outlying islands. (Quoted in Muirson, 1974, p. 76)

This Highlands/Lowlands dichotomy, already evident in the late fourteenth century, would become much more pronounced by the sixteenth. Yet while the Gaelic regions would be overwhelmed in the early modern era, in medieval times no such radical opposition existed. The Gaelic language did not have specific words for either 'Highlands' or 'Lowlands'. Gaelic continued to be one of the languages spoken at court in the twelfth and thirteenth centuries. Multilingualism seems to have been common in medieval Scotland, at least among the elite (Dawson, 1998; Muirson, 1974).

Most important of all perhaps, and in sharp contrast to Ireland, there was no *legal* discrimination against the Gaelic language or people of Gaelic descent in medieval Scotland. People could shift from one to the other and be comfortable in both. The Celtic elite of the Lowlands – except for those opposing the Crown – was not eliminated; rather, they fused with the newcomers into a unified aristocracy. The Scottish monarchy could assert its Gaelic ancestry while in practice tilting towards first French and then 'Inglis', as Scots-English was referred to (Grant & Stringer, 1995).

The towns, or 'burghs', appear to have played a central role in the rise of 'Inglis'. Most of the early burghs were 'on land belonging to the Crown, enjoyed royal protection and had certainly or probably been founded by kings' (Barrow, 1981, p. 87). The patronage offered by the monarchy to the towns was based primarily on the resources that could be made available. Urban development could, through trade, increase the value of the agricultural surplus or, perhaps more importantly, 'monetise' it and in the process magnify royal power. Writing came to be used for keeping records of surplus extraction and trade in these centres. As the feudal order spread across lowland and eastern Scotland, towns came to proliferate, encouraged not only by the Crown but also by local seigniorial lords, conscious themselves of their economic value. Given the Gaelic aversion to urban life, Scottish towns drew on the 'Inglis' speakers of Lothian for their population, and with the spread of urban centres, the language of Lothian spread too (Barrow, 1981; Muirson, 1974).

In the twelfth and thirteenth centuries, the seigniorial order expanded in Scotland, as elsewhere in Europe, with tillage agriculture pushing the boundaries of arable land. Scotland was likewise hit by the fourteenth-century crisis, though detailed evidence of economic conditions appears limited. Nonetheless, there was a clear contraction of the manorial order: demesne farming disappeared and serfdom collapsed. The historian Keith Grant has noted a certain similarity between the contraction of the Scottish core and the situation of the Irish Pale, but also a crucial difference. The Scottish core region was never as fragile as the Pale. The existence of an autonomous Scottish monarchy may have been crucial here (Grant, 2000).

A Scottish legal system grew up alongside the Scottish Crown. Scottish law was heavily influenced by the Anglo-French influx and by a more general borrowing from English law. It was developed, like its English counterpart, from the practice of the court. In the thirteenth century, Scottish jurists regarded themselves as sharing a common law with the English. Yet the two legal systems were not identical; some elements of Celtic law survived for centuries. On the key issue of land inheritance, however, primogeniture had become the norm in Scotland by the late thirteenth century (Sellar, 1989).

The royal government had encouraged the 'stabilisation of norms' regarding land use precisely because it helped to secure the status quo and minimise disorder. This involved interventions within lordships to uphold law. One effect of this was to establish relations between the local community (of landholders) and the royal government, bypassing the local lords. Written legal documents came to be considered as better witnesses because they had a longer purchase, while the idea of 'ownership' encouraged the notion that land could be a commodity. The Scottish monarchy, however, lacked the resources of their English counterparts. In England, a distinct legal profession had come into existence before the end of the thirteenth century; there are no signs of this happening in Scotland before the fifteenth century (MacQueen, 1995; Sellar, 1988).

In Wales, the Edwardian conquest inaugurated a legal order whereby English criminal law was imposed, but the Welsh were allowed to maintain their own civil law. In Scotland, the reverse seems to have occurred. English or Anglo-French civil law was introduced by a Gaelic monarchy, but older traditions of criminal law persisted for centuries. The principles of 'blood feud' and compensation for criminal injury continued not only in the Highlands but also in Lowland Scotland up until the late sixteenth century. The survival of a system of private justice might have been viewed as an implicit challenge to the system of royal justice, but the Crown's response was not to prohibit it, but rather to take its share of the compensatory payment. It certainly reflected the administrative and financial weakness of the Crown, and the enduring strength of kinship ties (Wormald, 1980).

The weakness of the Scottish state was not simply the product of aristocratic hostility to royal power. The Scottish magnates were not seeking to subvert the Scottish monarchy; rather, they viewed the kingship as a focal point holding Scotland together. They resorted to systems of private justice because royal justice was unable to provide them with protection (Wormald, 1985).

The weakness of the Scottish Crown in the late medieval period was in large measure due to the effects of warfare in the fourteenth century. If the fourteenth century gave Wales its long era of peace, and Ireland its Gaelic revival, it gave Scotland its 'Wars of Independence'. The generalised crisis of the feudal order in the fourteenth century took its toll on Scotland, but it tends to be overshadowed by these wars. From another perspective though, the 'Wars of Independence' can be seen as an aspect of the general crisis. The English monarchy, its home resources depleted by the agrarian crisis, needed to expand its territorial base to make up the shortfall. The Scottish feudal aristocracy, closely allied to France, proved capable of successfully resisting the English kingdom's efforts at expansion. Scottish military resistance to English expansion was not confined to the warrior aristocracy. Keith Grant argues that it was 'essentially a "people's war", fought primarily by the wealthier peasantry. Its leadership, however, was aristocratic'. The key role played by the wealthier Lowlands peasantry in the Wars of Independence had important long-term consequences for Scottish development (Grant, 2000, p. 350).

The Scottish Reformation

Religious division and war dominated Europe in the sixteenth and seventeenth centuries. The religious movements of the period, the Reformation and the Counter-Reformation, were to have a huge impact on the spread of literacy, and on much else besides. In Lowland Scotland, like in the Irish Pale, the initial reception given to the Reformation was less than decisive. Protestant zealots, while more numerous in Scotland than in Ireland, were very much a minority; so too were upholders of the Roman Church. But by the turn of the seventeenth century the population of Scotland was firmly on the side of the Reformation and the population of Ireland firmly against it. How can this difference be accounted for?

If the Reformation is seen as a decisive contributor to the diffusion of literacy, it is also the case that the Reformation itself would have been inconceivable without an earlier base of a literate laity. It is not necessary to exaggerate here. It is true that visual imagery played an important part in the spread of Reformation propaganda in Germany; it is also true that the Counter-Reformation drive significantly increased levels of literacy in Catholic countries and regions. Nonetheless, it was the phenomenon of huge numbers of lay people reading the sacred scriptures for themselves that truly transformed the Western Christian Church.

Here we see a decisive difference between Lowland Scotland and the Irish Pale. Despite the weaknesses of the Scottish state, written contracts had become quite widespread. A significant section of the peasantry – albeit a minority – had written leases for their landholdings and it seems reasonable to conclude that a certain level of basic literacy would have become important for them. Among the lairds – the lower landowners – literacy seems to have been widespread at least since the fifteenth century (Whyte, 1995a).

Through 'feu farming', land exchange was circumventing feudal restraints and becoming a matter for commerce; written records of these transactions needed to be preserved. The lairds, as the main beneficiaries of these transactions, needed at least to be able to read. In the Irish Pale by contrast, landholding tended to be on a customary basis, and there is little to indicate that literacy had permeated downwards in the late medieval era (Robertson, 1977; Whyte, 1997).

This process of commercialisation had become more pronounced by the sixteenth century when Scottish society,

> becoming more literate, better educated, began to turn its attention away from the amateur to the professional. The so-called 'Education Act' of 1496 which directed eldest sons of landowners to learn 'perfyte Latyne' and then study law was an early attempt to provide the local courts with judges with a training which enabled them to do more than apply common-sense rules. A century later there was a clear distinction between the school- and university-educated lairds who rose in government, administration and the law, and those who remained in the relative isolation of their estates. (Wormald, 1980, pp. 90–1)

No less important than a level of literacy was the language in which literacy was delivered. The Reformation sought to bring the spirit of religion back into the lives of the people. To do this the Christian message had to be delivered in a language the people understood. Latin could not do that. Luther's decisive achievement in Germany was the publication of printed German translations of the Bible. For a long period after, Luther's Bible was the best selling book in Germany. The effect of Luther's Bible was not merely to consolidate Protestantism in Germany; it was also crucial in establishing a standard written German (Scribner et al, 1994).

In Scotland, the message came in 'standard English', not in 'Scots'. The differences between 'standard English' and 'Scots' were probably not much greater than those between the various dialects of sixteenth-century German. They were certainly sufficiently close to enable Lowland Scots readers to understand what they were reading. By contrast, to a monoglot Gaelic speaker in Ireland or Scotland, English (or Scots) would have been wholly incomprehensible.

Wherever the Reformation was successful, it would seem that cities – the centres of commerce and administration – played a leading role. The cities were not, however, in a position to impose the Reformation on a hostile countryside. To do so would have been to court isolation and defeat. The demographic weight of pre-modern Europe was overwhelmingly rural. For the Reformation to succeed it needed allies in the countryside, preferably among the elite. The Scottish nobility for the most part supported the Reformation. Concerns they might have had about disturbing traditional religious practices were no doubt eased by the sharing out of monastic lands among them (unlike in Ireland, where the government gave most of the monastic lands to English settlers) (Goodcare, 1994; Whyte, 1997).

There was no question of Protestantism being imposed from the outside on Scotland. On the contrary, the Reformers were able to use resentment towards French dominance at court to buttress their case. Moreover while the Reformers relied on English religious scripts and on English military aid to secure their victory, they were certainly not imposing English religious orthodoxy on the Scottish population. Quite the contrary. The Scottish Reformation took its message from the French world. Geneva, Calvin's base, while politically part of the Swiss Confederation, was linguistically and culturally part of France. It was in France that Calvin's adherents would fight and lose one of the great battles of the Reformation. Despite its use of 'standard English', the Scottish Reformation was unquestionably Scottish, and once it achieved dominance, it was immeasurably strengthened by patriotic sentiment (Goodcare, 1994; Whyte, 1997).

It is generally accepted that the Reformation expressed a more individualistic approach to religious belief. The individual's direct relationship to God, unmediated by cleric, saint, ritual or imagery was central to the Protestant message, or at least to its Calvinist variant that Scotland embraced. It seems paradoxical then that this individualist message should have had such an impact in a society where urban development and a money economy were still quite limited, and where kinship and lordship were still quite powerful. This paradox may have been the secret of Calvinism's success in Scotland. The Reformation in Scotland involved a good deal more than the elimination of one Church and its replacement by another. Rather, these events themselves initiated a cultural and social process which transformed Scotland. The very extremism of Calvinism may have been its attraction.

The strongest support for the Reformation in Scotland came from the lairds, Scotland's equivalent to the English gentry. Already largely literate by the fifteenth century, they were open to influences coming through the towns. The lairds played a major role in the new church assemblies – the kirks – which sought to impose a collective puritanical discipline on their local communities. As leading literate laymen, the lairds' opinion carried great weight and the kirks gave them considerable power over their local communities.

> Calvinist emphasis on discipline, imposed in Scotland by a hierarchy of church courts, from the kirk session at parish level to the general assembly at national level, did cut across the traditional social hierarchy; for it was the lairds and burgesses, not the nobles, who sat on local church courts, so that the nobility was now at least in theory, subject to discipline by their social inferiors. (Wormald, 1980, p. 94)

The Scottish Reformation appears to have compensated for the weakness of the Scottish state by introducing a locally imposed culture of restraint, and empowering a social agency with the power to enforce it: the lairds and the burgesses. Despite its individualistic theology, Scottish Calvinism did not seek to undermine social authority or cohesion but rather to impose a more powerful form than that offered by the traditional nexus of lordship and kinship (Goodcare, 1994; Whyte, 1997; Wormald, 1980).

Education was to play a key role in this process. Towards the end of the fifteenth century, parliament had passed an act encouraging the education of the nobility. A century later the educational ambitions of the Scottish state had expanded sufficiently to include a project for the provision of education in every parish, though the full implementation of this programme would take a good deal longer. The driving force behind the educational programme was religious in motivation: the scriptures should be accessible to all. Saving one's soul had social repercussions, of course: the God-fearing lived orderly lives (Whyte, 1997).

Whatever difficulties Calvinism faced in the Lowlands, these were minor compared to the barriers that confronted it in the Gaelic-speaking Highlands and Islands. Literacy levels were very low in the Gaelic areas, and the language obstacle further widened the gulf between the Lowland reformers and their potential audience. Settlement patterns increased the difficulties. There were no towns worth speaking of and most of the churches had been built, quite deliberately, in the most remote of places. Kinship was pervasive. Gaelic spiritual beliefs bordered on the polytheistic; spirits abounded, some good, some bad, and their strongest orthodox religious attachment was to their saints. Traditional customs were also at variance with the austerity of the Calvinist ethos; the Gaelic communities extolled generosity and largesse and despised frugality (Dawson, 1994).

The scale of these obstacles makes the success of Calvinism in the Scottish Gaidhealtachd all the more impressive. By the 1620s when Irish Franciscan friars arrived in the 'Highland and Island' region of Scotland on a mission to win over Gaelic Scotland to the Catholic cause, they discovered Protestantism to be so entrenched that the battle was in effect already lost (Bradshaw, 1998).

Behind the contrasting fates of the Reformation in Gaelic Scotland and Gaelic Ireland lay the wider political context of their societies. There had been no *legal* discrimination against the Gaelic community in Scotland. Much of the Scottish Gaelic elite seems to have been at home in both worlds. In the fractious world of Scottish Gaeldom, it suited many of the Gaelic elite to maintain close relations with the monarchy and with the commerce and society of Edinburgh. 'There is no sense that the Highlanders were outside the national community' (Grant, 1988, p. 120). Scottish Gaeldom combined cultural unity with the Irish Gaelic world and political allegiance to the Scottish monarchy. There seems to have been no discrimination against the Gael within the medieval Scottish Church, and as a result there was not the same need for the Observant orders of friars in Gaelic Scotland, as there had been in Ireland. Finally, the process of social transformation from a clannic society occurred more gradually in Scotland than in Ireland. It seems to have begun earlier under the influence of the Scottish monarchy, and was not finally completed until the eighteenth century.

The most powerful Gaelic sept in the late medieval period were the McDonalds, who dominated the Hebrides, but it was the Campbells, controlling Argyll, who occupied the most strategically important area at the border between the Highlands and Lowlands in the west of Scotland. Their politics and culture mirrored their frontier position: the earls of Argyll were careful to maintain the institutions of Gaelic literacy, not least the loyalty of the poets, while also retaining strong links to the Scottish monarchy (Dawson, 1994; MacCraith, 1995).

The support of the Duke of Argyll, head of clan Campbell, was essential for the success of the Protestant cause. Argyll encouraged the publication in 1567 of the *Foirm na n-Urruidheadh*, a Gaelic translation of the *Book of Common Order*, the first printed work in Gaelic. Its use of 'Classical Common Gaelic' rather than the 'Scottish Vernacular' would suggest that it was intended for dissemination not only in Scotland but also in Ireland. In the event, Calvinism made little headway in Gaelic Ireland, and it would be another century before a Gaelic translation of the full Bible was published. A Scottish Gaelic translation was not produced until 1801 (Dawson, 1994; MacCraith, 1995).

In the Middle Ages, Latin had been the language of government in the Highlands, but by the sixteenth century it was being displaced by Scots-English. Being literate in the three languages became imperative for members of the Gaelic learned stratum. It was these traditional learned orders who played the crucial role in the dissemination of Protestantism in the Scottish Gaidhealtachd. Most of the clerics in seventeenth century Argyll came from the traditional learned families. As well as their multi-lingual skills, they were also able to combine the vernacular and the literary variants of Gaelic to memorise and orally transmit Calvinist beliefs. Poetry and song were widely employed. The parish was not regarded as the primary unit of church organisation, rather churchmen tailored their approach to local practices. Many services were held, as was customary, in the open air, and ministers travelled considerable distances to reach their flocks (Bannerman, 1983; Dawson, 1994; McCaughey, 1989).

Gaelic Calvinism did not only adopt traditional modes of communication, it also adapted its message to its local environment. Popular belief in supernatural activity was tolerated, though Catholic reverence for saints was repudiated. Likewise traditional funeral practices, including wakes, were acceptable to the Gaelic ministers, though the funeral service itself was altered. In the event, a distinctively Gaelic Calvinism proved short lived. The social and cultural transformation of the Scottish Lowlands, occasioned by the Reformation, also radically changed the relationship between the regions of Scotland: in effect it created the 'Highlands' as a distinct entity (Dawson, 1994).

Divergence between Highlands and Lowlands

In late medieval Scotland social practices in the different regions shaded into one another, rather than contrasted in black and white terms. However, by the sixteenth century social changes in 'Lowland' Scotland were sufficiently rapid to create an intensified sense of difference between it and Gaelic Scotland. It seems clear enough that the new structures of social control which emerged from the Reformation had the effect of accentuating the geographical and linguistic disparities. Jenny Wormald noted that 'with the decline of the bloodfeud in the lowlands went an increase of suspicion and hatred of the highlander" (Wormald, 1980, p. 97).

The Scottish Highlanders came to be seen as wild and barbaric in contrast to the orderly, God fearing and civilised Lowlanders. Endorsing the Reformation was not sufficient to ensure the Highlanders' place in the emerging national community. In a cultural landscape where the 'Highlands' came to be seen as a bastion of barbarism, the experiment of transmitting the Reformed doctrines and liturgy through Gaelic, had to be abandoned. A Scottish Gaelic Bible could not play the role of its Welsh equivalent as a harbinger of a popular literacy in the community's vernacular (Dawson, 1998).

England

The (Norman) French conquest of England in the eleventh century was mainly an aristocratic affair involving knights and clergy. The invaders brought with them a tight administrative system which had already been developed in the French kingdom. The new administrative cadre was recruited from the ranks of the clergy, and the language they wrote in was Latin. The first major fruits of this system were to be found in the *Domesday Book*, where the conquerors set out a detailed account of their new kingdom's resources. For William the Conqueror this served a double function: to assess the total social surplus available for distribution within the elite and the amount available to the monarchy (Britnell, 1996).

Literacy was of course central to religious practice and beliefs. It was from the ranks of the Church that the monarchy drew its administrative officials, while canon law heavily influenced the development of the wider legal system. Outside of the clergy literacy was very limited indeed, and literacy skills were not considered necessary for normal life, even by the nobility, very few of whom could read or write. In the centuries that followed, writing and literacy spread widely through English society.

Religion aside, three key areas of social practice have been identified as being associated with the use of writing in this era: law, administration and commerce. While apparently distinct, the three overlapped in a variety of ways. The 'commercial revolution' of the twelfth century, as it is sometimes called, was closely linked to changes in the social organisation of agriculture. Landlords began to manage their estates directly and to sell surplus produce in towns which, as well as acting as market centres, also became centres of craft production. With the development of manorial administration and urban commerce, the keeping of written records became much more widespread (Clanchy, 1993).

There were legal implications to these changes. Codes and regulations had to be drawn up: 'Estate management and the common law evolved in parallel: they came together here' (Hatcher, 1981, p. 30). As the thirteenth century progressed, tenants' obligations came to be defined more tightly by manorial officials drawing up tenants' rentals and customals (Hatcher, 1981).

The problem with customary agreements, and custom in general, was its tendency to freeze rents. The landlords were well aware that in an era of expanding population and production, and of rising prices, it made sense to abandon custom and increase their income by transferring land from villeinage into more profitable leaseholds or competitive tenancies at will. Many tenancies were converted from labour rents to monetary rents. The tenants for their part regarded this process as enfranchisement, though at least half the English peasantry remained unfree (Hatcher, 1981).

The demographic collapse of the mid-fourteenth century transformed the balance of power between landlords and peasants in England as elsewhere in Europe. It led to a sharp rise in the land/labour ratio with tenants in a position to force down rents and increasingly resist other forms of seigniorial exactions. Attempts by lords to retain unfree peasants on their manors by force proved ineffective. The Peasants Revolt of 1381, though a failure, was followed by a massive flight of peasants in England from conditions of unfreedom. Landlords were no longer in a position to preserve traditional patterns of authority: labour services were becoming difficult to impose. More and more, landlords' relations to their subordinates became governed by contract.

> The need to keep a written record of new contracts, in circumstances where long memory was no longer a guide to current terms of tenure was the main reason for the development of hereditary copyhold which developed in parallel with copyhold leases. ... On some manors the issuing of copies to customary tenants became the normal procedure. This practice carried even further the modification of customary relationships by record keeping. (Britnell, 1996, p. 222)

The diffusion of money and writing were closely linked because once customary traditions were broken – to be replaced by money rent – a written security of tenure became more necessary. By the same token the development of written contracts extinguished the social relationships of custom. While there were significant parallels between the process of 'literisation' and commercialisation, it would be mistaken to see one as simply a byproduct of the other. In the century following the Black Death, there was a significant decline in the level of 'commercialisation' as measured by a number of key indices. Agriculture seems to have become less market orientated, wage labour on the land reduced and the units of production had become smaller. Yet this period, which saw a decline in the levels of 'commercialisation' (as usually computed), also saw a crucial – arguably *the* crucial – expansion in the use of literacy. Land came to be rented out by means of *written contract*. This more widespread use of written contracts in the period occurred alongside the development of a growing differentiation within the English peasantry (Britnell, 1996; Byres, 2006; Hatcher, 1994).

The gradual diffusion of literacy was accompanied by a transformation in the patterns of social power. The weakened social power of landlords in relation to tenants in the period of demographic collapse following the Black Death was countered by the increasing centralisation of justice. With the collapse of serfdom, the English elite found themselves in a much weaker position in relation to the broader population; they needed to integrate them into a law-based system if the social order was to survive. The second half of the fourteenth century saw an enhanced power of local royal officials – the Justices of the Peace – and the increasing use of royal courts. While the Justices of the Peace were not paid officials, they were the local representatives of an increasingly professionalised legal system: it was in this period that a centrally organised legal profession emerged (Coss, 1995).

The Rise of English

In the context of the twelfth and thirteenth centuries, being literate primarily meant to be able to read or write Latin. Writing was distinct from, and rarer than, reading because of the difficulties involved in the use of parchment and quill. Because of the major role played by the Church in medieval life, some oral knowledge of Latin liturgy would have been quite widespread; and most likely some basic reading knowledge of Latin would also have been in existence, even among the peasantry (Clanchy, 1993).

Prior to 1300, neither (Middle) English nor French was sufficiently standardised or developed as a written language to be suitable for basic instruction in reading and writing. As the vernacular languages came to be written down more, English and French were in competition with each other for ascendancy, French initially being more popular with lawyers and government officials, English being used more for 'literary' purposes. French remained the language of court until the early fifteenth century but its decline is evident from a much earlier period (Baugh & Cable, 1993; McCrum et al, 1986; Price, 2000; Wolff, 1971).

Two crucial factors worked against French: the demographic weakness of the French speaking community and the persistent conflict between the English and French monarchies. The Norman-French conquest of England was essentially an aristocratic affair, involving military and clerical elites, but not – for the most part – any larger plebeian settlement. A manorial type economy already existed in much of Anglo-Saxon England; the Norman-French conquerors only needed to take control, not to establish it. The conquerors found themselves surrounded by English speakers, with whom many intermarried. While the wars against France encouraged a greater tolerance towards the use of the English language, French remained the language of prestige in late medieval England, as indeed it was across much of the rest of Europe. Even where English was becoming the 'mother' tongue, the children of the nobility were being instructed in French, and some of the Oxford colleges included in their statutes (in 1326 and 1340) a requirement that undergraduates converse in French and Latin. Despite these elitist measures, the functional requirement that the rulers be able to effectively communicate with those they ruled pressed home the case for English and from 1356 onwards the proceedings of the sheriffs court in London and Middlesex were held in English rather than in French (Baugh & Cable, 1993; McCrum et al, 1986; Price, 2000).

There is considerable debate among historians as to the extent of popular literacy in late medieval and early modern England (Cressy, 1980; Poos, 1991). The wider use of writing certainly created a situation where people would have different degrees of exposure to writing, and in consequence one finds shades of literacy and illiteracy (Goody & Watt, 1968). Despite the arguments about the *rate* of increase in levels of literacy (themselves reflecting problems with limited data and methodological issues about defining literacy) there seems little dispute that as the vernacular came to be more widely used for writing purposes, so literacy came to be more generalised among the population.

The crucial turning point here occurred in the 1430s when, from being an exception among written documents (the great bulk of which had been in Latin or French), English came to be widely used for official documents. The crucial institution in promoting this development was the Chancery, 'which alongside the closely allied Exchequer' comprised 'virtually all the national bureaucracy of England' (Price, 2000, p. 149). Because the Chancery was producing the greatest quantity of English texts, and because of its central position within the royal administration, it came to establish a *standard* written English. The establishment of England's first printing press in 1476 by William Caxton in Westminster greatly reinforced this standard, and contributed immeasurably to the spread of reading and writing (Price, 2000; Starkey, 1992).

Alongside the changed social and political landscape of late medieval England, English began to emerge as a literary language though Latin remained the prestigious language of scholarship into the era of the 'scientific revolution' in the seventeenth century. It is doubtful if Newton's path-breaking work in physics would have had the same impact if it had not been written in Latin.

The rulers of Renaissance England were acutely aware of the power of the written word, a power that went far beyond the simple transmission of messages. A widening band of literacy created dilemmas for them which could not easily be resolved. This was highlighted by the differences within the elite over the publication of the Bible in English in the early Reformation. The Archbishop of Canterbury stressed, in a preface to the 1540 Great Bible, that the scriptures should be read by all, rich and poor, men and women. Three years later an Act of Parliament sought to prevent the bulk of the population from direct access to the Holy Word. 'Reading the Bible was prohibited outright for women, artificers, journeymen, serving-men of the rank of yeoman and under, husbandmen and labourers; noblewomen and gentlewomen could read the Bible silently; only noblemen, gentlemen and merchants were permitted to read it aloud to others' (quoted in Sanders & Ferguson, 2002, p. 1).

Clearly direct access to the sacred scriptures by the lower orders was considered a threat to the social hierarchy. Such legislation of course proved impossible to police. This caution concerning popular access to the sacred texts proved to be percipient. In the seventeenth century the spread of literacy within the populace encouraged, or at least permitted, a multiplicity of interpretations of Christianity which led some currents of English society to draw upon their religious beliefs to question the legitimacy of all social hierarchies (Cressy, 1980; Hill, 1972).

The accumulation of these elements formed the essential background to what has been described as the 'educational revolution' of Renaissance England (Stone, 1964). New schools were created and existing ones enlarged. Literacy was no longer an optional extra for the upper strata, but an essential pre-requisite for social position. The transformation of social relations from ones of personal dependency (or personal inter-dependency) to ones mediated by the written word (and money) had the effect of transforming the very nature of social identity and power.

The integration of the elite into the state network was predicated on the emergence of a new mode of communication. This transformed not only the structure of the ruling class in England – the gentry became much more prominent – but also its self-conceptions. The shift from a predominantly military aristocracy to a predominantly civil one was accompanied by the formation of a new sense of collective identity. The reanimation of the classical tradition of learning in Renaissance Europe provided an alternative model of class, one more appropriate to the new environment. Gentlemanly virtue would best display itself through the effective wielding of the pen rather than the sword. Being cultured – being a bearer of civilised values – became a mark of high social position (Nauert, 1995).

The evolution of a reasonably stable polity in England – and its extension elsewhere – was closely linked to the development of its legal system. Not merely did the state enforce the rules, but the very belief that there were rules to be enforced, that some system of justice existed, provided a powerful vindication for the whole social order. Legitimacy in England came to be derived through the law. But for the law to be respected it needed to be broadly understood, and this could only be achieved through the vernacular language.

What was true of law was likewise true of culture: the audience was enlarged. 'The key figure of the English Renaissance in the fifteenth century was the same as that of the sixteenth: the amateur gentleman, who wrote in English, though he was inspired by Latin' (quoted in Starkey, 1992, p. 153). The newly cultured elite, especially the gentry, saw themselves not merely as rulers but as cultural leaders of society; a role magnified by the Reformation. However, this post-Renaissance mode of social power, powerful though it proved to be, was in some respects more porous. The greatest writer of the age, William Shakespeare, was of plebeian background with 'little Latin and less Greek'. Literacy and learning became potentially accessible to the lower classes. Whether this was a strength or a weakness of the new system of class power is debatable. In one definite respect though, it possessed a significant limitation: it could not be so easily transferred to other regions where a significantly different vernacular language pre-dominated.

The Social Origins of Conquest

This brief overview of developments in Scotland, Wales and England is intended to highlight their differences from the Irish trajectory. The contrasting paths taken by England and Ireland in the late Middle Ages were rooted in their divergent responses to the general crisis which the feudal social order experienced in the fourteenth century. In late medieval Ireland, two distinctive systems of social organisation operated, and the interaction between the two was crucial in shaping Ireland's historical trajectory. In Anglo-French Ireland, a seigniorial-manorial system existed very similar to that of England and much of the rest of Europe. In Gaelic Ireland, a clannic-pastoralist system persisted, similar to Wales and Gaelic Scotland. Both Anglo-French Ireland and England evolved along similar lines in the twelfth and thirteenth centuries, with commercial and urban development playing a key role. Both underwent a deep structural crisis from the end of the thirteenth century, a crisis that had its roots in the feudal order reaching its technical and ecological limits. While both the Irish and English responses were specific, they form part of a much wider pattern of European societies engaging with a systemic crisis whose outcomes would have deep and long-term historical consequences.

One of the key distinguishing features between England and Ireland in that period lay in the social character of the Norman-French conquest. In England the colonisers were mainly aristocratic; in Ireland the colonisers included a substantial popular element. The divide between native and settler popular communities was an important element in the structuring of power in Anglo-French Ireland and it impacted on the way the fourteenth-century crisis was experienced there. The indigenous population – with few exceptions – had been subjected to serfdom and were excluded from royal law. Legal and 'ethnic' distinctions overlapped, but it is clear that the 'ethnic' was not an absolute; in the late medieval period ethnic identities were being transformed across much of Ireland. The survival of a clannic-pastoralist order at the margins of the seigniorial system was another key feature that distinguished 'high' medieval Ireland from England in that period. These two elements together ensured that the outcomes to the fourteenth-century crisis would be very different in the two countries. In the case of Ireland the fourteenth-century crisis resulted in the reinvigoration of the

Gaelic social order, which by the fifteenth century had come to dominate most of Ireland.

In Anglo-French Ireland a system of government and social organisation was introduced, modelled on that of England. The chief lords or kings issued charters of land to their followers, which in turn provided the basis for tribute/revenue or military support or both. They needed people to work the land of course, but once an agricultural system was in place the lords had the upper hand, because if peasants left their plots of land they could not easily bring the crops with them. This pattern of power at the micro level of society established the contours within which a concentration of power at a higher and wider level could develop. Selling on the agricultural surplus became an important form of revenue, and this encouraged the growth of towns which developed their own commercial practices of literacy. The early literate practices of Anglo-French Ireland were very similar to those of England. Latin was the major language of literacy, followed by French. While English was widely spoken in thirteenth-century Ireland, it was rarely written. By the time English came to be used as the official written language of government, it was hardly spoken at all in Ireland outside of the towns, and even there it seems that the poorer inhabitants were Irish speaking. This linguistic transformation was a product of the fourteenth-century crisis that saw the English colony decimated. Faced with increased seigniorial exactions, and structural collapse, most of the English-speaking population of the countryside either fled Ireland or became gaelicised. The English-speaking towns also witnessed major demographic decline. The position of the indigenous population was strengthened in the wake of the fourteenth-century crisis, but because they were excluded from royal law, they had no need to acquire knowledge of pragmatic literacy; they operated instead within practices of customary law. So at the very time that a vernacular literacy began to spread in England, English itself was little spoken in Ireland and literacy remained highly restrictive.

Cultural forms in late medieval Gaelic Ireland were closely related to structures of social organisation. A characteristic feature of virtually all cultural forms in Gaelic Ireland was their preoccupation with the past, or with maintaining a sense of continuity with the past, which placed the Gaelic world at odds with the emerging Renaissance culture characterised by a new sense of time. This pervasive stress on continuity with the past makes sense in a context where institutions of power were weak and central authorities absent; in such a context, tradition was crucial for legitimating all operations of power. The weakness of Gaelic rulers was closely linked to the problems involved with surplus extraction. There was very little room here for the intensification of labour that characterised the feudal order. Herders could depart from the *tuath* with their wealth (cattle); for the Gaelic chiefs to pronounce against such flight carried little weight because they lacked the power to enforce it. Alongside these difficulties, pastoral production encouraged the dispersal of herds which in turn gave priority to maintaining close bonds across society. The difficulties that Gaelic chiefs had in controlling the population of their own territories in turn militated against the formation of any central power controlling Gaelic Ireland.

In Scotland, Wales and Ireland, divergent social orders coexisted, but did so in very different combinations. In Scotland the two orders were formally unified within a single polity, though in actuality they remained quite distinct. These differences were amplified by the tendency of Lowland Scotland to develop along similar lines to England. In Wales, though the English monarchy exercised military and political supremacy, it relied upon the intermediary role of a section of the old Welsh elite to secure its power. This layer, and the territory they dominated, was gradually absorbed into the English power system, adopting pragmatic literacy in the process.

A clear contrast is apparent between patterns of literacy in regions where a clannic-pastoralist order was dominant and those regions where a seigniorial-manorial system prevailed. In the former, pragmatic literacy were barely present in the 'high' medieval era, while in the latter regions these practices were widespread and continued to expand during the era. This contrast seemed to flow from the relative ease in using written forms to control the social surplus in the manorial regions compared to the pastoralist economies. The more limited role played by kinship in the seigniorial regions also ensured that there was less resistance to the introduction of individual land-ownership, with its concomitant centrality of written records. Where pragmatic literacy did spread, it enabled new forms of political and social power to emerge. In the later Middle Ages these practices of literacy *deepened*, coming to regulate more and more areas of social life. Written records enabled land ownership to be separated from personal relations of power, transforming the relationship between the monarchy and the elite and in effect bringing a new form of elite into being: a class of landowners.

In neither England nor Lowland Scotland did the language of the elite come to be spoken by the wider population. Instead it was the elite who adopted the popular vernacular. This process was closely linked with the more widespread use of writing. It clearly reflected the elite's need to communicate their rules and regulations from above, and to secure popular consent from below, for the effective functioning of the social order. While the earlier diffusion of literacy in England was driven by the need to regulate relations between the monarchical elite and the landed elite, by the later Middle Ages it was increasingly important for regulating relations between the elite and the peasantry (or at least its upper stratum). Once access to land was governed by the written word, then access to the written word became vital to obtain any level of prosperity. It seems clear that this earlier spread of a vernacular literacy in both England and Lowland Scotland contributed to the positive reception accorded to the Reformation, which in turn encouraged larger numbers of people to learn to read.

In Ireland, low levels of literacy limited the potential indigenous support base for religious reform. The fact that the Reformation was promoted through the English language, spoken by very few people in any part of Ireland, did little to advance its cause. In practice, the religious changes sponsored by the Tudors in Ireland were part of a much wider programme of social and political engineering. While this reform project achieved a degree of initial success, English law was at such variance with Gaelic custom and law that its imposition resulted in widespread social disruption and deepening opposition. Antipathy to the English government's secular policies encouraged opposition to the religious reforms. Latin remained the 'bridge' language between the literate groups in both Gaelic and Anglo-French regions, and facilitated the Counter-Reformation response. In Gaelic Ireland, the two key traditional literate groups, the poets and the friars, helped unify the opposition to religious and political changes. Increasingly over the course of the sixteenth century, the English state resorted to coercive measures to maintain control. Intensified coercion in turn alienated the population of the towns, which had been traditionally loyal to the English crown.

Though sharing similar forms of social organisation to Gaelic Ireland, neither Wales nor Gaelic Scotland were subjected to the Irish type of conquest in the Renaissance era. Similar social tensions were minimised in Wales and Scotland because the social transformation took place *over an extended period of time*, and the elites were able to adapt to the new system of social power. The attempted integration of the Irish elites, both Gaelic and Anglo-French, into the English power system took place in the much narrower time range of the sixteenth century, and in a time period where the earlier forms of compromise and ambiguity were being replaced by a system of legal, and increasingly cultural, uniformity.

The Tudor reform project in Ireland involved a comprehensive social engineering programme. Changing the rules of social organisation impacted across society: it was not merely of concern to the elites themselves. Upturning the social order inescapably involved undermining traditional patterns of hegemony, the ways in which ruling groups secured consent for their rule. The main way in which hegemony was traditionally secured – and this was especially true for the Welsh and Gaelic lands – was through upholding custom, maintaining a continuity of social practices across time.

In Wales and Gaelic Scotland, social transformation occurred over centuries. The Welsh elite continued to use Welsh civil law long after the Edwardian supremacy. While some features of (Lowland) Scottish law became generalised in Scottish Gaelic areas in the medieval era, other elements of Gaelic law and practice survived at least into the seventeenth century. The Welsh and Scottish Gaelic elites could reach into both cultures. In neither society was external dominance in the late medieval or early modern periods experienced as a sharp rupture. The very gradualism of the changes enabled the local elites to maintain much of their influence throughout the transition from one system of social power to another.

The Reformation accentuated the problems of hegemony, as the contrast between Ireland, and Scotland and Wales, makes clear. The Reformation concerned much more than differences of religious doctrine: it expressed the collapse of Latin Christendom and its replacement by a system of national cultures based on vernacular literacy. This was most clearly evident in England where the establishment of a *national* church occurred before doctrinal divergence emerged. Even in Scotland, where doctrinal differences were much sharper, the Reformation was very clearly accompanied by major shifts in the forms of social power, with the lairds and burghers achieving much greater prominence, and with the nature of social power itself becoming increasingly mediated through writing and money.

The Welsh and Scottish Gaelic elites were able to draw on the services of the traditional learned strata to give legitimacy to the religious changes. The fact that this was done through the Welsh and Gaelic languages was of crucial importance. In Ireland, the deep social crisis that followed on from the Tudor reform project left little room for this option.

While the Nine Years War formally ended in a compromise agreement – the Treaty of Mellifont – in reality it marked the accession of an English monopoly of military power across Ireland. The New English elite used their military supremacy and their dominance of the state to roll back the power of the Gaelic and Old English lords. Civil law was circumvented to push through dispossession programmes, and the New English elite used the judicial system to accumulate extensive territory. After the flight to Spain by key members of the Gaelic elite, a full scale plantation programme was introduced in Ulster involving massive population displacement. The removal of the Gaelic elite did not resolve the problems facing the English conquerors. The State Papers of the early seventeenth century recount continued resistance by the Gaelic population to government attempts to impose English social practices. In many cases collective ownership of land persisted until the 1640s. Elsewhere, Gaelic families sought, often with the assistance of 'Old English' elements, to evade English law and continue with traditional practices by registering the ownership of family land in the name of the head of the *slíoght* (the extended family). These social conflicts formed the background to the 1641 Revolt, which in turn precipitated civil war and revolution across the Atlantic Isles. While the revolt began as a protest by elite groups it quickly acquired a mass character, and was seen very much as a 'lower class revolt'. There appears to have been a close correlation between the intensity of the revolt and the scale of population displacement as a result of plantations (Butler, 1925; Calendar of State Papers, 1860–1912; Canny, 2001; Gillespie, 2006; Pawlich, 1985; Smyth, 2006)

The Irish revolt intersected with a growing tension within English politics between the monarchy and the bulk of the landed elite, represented by Parliament. The English agrarian elite had become a landowning class and were consequently less dependant on the monarchy and reluctant to allocate it greater power or resources. This fissure coincided with religious tensions, with most of the landowning class seeking a more overt commitment to the Protestant cause in Europe, and the monarchy attempting to retain a greater level of flexibility in foreign policy. The Irish revolt helped bring matters to a head. The Parliament was unwilling to allocate resources to the king to raise an army to suppress the Irish rebellion, lest it be used to advance royal interests closer to home. While most of the London mercantile elite supported the monarchy, a section of them was closely linked to the radical Puritan faction in Parliament led by Oliver Cromwell, and they helped finance a force to suppress the Irish revolt: religious zeal and material interest overlapped. Significantly, the faction of London merchants that supported Parliament consisted primarily of those involved in organising colonial settlements and commerce in North America and the Caribbean (Brenner, 2003).

In a seminal study, William Smyth has mapped, literally, the process of the colonisation of Ireland in the sixteenth and seventeenth centuries, pointing out the close connections between the patterns of conquest in Ireland and the Americas. Like the colonisation of the Americas, it involved much more than military confrontation: the destruction of the means of living of the indigenous population played a crucial role in the conquest, though the ultimate outcome in Ireland would be a colonial pattern closer to that of Latin America than to North America. William Petty, the Cromwellian official who carried out an extensive mapping of the country in the 1650s, concluded that Ireland lost around a third of its population over the course of the rebellion and conquest, a figure broadly supported by later historians. These transformations were perhaps most striking in the urban centres where the older mercantile and artisan communities were disposed of. The figures for land ownership are one index of the changes which occurred in Ireland over the course of the seventeenth century. In 1600, more than 80 per cent of Irish land was owned by Catholics, in 1641 Catholics owned 59 per cent; this figure had fallen to 22 per cent in 1688 and to 14 per cent in 1703 (Canny, 2001; Edwards et al, 2007; Smyth, 2006).

2
Roots of Capitalism and Nationality

AGRARIAN SOCIETY AND CAPITALIST DEVELOPMENT IN SCOTLAND AND IRELAND

It seems clear enough that the Industrial Revolution in England had a huge knock-on effect on Ireland, as it did on Scotland. So why then did Ireland, unlike Scotland, not experience a general wave of industrialisation?

The question of Ireland's failure to industrialise was widely discussed in the nineteenth century, and the discussion tended to be a highly charged one. For many English commentators the absence of industrialisation could be taken as evidence of the innate backwardness of the population. Others saw it as a symptom of the general adherence to Catholicism, a view given added credence by the fairly successful industrialisation of the northeast where most of the population was Protestant. Radical nationalists argued that Irish economic stagnation was a product of English political rule, and pointed to various measures that had been taken to restrict Irish industry in the formative stages of the industrial era.

Later economic historians tended to favour more neutral explanations, avoiding either cultural stereotyping or political judgements. The absence of mineral resources in Ireland, especially coal, was a common explanation. This theory, though, has its own problems. While there was little coal, there was an abundance of peat. Some capital investment and a little technical innovation could surely have turned this into a ready source of energy. Even without using peat, maritime transport was cheap and easy. If cotton could be shipped across the Atlantic, why could coal not be shipped across the Irish Sea? Besides, the region in England which had the least mineral resources – the southeast – became and remained the most prosperous one. Why did Ireland not develop an industrial base focused on lighter goods, for example the production of food?

Historians have also pointed to other 'internal' factors, especially the absence of capital. However, this explanation is also problematic. In the 1840s and the following decades Ireland experienced a wave of railway building which gave the country one of the most extensive rail networks in the Europe of its time. Joseph Lee has shown that, while most of the initial capital came from England, once the venture proved successful capital flowed from within Ireland to build the remainder. Clearly there were stocks of capital in Ireland, and clearly too those holding them were reluctant to invest in enterprises unless they were sure of a safe return (Lee, 1969).

More recently Dennis O'Hearn has taken up the debate again, emphasising the importance of external factors in bringing about Irish underdevelopment. O'Hearn argues that the Irish economic fate needs to be seen in the context of the Atlantic economy as a whole, which turned some regions into underdeveloped peripheries and others into core areas of growth. O'Hearn enumerates some of the restrictions on trade and manufacturing which the English state imposed on Ireland in the seventeenth and eighteenth centuries. He particularly emphasises a point rarely noted by economic historians: the long-term effects of the destruction of the old urban mercantile stratum in the Cromwellian era (O'Hearn, 2001).

There can be little doubt that restrictions imposed on Irish trade had a damaging effect on Irish development; quite how damaging they were is more difficult to assess. There is, however, a problem with O'Hearn's emphasis on 'external' factors in explaining Irish retarded development. Why was Scotland able to industrialise when Ireland was not? While the Industrial Revolution did not originate in Scotland, its knock-on effect there was beneficial, whereas in Ireland the opposite was the case. Moreover Ireland, with its own parliament, might seem to have been in a better position to benefit than Scotland. Of course, the Irish Parliament in the eighteenth century only represented a small elite, but the Westminster Parliament itself was hardly a democratic forum. It is also true that the elite in Ireland were mainly descendants of English settlers, but so too were the elite in North America, and such ties did little to inhibit them upholding their own interests. The contrasting trajectories of Ireland and Scotland clearly need some explanation.

The Highland/Lowland Ratio

An earlier chapter noted significant parallels in the history of Scotland and Ireland, despite great differences. In the early modern period the similarities and the contrasts became even more pronounced. Over the past couple of decades there has been an interesting collaboration and debate between Scottish and Irish historians of the early modern period in an attempt to explain why there was such a sharp divergence between the two countries following the Industrial Revolution.

One hypothesis put forward sought to explain the contrast in terms of the balance of highland to lowland regions, with Ireland being more dominated by its highlands than Scotland (Cullen, Smout & Gibson, 1988). In terms of purely physical geography this explanation is unconvincing; a glance at a map will show that Scotland is the more mountainous of the two countries, while its islands are far more numerous and substantial than Ireland's. It is true that prior to the Elizabethan conquest, the autonomous Gaelic areas of Ireland were much more populous than Gaelic Scotland: a recent estimate puts the population of Gaelic Ireland in the sixteenth century at 800,000, four times that of Gaelic Scotland (McLeod, 2004). However, Wilson McLeod notes that Gaelic Ireland included more substantial fertile lowland regions than Gaelic Scotland.

Aside from the issue of physical geography, there is another difficulty with this hypothesis. Social developments in Scottish and Irish agriculture diverged radically in *both* 'highland' and 'lowland' regions, as we will see. The Gaelic elite continued to dominate the Scottish 'Highlands and Islands' into the eighteenth century, and elements of the clannic order survived at least until the Jacobite uprising in 1745, whereas the Gaelic social order was extirpated in Ireland in the sixteenth and early seventeenth centuries. If it was remnants of the Gaelic order that are supposed to have retarded the growth of capitalism in Ireland, surely such influence would have been greater in Scotland?

Had these historians posed their hypothesis somewhat differently and focused on the relative weight of the Gaelic-speaking and English-speaking regions within their respective societies, then the whole issue would have taken on a very different colour. It certainly was the case by the mid-eighteenth century that Gaelic speakers were more numerous in Ireland, in both relative and absolute terms, than their counterparts in Scotland. The implications though, of an approach which focuses on language communities, are quite different to one centred on physical geography.

Divergent Economies

There was a sharp divergence in demographic patterns between the two countries. Historians do not have exact figures for the eighteenth century, but whatever estimates are used the contrasts between Scotland and Ireland are striking. The most recent estimates suggest that in 1700 both Ireland and Scotland had a similar proportion

– 5.3 per cent – of their populations living in towns with over 10,000 inhabitants. A century later these proportions were radically different: a little over 7 per cent for Ireland and over 17 per cent for Scotland. In absolute terms, the urban population of Ireland had continued to grow over the course of the eighteenth century – it was significantly larger than Scotland's – but urban growth could not keep up with the rapidly expanding rural population (Whyte, 1995b). By 1850 the contrast was even more marked, with Scotland having 32 per cent of its population urbanised and Ireland having slightly over 10 per cent. These figures seem to suggest that two key factors need to be taken into account in any explanation of the divergence between Scotland and Ireland in this era: the contrasting population growth in the countryside and the disparity in urban evolution.

The Scottish historian Tom Devine has recently pinpointed two key differences between Scotland and Ireland in this era: the successful development of agrarian capitalism in Scotland and the profitable involvement of Scottish merchants in colonial trade. This observation touches on issues addressed in a wider debate, between contrasting theoretical approaches, for explaining the origins of capitalism. One of those is 'world systems theory', inspired by the work of Immanuel Wallerstein, which emphasises the central role of the establishment of a global market and how different countries and regions become allocated positions within this framework. An alternative theoretical framework has been elaborated by Robert Brenner which emphasises the role of changing social property relations in determining long-term social and economic development (Brenner, 1985; Wallerstein, 1974).

The Commercialisation of Agriculture in Scotland and Ireland

From about 1760 onwards, the agricultural sector in both Scotland and Ireland underwent major changes which had profound effects on both societies. In both cases the dynamic for change came from the English Industrial Revolution, and the opportunities for maximising profits which flowed from it. In Scotland the process seems to have encouraged capitalist industrialisation, whereas in Ireland it did not.

In both Ireland and Scotland the commercialisation of agriculture involved the imposition of higher rents and the concentration of land holdings. It also necessarily involved the enclosure of land, and the exclusion of many who previously had access to land usage. In the Scottish Lowlands a social structure similar to England's emerged in this period, characterised by a triadic pattern of landowner, capitalist farmer and landless labourer. In Ireland this pattern did not emerge, or if it did only on the margins.

Why did an agrarian capitalist order develop in Scotland but not in Ireland? After all, the conquest of Ireland has been described as instituting a capitalist property system and it is quite clear that merchants were heavily involved in the plantations (Canny, 2001; Wood, 2003). Both Elizabethan and Cromwellian conquerors were steeped in the Puritan ethos, and were reviled by contemporary Irish writers on these very grounds. Yet by the eighteenth century their descendants were imbued by a thoroughly aristocratic spirit, though many shared with their Scottish counterparts an enthusiasm for the ideas of agricultural improvement which were current at the time (Barnard, 2003; Dickson, 2005). What factors encouraged the formation in Scotland of a class of capitalist tenant farmers, who cooperated with the landowners to raise the productivity of their holdings, and why did a similar process not occur in Ireland?

The Transition to Agrarian Capitalism in Scotland

By the mid-nineteenth century, both the Highlands and the Lowlands had developed a system of capitalist agriculture, though with significant differences between them. In the Lowlands, agricultural production tended to be either arable or mixed arable/pastoral, and a social pattern developed akin to England. In the Highlands, sheep raising became predominant with the owners renting large tracts of land to a small layer of tenants, who in turn hired only a very small labour force to tend the sheep. Both transitions involved the removal of population from the land, particularly in the Highlands where the 'Clearances' drove most of the population from their ancestral lands.

The Gaelic social order in the Scottish Highlands and Islands had undergone significant changes over the course of the sixteenth and seventeenth centuries, but substantial elements of earlier clannic practices survived down to the eighteenth century. The major lords of the region had for a long time operated between two cultures and two conceptions of law, being at once Gaelic clan chiefs and anglicised landowners. At the apex of Highland society rents were paid in money form, but lower down the social hierarchy rents in kind were commonplace. Traditional agricultural patterns, including joint tenancies, pasturage in common and cooperative working of the land had persisted. Cattle rearing, on a small scale, remained at the heart of the Highland economy. So too had older settlement patterns, with most of the population living in townlands, the *bailie*. In some, though not all parts of the Highlands, landholding remained linked to military commitments. Clansmen were expected to rise up in support of their chiefs. Holding these social practices together was the traditional notion of *duthchas*: the notion that being part of the clan network involved a set of responsibilities and duties, and that the clan leadership had a duty of care for clan members in periods of distress. The key intermediary figures were the *tacksmen* – the tenants of the chief who not only collected rent from sub-tenants, but also acted as the political overseers of their areas. The tacksmen were literate, had written leases and paid their rents in money form. Below them were the mass of the peasantry, who were mostly illiterate and who paid much or all of their rent in kind, rather than in cash, and who also performed some labour services. In times of economic distress, usually a consequence of bad winters, the tacksmen provided assistance to those in difficulties and held back from rent demands (Davidson, 2004b; Devine, 1994).

The first challenge to this Highland order came in the 1730s in Argyll where the landowner, the Duke of Argyll, finding himself burdened by debt, sought to eliminate the tacksmen from the social frame. Labour services were commuted and the peasants were to pay rent directly to the Duke. The peasants themselves were not too enthusiastic about the new dispensation especially as it involved a significant increase in rent. Over the course of the decade, the new regime turned out to be something of a disaster. Bad weather and low prices for cattle left many unable to pay rent, their difficulties exacerbated by the absence of relief or credit from the tacksmen. While this particular experiment proved costly for the Duke, it presaged larger changes to come.

The really dramatic transformations in the Highlands came in response to the new urban demands produced by the Industrial Revolution in England. Many of the larger landowners, like Argyll, were resident in England; all were aware of the huge new opportunities for profits to be gained by landowners. Many found the costs of keeping up appearances among their peers to be increasingly onerous and provided a ready audience for the burgeoning literature on agricultural 'improvement'.

The campaign for agricultural 'improvement' was a key part of a much wider intellectual renaissance: the Scottish Enlightenment. Scotland had for a long time possessed a thriving intellectual culture; even before the Reformation it had three universities. By the middle decades of the eighteenth century the intelligentsia of the Scottish

Lowlands found themselves in a singular position. The Scottish ports, especially Glasgow, were integrally involved in global trade, exchanging not only goods, but an awareness of the wider world. To their south lay Europe's most vibrant economy, possessed of the most productive agriculture, its cities and industries on the verge of a world-changing Industrial Revolution. To their north, in the Highlands and Islands, one of the last clannic orders in Europe persisted. If this contrast was not stark enough, in 1745 the Highlanders rose up in support of the Stuart contender for the crown, easily overcame the Scottish state, and pushed down into England. Their eventual defeat, and the repression in the Highlands that followed, broke the residual power of Jacobitism, but also concentrated the minds of landowners and intellectuals alike (Davidson, 2004a; Devine; 2000). The defeat of the Jacobite rebellion enabled the landowners to cleanse the Highlands of most of its population to make way for sheep.

The transformation of the Scottish Lowlands was less dramatic than that of the Highlands, and less catastrophic for its inhabitants, but it was arguably much more critical for the development of industrial capitalism in Scotland. Long before the 'Improvers' campaign, Lowlands agriculture was becoming more commercialised. From the early eighteenth century, written leases were becoming the norm, and there was a gradual shift towards single-occupier tenancy. New systems of crop rotation were also being introduced.

Having said this, the intervention of the 'Improvers' was essential for bringing about the radical changes that did occur in Lowlands rural society in the decades after 1760. The major changes were initiated by the landowners. Believing that there was an optimal size of landholding, they began to systematically reduce the number of tenants on the land. The key to achieving this was rental contracts. These were highly detailed affairs outlining exactly what changes the tenant was supposed to introduce, and in what manner and by what time. Nor were these contracts mere statements of intention. The Scottish courts had no compunction about evicting those who failed to comply with the terms of their contract (Davidson, 2004b).

Written leases became widespread in Scotland long before the 'age of improvement'. The crucial point about written leases was that they helped bring about an increased differentiation within the peasantry. Differences within the English and Scottish peasantries had long existed but the spread of written legal forms to agrarian social relations both widened these differences and hardened them. It enabled the stabilisation of a more prosperous stratum of peasant farmers. The consolidation of this layer came at a double cost: to those above them and those below them. Landlords were not only prohibited from behaving in an arbitrary manner, but were pressed to engage in longer-term economic calculation to ensure that they did not incur future financial losses through these leases. In this context it made more sense for landlords to switch to a strategy of 'output maximisation', rather than 'surplus maximisation'.

The poorer tenants in Scotland, like their counterparts in England, found themselves increasingly dependent upon their more prosperous neighbours. Without direct access to land, they had little choice but to work for them. The emergence of a capitalist class in the countryside was not only of great socioeconomic significance, but of sociopolitical importance too. From the latter half of the seventeenth century in England, and from the eighteenth century in Scotland, there now existed a much larger segment of the rural population that had a vested interest in upholding the rights of property and the existing social order. In the event of threats from abroad or social rebellion from below, the loyalty of the yeomanry was rarely in doubt. In Scotland, while

> the social gulf between tenant and landowner was often wide, particularly where estates were large, there are indications that in some areas at least the upper ranks of the tenantry were identifying themselves more closely with the interests of landowners than with the lower ranks of the peasantry by the end of the seventeenth century. (Whyte & Whyte, 1983, p. 39)

In Scotland, the commercialisation of agriculture occurred with limited social disruption:

> The capacity of Scottish society south of the Highland line to adjust to profound social change without visible internal conflict was in part at least a reflection of the tightness of social control within the affected communities ... the old-established governing classes were also enthusiastic innovators and were able to exploit their inherited authority to gain social acceptance for agrarian change. (Devine, 1988, p. 128)

The Consequences of Agrarian Capitalism in Scotland

The emergence of a three-tiered capitalist agricultural system contributed to the development of industrial capitalism in a number of ways. The development of a prosperous layer of capitalist farmers had the effect of providing an enlarged market for manufactured goods, compared to a highly restricted luxury market geared towards the landowning classes (Devine, 2000).

The social transformation of the countryside, by pushing large numbers of people off the land and into the cities, created a supply of labour willing to work in factories under conditions that a landholding peasant might have been very reluctant to engage in. By lowering the price of food – and consequently of labour – capitalist agriculture created greater opportunities for new industries to emerge. However, the existence of a huge supply of landless labour does not automatically bring about industrialisation, as can be seen from the situation in nineteenth-century Ireland, or in much of what is euphemistically called the 'developing' world today. In fact, an excessive supply of 'free' labour can inhibit industrial development because the low wages prevalent in such an economy both limit the domestic market and leave little incentive for employers to engage in technical innovation. Such innovation, however, is the real spur to industrial advance (Dobb, 1963).

Scottish landowners played a significant role in financing the manufacturing industry and especially mining, which was often seen as an extension of estate improvement. Agrarian capitalism contributed to industrialisation in other ways too, some of the most important of which were political. One of the consequences of this commercial involvement was that the landed elite came to have a vested interest in removing restrictions on trade, commerce, banking etc. as well as providing economic aid to industry (Devine, 2000).

Obstacles to Agrarian Capitalism in Ireland

In Ireland, by contrast, the commercialisation of agriculture met with fierce opposition. From the 1760s agrarian resistance movements spread across the Irish countryside, especially in those areas where commercialisation was most advanced. These loosely knit networks were characterised in the main by 'conservative' demands; they did not seek agrarian or political reform, but rather sought to uphold the agrarian 'status quo'. They operated mainly within their own communities, where they attempted to protect 'communal' values over 'individualistic' ones (Beames, 1983; Donnelly, 1978).

To say that the agrarian resistance movements battled for communal values is not to imply that there were no socioeconomic differences within the peasantry, or that they sought to achieve social equality. What they did seek was to maintain an order – real or imaginary – where the more prosperous inhabitants looked out for the poorer ones and where everyone in the community was guaranteed a living. To use Edward Thompson's description of popular consciousness in eighteenth-century England, they sought to uphold a 'moral economy' in opposition to the emerging commercial one (Thompson, 1993).

It is debatable how successful this agrarian resistance was. To contemporary observers it certainly seemed to be a formidable force:

> The Whiteboy association may be considered a vast trade union for the protection of the Irish peasantry; the object being not to regulate the rate of wages or the hours of work, but to keep the actual occupant in possession of his land, and in general to regulate the relation of landlord to tenant for the benefit of the latter. (Lewis, 1836, p. 99)

A cottier class battled to cling onto a share of the land, but the process of consolidating landholdings continued and with it came a much greater social differentiation within the peasantry. Despite this, capitalist social relations never came to dominate the Irish countryside in the same way they did in the Scottish Lowlands. In part this was due to the success of the agrarian resistance in maintaining some grip on the land, at least up until the Great Famine. To use a different language, the primary producers could not be fully separated from their means of subsistence. Why were the outcomes of agrarian change in Ireland and Scotland so divergent?

The Social Dynamics of Eighteenth-Century Ireland

To all appearances the Anglo-Irish elite possessed a monopoly of power in eighteenth-century Ireland. They owned almost all the land. They monopolised parliament and local government. They monopolised the legal system, and they dominated the educational system. Yet this concentration of power did not in itself resolve what had been the basic problem facing the lords in the late medieval era: how to extract an income from the soil. Someone had to work the land, and from the mid-seventeenth century at the latest it had become quite clear that there were not going to be enough settlers from England or Scotland to do the labouring, at least not outside of Ulster, and even there only in parts (Canny, 2001). It is not that the Anglo-Irish elite lacked a commercial cast of mind. They had no problems clearing forests and selling off the timber or extracting minerals; what they lacked were the numbers on the ground to organise agricultural production. Whatever their original intentions, the new landowners were not in a position to redesign the Irish countryside in their own image. Historical experience demonstrates again and again that military ascendancy does not guarantee regular revenue from a conquered territory. To achieve that, a deeper level of social control is necessary.

The Anglo-Irish elite's problems here were accentuated by demographic constraints. The Elizabethan conquest and the Cromwellian war both took a fearsome toll on the Irish population, with warfare bringing hunger and disease in its wake. It has been estimated that Ireland had a population of 1.4 million in 1600, that this had risen to 2.1 million by 1641 and fallen again to 1.7 million by 1672 (Gillespie, 1991).

> Economic factors such as a shortage of suitable tenants acted as constraints on landlords charging the full economic rents for holdings during the seventeenth century ... landlord-tenant relations were governed by factors other than economic ones. (Gillespie, 1991 pp. 25–6)

Throughout the seventeenth century, labour was a scarce commodity in Ireland. To secure revenue from their property landowners needed to make accommodations with those who would work it. They also needed intermediaries to turn the agricultural surplus into money: what became known as middlemen. Problems arose here too.

Most of the middlemen came from the junior branches of landed families. In many cases, especially in the west and southwest, they came from elite Catholic families, both Gaelic and Hiberno-English, who had been dispossessed in the seventeenth century. Excluded from public office, these families maintained close links to the Irish Catholic diaspora on the Continent, providing a steady stream of recruits to the Catholic Church and to the armies of France and Spain (Cullen, 1981; Whelan, 1996).

Whatever their origins, the middlemen faced the same issue of trying to secure an income sufficient to cover the rent and their own needs. This was best achieved by establishing cordial relations with those working the land, whether pastoral or arable or, as was increasingly the case, a combination of both. The demographic advantage that the peasantry possessed in the seventeenth and early eighteenth centuries enabled them to maintain their traditional way of life to a very considerable extent. Communal decision making about land use and work sharing remained the norm across much, if not most, of Ireland throughout the 'Penal' era. Most important of all, the belief that every family ought to have some access to land remained deeply rooted.

It was this social context which helps explain the apparent paradox of the Penal era, the combination of draconian laws and social peace. For most of the eighteenth century, social conflict was muted in Ireland and rates of criminal prosecution were not excessive by the standards of England or Scotland (Connolly, 1988; Garnham, 1997). A large measure of social tranquillity was achieved precisely because the landowners were effectively excluded from the process of agricultural production, and a traditional way of life persisted little disturbed by the workings of law or government. This is not to suggest that the Penal Laws were without socioeconomic effect; indeed, the full scale of their impact only becomes apparent at the moment when the harmonious order begins to break down.

The Penal legislation against buying land, and the time restrictions on leasing, clearly inhibited the development of a legally-backed social framework within which a more efficient agricultural system might have emerged.

> For much of the eighteenth century, the opportunity for Catholic tenants to participate in the tenurial process was formally limited by purely political legislation in a way which would have limited their incentive to engage in productive agricultural improvement. (Proudfoot, 1993, pp. 229–30)

For the most part, neither landlords nor middlemen invested capital in their estates, in sharp contrast to the situation in Scotland or England. Middlemen in the southwest did supply many of their sub-tenants with cattle. This could be seen as a more commercialised form of the older Gaelic system of 'lending' cattle. Significantly though it was not dependent on making improvements to the land itself. Some large tenants did farm their own land, but in general it seems that they could make more money by sub-letting it (Dickson, 1979).

By the late eighteenth century, when the key socioeconomic restrictions of the Penal Laws were removed, the land/labour balance had drastically changed. The ubiquity of the wonder crop from the western hemisphere – the potato – had encouraged a population explosion. The Irish population rose from an estimated 2.8 million in 1712 to 5 million in 1800 and 8.5 million in 1845. Demography was now on the side of the landlords. The middlemen stratum was gradually squeezed out, eliminating not only the Catholic 'underground gentry' but also the privileged position occupied by substantial Protestant tenants.

The Penal Laws seem to have contributed to preventing the development of a social layer within the Irish peasantry that could have established an alliance with the landowners, over and against the labouring stratum. Only in parts of Ulster did a somewhat different picture emerge.

Ulster: A Mirror of Two Societies?

One historian has described Ulster as a mirror of the two societies, Ireland and Scotland. While it is certainly true that Ulster combined elements present elsewhere in Ireland and Scotland, the mirror metaphor may not be sufficiently precise to capture the particular configuration of elements that came to determine its future (Crawford, 1983).

Literacy was more widespread in eighteenth-century Ulster, especially in east Ulster, than elsewhere in Ireland. While there was a close association between the Presbyterians of northeast Ireland and Scotland, the two societies were by no means identical. Irish Presbyterians did not possess the civil liberties enjoyed by their Scottish counterparts. Another important factor that distinguished Ulster from either Scotland or the rest of Ireland was the presence of a substantial number of Anglican peasants and artisans, most of whom originated in the north of England rather than Scotland. This community would substantially impact on modern Ulster's political history.

At a socioeconomic level too, there were significant differences. Eighteenth-century east Ulster did not see the emergence of an agrarian capitalism along the lines of Lowland Scotland or England. Written leases were certainly common enough in eighteenth-century Ulster. What is really significant about them is that they were not the sole basis for the tenurial relationship between landlords and peasants. Tenants insisted that there also existed an older customary reciprocal relationship between the two, and landlords accepted the thrust of their argument. This customary relationship was based upon the existence of a reciprocal understanding – presumably oral – between the ancestors of both tenant and landowner dating back to the plantation era or to acts of loyalty shown at later periods of rebellion or war. By the nineteenth century the practice had become known as the 'Ulster Custom' (Crawford, 1983; Dowling, 1998).

What distinguished Ulster from both Ireland and Scotland in the eighteenth century, according to one historian, was the 'evolution of a society of small tenant farmers' (Crawford, 1983, p. 62). This evolution would seem to have been a consequence of the Ulster Custom. The Custom permitted some capital to be accumulated by tenants, which could be used to set up relatives in the linen industry. Perhaps equally important, the Ulster Custom ensured that a quite distinctive relationship between landlords and tenants existed in the region. Many Ulster landlords encouraged improvements aimed at increasing agricultural productivity and also made more general investments in regional infrastructure. The existence of a more cooperative relationship between landlords and tenants also encouraged the development of the linen industry, though it would be the 1830s before this developed into a mechanised capitalist industry (Crawford, 1983; Dowling, 1998; Ó Gráda, 1994).

The transition to capitalist industrialisation was not without difficulties. The ending of property restrictions against Catholics enabled them to compete more openly, both in the linen trade and for farming tenancies, upsetting the confessional hierarchy, especially in central Ulster where Anglicans were most numerous. For the lower strata of Anglicans, especially the linen weavers, this breakdown of the confessional hierarchy was deeply disturbing because it removed the only real protection they had, and it appears to have been a significant factor in the rise of communal conflicts, especially in Armagh, culminating in the formation of the Orange Order in the 1790s (Miller, 1983; Whelan, 1996).

At a more general level, linen in its proto-industrial stage employed far greater numbers than in its more modern industrial stage. Linen always remained something of a luxury textile industry and this impacted upon its potential for expansion (Cullen, 1972). One agent for a landowning company remarked about the poorer residents of a mid-Ulster region in the 1840s:

> In former times they were able to support themselves comfortably by the spinning wheel, but machinery for spinning linen yarn has knocked [out] almost entirely the hand spinning, and although the mill work gives employment to many hands, still it cannot employ the multitude. (Quoted in Dowling, 1998, p. 156)

The Anglo-Irish Order: Domination Without Hegemony

Why was it that the Anglo-Irish elite had failed so spectacularly to establish a system of hegemony by the late eighteenth century?

The Gaelic myth of origins is contained in a text called *Leabhar Galldha*, the Book of Invasions, which details the successive waves of invaders to Ireland from pre-historic times. The history of conquest provides its own legitimation. In principle a newly colonising ruling class could insert itself into this narrative and come to be accepted as legitimate rulers in their own right. Had not the Anglo-French invaders of the twelfth century adopted this very course, despite taking a few centuries to accomplish?

One possible explanation for this failure was the short time-period involved since the conquest. As Terry Eagleton puts it, the Anglo-Irish elite 'had simply not been around long enough for their expropriations to have been mercifully eroded by the passage of time' (Eagleton, 1995, p. 42). Arguably though, the more crucial issue was not the *length* of time involved but the *character* of the time in which the construction of a post-conquest order took place. The Anglo-Irish aristocracy was attempting to establish a stable agrarian order in Ireland at the very time that in England itself a radically new social order was beginning to emerge. Moreover, this new social order developing in England would not be characterised by stability, but by incessant change.

The failure of the Anglo-Irish elite to convert the indigenous population to the reformed faith has already been noted. The unwillingness of the Anglo-Irish elite to cross the linguistic divide was clearly crucial here, which in turn accentuated the alien character of the new religion, giving credence to the Counter-Reformation claims, just as the Welsh reformers' use of their own language confirmed the Welsh character of Protestantism.

This failure to convert the population did little to boost the authority of the new ruling class, but in itself it was arguably less important than their failure to tolerate religious difference. The purpose of the Penal Laws was not to convert the population but to secure a monopoly of social and political power for the Anglo-Irish. By promoting religion to the post of guardian of the elite's frontier, the Penal Laws greatly consolidated communal divisions. The fact that the Penal Laws were unable to break the hold of Catholicism on the majority of the Irish population is often taken as evidence of their more general failure. In fact, they proved highly successful in consolidating the power of the Anglo-Irish elite and in shaping the whole direction of early modern Ireland. The percentage of Irish land owned by Catholics fell from around 30 per cent in the 1690s to less than 10 per cent by the mid-eighteenth century (Foster, 1988).

One major effect of the Penal Laws was to prevent the legal system itself coming to play the central role in early modern Irish society that it did in England or Scotland. In an ironic and surely unintended manner, the Anglo-Irish rulers ended up reproducing a system of legal exclusion in the early modern period analogous to that which the Anglo-French rulers introduced in the medieval period. The medieval system of exclusion was based upon national/racial grounds, the early modern upon religious ones. In the former case the purpose was to reduce the native population as a whole to servile status (though with some exceptions). In legal terms the status of the native population was the same as that of serfs in England, with the terms *hiberni* and *servi* being used interchangeably. In the early modern scheme, Catholics were permitted to appear before royal courts, and could take cases before them. Two thirds of all cases before the High Courts in Dublin were connected with Penal Law issues concerning land ownership or inheritance. However, Catholics were not only excluded from the legal profession, they were also excluded from sitting on juries in civil law cases; the legal system was stacked against them (Kenny, 1987; Osborough, 1999).

Religious intolerance was normal enough in early modern Europe, the crucial difference in Ireland being that it was adherents of the majority faith – not a minority one – who were excluded from public office. However, religion was a barrier that was crossable, and many did cross. Initially there was great enthusiasm at the prospect of converts from the incorrigible natives, but this waned when it became apparent that most converts had opportunistic rather than spiritual motives. Given the legal minefield that faced Catholics hoping to inherit land, it made eminent sense to swear allegiance to the state Church, and by the mid-eighteenth century there existed a recognisable 'convert' community who acted as intermediaries between the Anglo-Irish elite and the Catholic population, not quite trusted by either.

The analogy, which is not to say identity, between the medieval and the early modern pattern of legal exclusion has already been noted. Most ironic of all perhaps is that in both situations there was a similar outcome. Exclusion from the route of the written legal system had the long-term effect of reinforcing oral customary law, and the social practices implicit therein. This in turn had crucial socioeconomic and political-ideological consequences. The peasants' best defence against depredatory landlords was to maintain tight networks of solidarity, and the best guarantee of equitable grounds within their own community was upholding tradition: this is how it was always done in the past and so it must be right. In the 1780s Sir Edward Newenham sought to engage the peasants of East Galway:

> I explained the whole system of agriculture to them, and promised that their landlord would give them a long lease: I stated to them the comfort of warm clothing and comfortable houses; no answer but that if such things had been possible, their fathers would have done so. (Quoted in Dickson, 1987, p. 125)

For the peasantry it would seem that social relations were considered a zero-sum game: any gain for the landlords would be a loss for them.

In the late medieval colony, the lords were forced to adapt to peasant custom. With labour shortages and an insecure environment, their best policy was to win the loyalty of their peasant communities. It was these conditions that led to the formation of the distinctive 'Old English' elite in the Pale: a group which sought to uphold English law and custom among themselves while accommodating peasant tradition, and so the Pale developed a gentry but not a yeomanry.

The early modern context was very different. For one thing, improved systems of communications – in both senses of the word – meant that the Anglo-Irish elite was much more absorbed into mainstream English upper-class culture. From the beginning of the Tudor plantations, land was already seen as a commodity, though in practice matters were a little more complicated. The new landowners, still short of labour, had to accommodate peasant custom, or at least to rent the land to those who would. With the rise of industrial capitalism in England the whole picture was transformed. The potential profits to be gained from providing food to this newly urbanised population were enormous. Moreover, there was no longer a labour shortage, but thanks to the life-sustaining power of the potato, a growing labour surplus. From the 1760s onwards the landowners attempted to adopt a more commercial orientation. The more prosperous of the peasants, for their part, were anxious to take advantage of the changed situation to enlarge their holdings, but they were not in a strong negotiating position. The structures of the confessional state hardly gave them confidence in the workings of the law, even if they had a written contract. They also had to exercise caution. Anyone taking advantage of someone else's misfortune fell foul not only of communal ire, but also of a set of cultural values which they themselves would most likely have absorbed.

The situation in Ulster had some parallels, and significant differences, to the rest of Ireland. Throughout the seventeenth and eighteenth centuries, Ulster had three – not two – denominationally distinct communities. The smallest of these, the Anglicans, dominated land ownership, the professions and the institutions of the state. They also included a substantial popular community. The Anglican ruling elite succeeded in establishing a secure basis of hegemony only over their own community. Neither the Presbyterians nor the Catholics gave much in the way of consent. Significantly though, their one solid base of social leadership was secured, to a large extent, on the basis of a pre-modern set of loyalties. It was not the written law and a clear commercially based tenure that established the ground rules for the social order in eighteenth or early nineteenth century Ulster. Rather, these overlapped with a much older form of hegemony based upon direct personal relations. In broad historical terms the social context of eighteenth-century Ulster could be seen as one in transition from oral custom and personal dependence to one based on written law and market relations.

The Scottish transition to agrarian, and later industrial, capitalism was not based simply on favourable economic conditions, but upon a particular sociopolitical context: the emergence of a three-class bloc combining 'improving' landlords, commercial farmers and urban merchants. While this bloc was never formalised in organisational terms, it was given theoretical shape by the Scottish Enlightenment intellectuals, who sought to imitate in a more or less planned way what had happened earlier in England, over a more extended period and in a more *ad hoc* fashion. Within this bloc, the commercial farmers were of course the least prosperous, and they were also the least 'activist', responding to the new situation rather than pioneering it. However, they were the most numerous, and it was their ability to carry through the programme of change that was critical for its success. Literacy would seem to have played an important role in the process.

While Scotland had a high rate of literacy in the seventeenth and eighteenth centuries, it was far from having a system of universal literacy. Quite apart from the Highland regions, uneven patterns of literacy persisted. For both centuries, a substantial majority of yeoman farmers were literate, while a substantial majority of labourers were illiterate (Houston, 1988). The literacy/orality divide overlapped with the class one, and placed the Scottish yeomen on the same side as the upper ranks of Scottish society. The singular character of Scottish religion would most likely have contributed to this process. If the kirk enabled the lairds to control wide areas of social life in the Lowlands, the close cooperation with the more prosperous, and industrious, farmers was essential to this achievement. Those who had direct access to the Word of God were of course in a better position to make objective moral judgements.

Tom Devine's description of the 'parish state' captures it very well. The Church of Scotland had important civil and jurisdictional powers in the eighteenth century. Aside from supervising the social and sexual mores of the parishioners, the kirk also supervised the movement of population (and labour): men and women needed a certificate of good behaviour signed by the minister to move parishes. Historians have noted that up until the late eighteenth century the majority of the Lowlands population seem to have accepted the discipline of the Church. Given the weight of forces stacked against them, it is hard to see how the Lowlands' poor could have done otherwise (Devine, 2000).

Hegemony and Industrialisation

The divergent sociopolitical contexts might seem tangential to the question of why Scotland underwent industrialisation, and Ireland largely did not. There are grounds though for suggesting that they are closely linked.

The emergence of a capitalist farming class created a mass market in the Scottish countryside, which in turn stimulated industrial growth in Scottish towns. By contrast the internal market in Ireland was much more limited. Even farmers with larger holdings appear to have had much less disposable income in Ireland than in Scotland (Cullen, 1981). Another crucial area of difference was colonial trade, from which Irish merchants were largely excluded in the eighteenth century. Superficially it would seem that the Irish elite were in a much stronger position than their Scottish equivalents to press home their case for establishing a share of colonial trade: they had their own parliament. However, the Irish Parliament was subordinate to Westminster, and was consistently overruled on issues of trade. Irish merchants were excluded by law from participating in the tobacco, sugar and rum trade, all of which proved lucrative for Scots merchants (Devine, 2003). Scottish entry into colonial commerce had been a key condition which the Scottish elite had insisted upon for the passing of the Act of Union in 1703. Why was the Scottish elite able to impose terms on London that their Irish counterparts could not?

If we consider the issue from the angle of social power, their contrasting destinies become more explicable. The Anglo-Irish elite lacked the *social weight* of their counterparts in Glasgow and Edinburgh. In any confrontation between the Scottish elite and London, the Scots could be reasonably secure in bringing in the Scottish nation behind them. The Anglo-Irish elite could not. On the contrary, they had reason to fear that the wider population would use the occasion of a divide between Dublin and London to challenge the existing order.

The clearest evidence of the social basis for the Anglo-Irish elite's political dependence on London comes from the great exception to it, the one point where Westminster's domination of the Irish Parliament was seriously challenged. In the 1770s, in response to the wars with France, the government encouraged the formation of the Volunteer corps to protect the country in the event of a French landing. Even though the Volunteers officially excluded Catholics (who were still prohibited from bearing arms) it quickly became a political movement demanding reform of government and an end to London's commercial domination of Ireland. The reform current within the Irish Parliament, the 'Patriots', also sought the removal of many of the legal prohibitions against Catholics. In effect, what the Patriots were attempting to do in Ireland was the same as the Scottish Enlightenment current had attempted and succeeded in doing in Scotland: to introduce a modern capitalist order in place of the semi-feudal one. This would have necessitated dismembering communalism and establishing Ireland as a centre of global trade. The effects of these changes, however, instead of stabilising the social hierarchy in Ireland, had the opposite effect of further undermining it and unleashing social forces outside of their control. It culminated in the formation of the United Irish movement which sought to bring about a revolutionary transformation, with Jacobin France as their model.

To make sense of the contrasting responses of Scottish and Irish societies to this double revolution of the late eighteenth century – the English industrial, and the French political – it is necessary to see them in the context of the earlier development of social power in Ireland and Scotland. In seventeenth-century Scotland, a modern form of hegemony emerged based upon religious literacy and the written law. This form of hegemony permitted and encouraged the growth of capitalist social relations in the countryside. It also ensured that in any conflict with London, the patricians of Edinburgh and Glasgow could rely upon a wider population base.

It is at this point that the contrast between Scotland and Ireland becomes most vivid, as does the role of the culture of writing in accentuating that contrast. The process of literisation in Ireland came much later (in the late eighteenth and nineteenth centuries). Spatially it was extremely uneven, and it was largely autonomously acquired. The elite failed to establish a religious-based hegemony in the crucial early modern period or to consolidate a universal system of law. The point about law is that its power comes from the belief that it acts as a *universally* applicable set of rules. In Ireland, by contrast, the Anglo-Irish elite needed, or thought they needed, to introduce a highly restrictive political/legal code in order to secure their ascendancy. The *social impact* and the *ideological impact* are really just different aspects of the same issue. This code inhibited the development of capitalist social relations in Ireland and acted as an obstacle to the evolution of a more modern form of hegemony. In any conflict with London, the Dublin based elite knew that they could not rely on a secure base of popular consent.

The successful Scottish Reformation established a mode of social control based upon the widespread use of reading and writing which enabled the upper strata of the peasantry to secure larger holdings through written leases, in the process eliminating smaller tenancies. The social control exercised by the Irish landowners was far too weak, and the degree of differentiation within the Irish peasantry too limited, for a similar operation to be successfully concluded in Ireland. The same relative weakness of the Irish elite, compared to their Scots counterparts, ensured that they had more limited bargaining power in dealing with Westminster, and the Irish mercantile elite was unable to carve out a lucrative place for themselves under the sun of colonial trade.

The existence of high levels of literacy in both England and in the Scottish Lowlands in the seventeenth and eighteenth centuries seems to have played quite a significant role in promoting a social makeover of the countryside. The development of written leases, in the case of England going back much earlier, appears to have contributed to the consolidation of a class of yeoman farmers who cooperated with the landowners in transforming agriculture. This had the dual effect of making agriculture much more productive (and food cheaper) and pushing 'surplus' labour off the land, forcing landless labourers, even if they stayed in villages, to find other ways of making a living, which in turn helped promote a profusion of trades and manufactures. This level of social disruption involved all sorts of risks for the society engaging in it, but Lowland Scotland pulled the feat off without any political cataclysm.

It was not merely that Scottish farmers were in a better position to read leases or improvement manuals, but more fundamentally the spread of a culture of writing had created a more modern mode of hegemony: one based upon the authority of written law and written religious practice. By the same token, this culture of writing had made it easier for the more prosperous Scottish farmers to develop a commercial mentality and to abandon traditional customary obligations. This more advanced form of social control had facilitated, if not encouraged, the development of capitalist social relations in the countryside. The similarities between developments in Scotland and England are striking.

The role of the commercialisation of agriculture in promoting civil war and revolution in seventeenth-century England remains a source of contentious debate within English historiography. By the eighteenth century, however, the English upper class, landed or mercantile, had established a firm grip over English society. The clearest test to their power came in the period of the wars with Revolutionary France. While the egalitarian ideals of Jacobinism had some following in both countries, the rulers of Britain never came close to losing their social control of the Scottish or English populations. There seems little doubt that the loyalty of the 'middling' stratum, not least in the countryside, had been won over an extended period of time. Nor was this loyalty simply one of deference to their superiors; this same stratum was quite capable of asserting its own interests if they considered it necessary. Their loyalty was to the social order as a whole, and expressed itself in a robust 'patriotism'. This social layer had sufficient weight, both numerically and in terms of direct influence, to maintain social cohesion and to marginalise the radical elements that did exist among the artisanate. The genesis of capitalism did not only involve compulsion, it also involved opportunities. Indeed it seems to be unlikely that this new social order could have consolidated itself had it not permitted significant numbers of people to acquire a level of prosperity that would have previously been far beyond their reach.

Emma's musings in Jane Austen's novel capture the distinctive social position of this stratum very well:

> The yeomanry are precisely the order of people with whom I feel I can have nothing to do. A degree or two lower, and a creditable appearance might interest me; I might hope to be useful to their

families in some way or other. But a farmer can need none of my help, and is therefore as much above my notice as in every other way he is below it. (Austen, 1994, p. 23)

To use a different language, the British ruling elite had established a system of hegemony over the middle ranks of society, but this was a modern form of hegemony, not one based upon personal deference. Literacy was central to it, at a number of levels. Being literate opened up a wider world for many people in the early modern era, and enabled them to move beyond customary practices. How their parents or grandparents had behaved could be seen as but one approach among many. Time and space are both extended. With literacy, the past acquires a greater distance. Places far away can seem much closer and developments elsewhere can have a great influence. The Scottish farmers were avidly reading tracts about improved agricultural techniques. The rise of a religiously inspired mass (but still far from universal) literacy deepened the social gap between the upper layers of the peasantry and artisanate, and the wider labouring population in England and Scotland, while establishing new grounds for engagement with the propertied classes. R. A. Houston had noted that in the early modern period literate people across Europe began to identify with one another (Houston, 1988). A shared literacy also gave the larger tenant farmers and the landowners greater opportunities to ensure that new written contracts would overrule any lingering customary rights of the poorer peasantry.

It does not follow from this that literacy should be seen as a *causal* element in the industrialisation of Scotland. It does appear though that there was a close *association* between the phenomena of literisation and monetisation. A similar association between literacy and the spread of money can be seen in Ireland, but both processes arrived too late to permit any easy capitalist transformation of social relations in the Irish countryside. The delayed development of societal literacy appears to have contributed to hindering the emergence of capitalist industrialisation in Ireland. The key factor here was not the absolute number of people in Scotland and Ireland who were literate, but rather the extent to which social relations had come to be mediated through writing and money.

THE PARADOX OF ANGLICISATION

In *Peasants into Frenchmen*, Eugene Weber showed how the development of a state-controlled education and a mass communications system in nineteenth-century France encouraged the development of linguistic homogeneity and the consolidation of a unitary national identity (Weber, 1979). In Ireland, by contrast, the rise of mass literacy was accompanied by a curious combination of linguistic assimilation and political estrangement. This chapter will explore how and why such a paradoxical situation arose.

The Rise of a Reading Public

The first really detailed overall picture of the diffusion of literacy in Ireland comes with the census of 1841. However, because the census organisers were anxious to find out more about the historical development of literacy in Ireland they also examined levels of literacy by 'age cohort' which enables historians to get a picture of literacy levels going back to the late eighteenth century. Information on the extent of literacy prior to this point is unavoidably patchy and impressionistic, but important nonetheless. Between census figures and these other sources, it is possible to sketch a general picture of the diffusion of literacy in Ireland in the time period when the 'early modern' shades into the 'modern' era.

Much of the pattern of literacy diffusion in Ireland in the late eighteenth and early nineteenth centuries is in line with wider European patterns, but some are more specific to the Irish context. In the 1841 census, males were twice as likely to be literate as females, though by the 1881 census young women had caught up and were now more literate than young men. The gender imbalance in the acquisition of literacy was consistent with the European pattern. Levels of literacy were significantly higher in the cities and towns than the countryside. Again this is consistent with the European pattern of an urban/rural dichotomy in literacy diffusion. It was an imbalance though that had an extra significance in the Irish context, given that Gaelic society did not produce its own urban centres. Literacy rates were significantly higher among Irish Protestants than among Catholics. This too was part of a Europe-wide pattern, though there were important exceptions. Protestant religious practice undoubtedly played a significant role in spreading reading and writing. Class differences were important too. Most of the wealthy were Protestant, and most of the poor were Catholic, and this obviously impacted on literacy rates. Nonetheless most of the Church of Ireland's adherents would have come from lower or middle social strata (Census of Ireland, 1841 and 1881; Cipolla, 1969; Houston, 1988).

According to the provisions of the Penal Laws passed in the early years of the eighteenth century, Catholics were prohibited from establishing schools. They were also denied access to Trinity College, the country's only university. In practice, the laws against running schools proved difficult to enforce, though this seems to have varied by region. In 1731 the Church of Ireland Bishop of Derry wrote:

> There are not any popish schools; sometimes a straggling schoolmaster sets up in some of ye mountainous parts of some parishes, but upon being threatened, as they constantly are, with a warrant, or a presentment by ye churchwardens, they generally think proper to withdraw. (Quoted in Adams, 1987, p. 11)

The exclusion of Catholics from public office, and discriminatory legislation against them regarding ownership and leasing of land, had a very significant impact on eighteenth-century Ireland and may very well have slowed down the pace of 'literisation' in Ireland.

The counties recording the highest literacy rates in the mid-nineteenth century were Antrim and Down. These were the regions where Scottish settlement was most concentrated, with most of the population adhering to Presbyterianism. Presbyterians – or Dissenters as they were more generally called – were in an anomalous position in eighteenth-century Ireland. Whereas in Scotland Presbyterianism was the state church, their Irish counterparts were subjected to many of the discriminatory measures imposed on Catholics. While unaffected by restrictions relating to land ownership and leasing, they were disbarred from holding civil or military office. Ulster Presbyterians maintained close links to Scotland throughout the century. Excluded from Trinity College, the University of Glasgow became their main focus for advanced education (McBride, 1994).

The census figures show a close correlation between the levels of literacy and the dominance of the English language. In part this is due to the patterns of seventeenth-century settlement. The settlers tended to be more literate, and in the areas where they were more numerous English was more widely spoken. The correlation though goes beyond this. Even in areas where descendants of settlers were thin on the ground, the use of English and the level of literacy were closely correlated. The diffusion of literacy was clearly accompanied by language change. County Kilkenny was something of an exception here, with a layer of prosperous farmers continuing to speak Irish into the nineteenth century.

A vibrant Gaelic literate tradition did persist into the modern era. The fact that it failed to consolidate itself into a *mass* literate practice needs some explanation. The collapse of the Gaelic social order following the Elizabethan conquest was accompanied by the disappearance of the bardic schools that had maintained the Gaelic literary tradition. These bardic schools had not only educated new generations of poets and other members of the *aosdana* but had ensured a standard literary language throughout Gaelic Ireland and Scotland. Without the patronage of the clannic system, and facing the wrath of the English state, the bardic schools could not survive. Yet a Gaelic literate tradition did persist – one which kept alive much of the older Gaelic culture, while breaking with it in significant ways.

The post-conquest Gaelic literate tradition was, like its predecessor, a predominantly poetic one, though not exclusively so. Like its predecessor too, it would, for the two centuries following the conquest, be primarily a manuscript literacy rather than a printed one. There were, however, printed works in Irish and they are worth noting. Most were religious texts, emanating from both Catholic and Protestant sources. Prose other than religious works tended to be traditionalist in orientation. Many folktales, and the classic Gaelic sagas, were written down, though many of these sagas remained in verse. Writings like the journals of Amlaoibh O Suilleabhain, which provided an account of daily life in the early nineteenth century, were rare in early modern Ireland (Ó Cuív, 1986).

It was in the field of Gaelic poetry that innovation was most apparent. Writing poetry was no longer a preserve of specialist families; many of the Gaelic poets of the eighteenth century were from labouring backgrounds. The themes addressed by the poets also expanded, while the rigorous metrical structures of bardic poetry gave way to a wide variety of poetic forms. If pre-Conquest Gaelic poetry displayed a sense of unbroken continuity with the past, the poetry of the later era reveals an abiding sense of a lost world. Traditional praise poetry was abandoned, and a new poetic genre developed – the *aisling* – which combined religious and millenarian themes. A saviour would come to redeem the land and end the oppression of the faithful. Walter Benjamin remarked that nothing is further removed from the spirit of the Counter-Reformation than millenarianism, but in seventeenth and eighteenth century Ireland this melange was precisely what dominated Gaelic poetic practice (Benjamin, 1977; Caball, 1998; Ó Cuív, 1986).

Over the course of the eighteenth century it became apparent that there was a rising popular demand for basic education prompted by pragmatic needs. The increased commercialisation of Irish society, not least of Irish agriculture, in the second half of the eighteenth century was accompanied by the increased use of English and rising levels of literacy.

> In 1684 there was an estimated 503 quarterly or twice annual fairs in the country, just under half of them in Leinster. By the 1770s this total had risen to almost 3,000, Leinster's share of which had fallen to just over a quarter. (Smyth, 1992, p. 25)

There was a significant increase in canal and, especially, road building. The second half of the eighteenth century also saw the rapid growth of Irish cities, which, with the exception of Kilkenny, were all located on the coast. With the new type of economy came a new type of learning.

In the early part of the eighteenth century, Gaelic scholars, poets and scribes were often supported by 'middlemen' of native origins, some of whom employed those scholars as tutors for their children. In the later part of the century this practice largely disappeared. Tutoring was replaced by schooling, still informal but catering for much larger numbers. Gaelic literacy seems to have declined, as did the teaching of the classical languages: the language in demand was English. The new English-language based popular education system was concerned with both legal terminology and with mathematics. The abolition of the Penal legislation regarding property and tenurial rights gave a whole new significance to questions of law, while the expansion of commerce increased the need for mathematical knowledge. Likewise, the ending of prohibitions on Catholics running schools opened up new opportunities for educated Catholics, as well as for Catholic religious teaching orders (Cullen, 1990).

While printing had been present in Ireland from the Tudor period, it only became a significant industry in the late seventeenth and eighteenth centuries. As literacy expanded in the later eighteenth century so too did the book trade, with the emergence of an extensive network of booksellers and travelling salesmen across the country (Gillespie, 2005; Ó Ciosáin, 1997).

The eighteenth century also saw the development of a newspaper industry in Ireland. For most of the century, Irish newspapers carried little political news. The Dublin papers paid little attention to events in the provinces, and by the latter half of the eighteenth century provincial newspapers became much more numerous. Much of their advertising revenue came from the Government, who could exercise effective control by the simple expedient of withholding advertising. Controversial opinion appeared in pamphlet form rather than in the regular papers. Jonathan Swift's satirical polemics were a case in point; the Government went after the printers of the *Drapier's Letters*.

In Ireland, as in Britain, coverage of parliamentary debates was prohibited for most of the eighteenth century. Only from the 1770s, when the battle had been won in Britain, did a couple of Irish papers begin to cover debates in the Irish Parliament. Their readership was small, and they were very much directed towards the country's elite:

> much of their limited readership consisted of country gentlemen who had very mundane reasons to consult the press and who were content to rely on their occasional visits to Dublin or the return of their cronies for news of the big world and for occasional gossip. (Cullen, 1984, p. 20)

In the 1790s it took five days for news from London to be reported in the Dublin newspapers, or longer again if the winds on the Irish Sea were heavy (Cullen, 1984).

The elitist character of Irish newspapers was accentuated by the introduction in 1774 of a government stamp duty of two pence a copy, placing papers outside the budget of the great majority of the population. The three pence that a daily newspaper cost in the 1790s was equivalent to half the daily wage of a rural labourer (Crawford, 1979; Cullen, 1984; Nowlan, 1984).

In the final decades of the eighteenth century the character of the reading public changed dramatically. Mass literacy emerged in the context of a world turned upside down. The combined effects of the American and French Revolutions transformed the political situation in Ireland: they created a mass politics. The American Revolution encouraged a growing demand for reform of the Irish Parliament and for greater autonomy from Westminster. Such sentiment had been widespread enough in Dublin (Protestant) middle-class circles since the time of Swift, but now acquired a wider resonance, especially among the Presbyterians of the northeast.

The impact of the French Revolution was even more dramatic. The reform movement had been in two minds about how to approach the 'Catholic Question' – the demand for civil equality for Catholics. Given that Catholic states were some of the most autocratic in Europe, and that Catholics were a majority in Ireland, the extension of the franchise to Catholics ran the risk of the new electorate voting for deeper reaction. The French Revolution showed that the Catholic world was far from impervious to the spirit of Enlightenment.

> The revolution provided the thrilling spectacle to reform-minded Protestants of French Catholics systematically dismantling the *ancien regime* equation between popery, despotism and political slavery. The Irish implications were obvious: if French Catholics could display such political maturity, so too could Irish Catholics. (Whelan, 1996, p. 100)

In 1791 the United Irish societies were formed in Dublin and Belfast with the aim of uniting people across confessional denominations for parliamentary reform and political independence. Initially middle class in composition, they quickly acquired a popular audience and membership, evolving from reform-orientated debating societies into a mass revolutionary movement. Literacy played a central role in the process. The United Irish newspapers, especially the Belfast-based *Northern Star*, achieved a circulation far larger than any of the established newspapers. Its audience was larger again. It is estimated that every copy of the paper reached an audience of at least ten times more. The movement was also able to draw on an extensive printing and publishing network, particularly in the northeast and the Dublin region. Radical books and pamphlets were widely circulated, including thousands of copies of Paine's *Rights of Man* and Tone's *Arguments on Behalf of the Catholics of Ireland*. In the cities and towns reading societies and book clubs sprang up, composed for the most part of artisans and small traders. Outside the cities republicanism found its core advocates among small time traders – shopkeepers and innkeepers – and among textile artisans who comprised the front ranks of popular literacy (Whelan, 1996).

Across the east coast of Ireland the United Irish movement organised and radicalised tens of thousands. What is striking is that the areas where the movement organised its mass support were the same areas where literacy was highest, and areas where the movement was weakest were the areas – predominantly Irish-speaking – where literacy was lowest: Munster, Connaught and the west of Ulster.

The rise of mass radicalism and the 1798 rebellion shocked the Irish elite and led many to identify popular literacy with sedition. These events formed the background to the debate which opened up in the nineteenth century about the prospects for mass education and the need to control it.

The Spread of Mass Education

A government-sponsored commission in the 1820s calculated that half a million children attended school in Ireland. One fifth of these received state aid; most were financed by the parents themselves. Some of these schools were affiliated to the Catholic or Protestant Churches but the majority of the estimated 11,000 schools were not supported by, or affiliated to, any institution, official or clerical. Most of the children were being educated in what was known, somewhat pejoratively, as 'hedge schools'. The ubiquity of these schools had become a source of concern to the Government, and the elite more generally. The teachers were suspected of having radical sympathies and it was feared that the hedge schools had become nurseries for sedition (Croker, 1824; Wakefield, 1812).

In the early nineteenth century, in both England and Ireland, there was much debate within the elite about the benefits or otherwise of popular literacy. The pessimists argued that providing education for the lower orders merely resulted in them acquiring ideas above their station, thus encouraging disaffection. The optimists felt confident that the education of the masses, provided it was properly controlled, could have a very beneficial effect, imbuing them with a sense of discipline and responsibility. 'Educate the rising generation and the gaols and barracks will not be wanted' (Wakefield, 1812, Vol. 2, p. 418). But by the 1820s the debate was becoming somewhat academic, as it became clear that many of the lower orders were acquiring an education for their children, one way or another.

Britain was one of the last states in western Europe to introduce a comprehensive system of public education. Across England, Scotland and Wales, the provision of basic education for the masses was organised on a voluntary basis, closely associated with one or other of the Protestant Churches. Reading the Bible was at the core of the curriculum; the skills of reading and writing were best acquired in conjunction with the precepts of faith. This confessional bent of British elementary education created some difficulties when it came to be applied to Ireland.

The events of the 1790s had traumatised the elite in Ireland and worried Westminster, encouraging a much more sustained effort to win the allegiance of the population. The unrest of the period was seen as a symptom of the moral deficiency that afflicted the country, itself a product of the failure of the earlier Reformation. The clear solution to the problem was the moral regeneration of the population, to be achieved through a 'Second Reformation' (Akenson, 1989).

A number of bodies linked to the established Church began to found schools with the specific purpose of converting the lower classes but, despite financial aid from the state, they failed to make significant inroads. The Catholic Church lacked the resources, both financial and personnel, to establish a comprehensive network of schools across Ireland. A government report from the 1820s estimated that there were between 40,000 and 50,000 children attending Catholic Church-run schools: the religious teaching orders were still at an early stage of their development. They did, however, have sufficient influence to prevent Catholic children attending any schools suspected of having a proselytising mission. The Government faced a dilemma: if they continued with the 'Second Reformation' project the effect would be to permit the children of the nation to be educated in a network of 'hedge schools' whose teachers were suspected of promoting sedition (Akenson, 1989; Coolahan, 1981).

In 1831 the Whig administration resolved the problem by introducing a system of 'National Schools' which marginalised the Church of Ireland and undermined the whole 'Second Reformation' project. The Government financed the building of these schools and paid for their upkeep and the wages of the teachers. Originally it had been intended that the schools be multi-denominational, but confessional discord prevented this, and in practice the national schools, though theoretically non-denominational, were associated with one or other denomination. The school managers, who had the power to hire and fire teachers, were local clerics (Coolahan, 1981).

The educational curriculum of these schools was to be determined at a national level by a government-appointed body, which produced a set of reading books that, while containing a high level of factual information, had 'a strong moralistic and socialising aura ... urging acceptance of the prevailing social, economic and political value system' (Coolahan, 1981, p. 20). The books had very little Irish content, being geared towards British cultural assimilation. They were so successful in this respect that they came to be used in British colonies around the globe. This educational system was designed not only to inculcate a spirit of order and obedience in the pupils, but in the teachers as well. The teachers' behaviour was to be strictly regulated. Obedience to the law and loyalty to the sovereign was expected. Teachers were prohibited from running public houses, or lodging in them. Nor could they attend markets, fairs, or engage in any political activity. Their governing maxim should be: 'A time and a place for everything and everything in its proper time and place' (quoted in Coolahan, 1981, p. 31).

Anglicisation and Cultural Homogenisation

The national schools have been sometimes blamed for the decline of the Irish language, and it is certainly true that in the decades following the creation of this school system the Irish language did experience huge erosion. It is also true that language change was part of the British Government's project of assimilating the Irish population. However, it seems clear enough that linguistic transformation was not simply a top-down affair. The children's parents wanted them to learn English. Irish might be the mother tongue, but English was the language of power. More than that: it was the language of survival. The Great Famine had shown the peasantry that one could not be guaranteed a living on an acre of potatoes and a few cattle. Engaging with the wider world had become a matter of necessity.

Alongside the decline of the Irish language, the middle decades of the nineteenth century also witnessed the decay of many traditional beliefs and practices. Foreign visitors had long remarked on the peculiarities of popular religious beliefs which bordered on the pantheistic, and the persistence of superstitions and magical practices into the nineteenth century. A striking example of this was the 'holy turf' phenomenon during a cholera outbreak in 1832. There were reports from much of the country of strangers arriving in towns with turf or ash, which had been blessed by the Virgin Mary and which, if distributed among the population, would prevent the spread of disease. Two decades later, William Wilde wrote a book on popular customs and beliefs in 1852, but by this point he was writing about a way of life in terminal decline: 'The old forms and customs too are becoming obliterated, the festivals are unobserved, and the rustic festivities neglected or forgotten' (Wilde, 1979, p. 14).

The success of the Fr. Matthew's Temperance Crusade, in the pre-Famine decades, was one indication of changing attitudes. Such campaigns were widespread in Protestant Europe but were new to Ireland; indeed the Catholic hierarchy were initially sceptical towards it because of these associations. The temperance movement, however, made a huge impact, especially in the urban areas of Munster. Frugality was encouraged as well as sobriety, and savings banks were promoted. Temperance reading rooms, including libraries, were established around the country to wean people away from their old habits and to encourage discussion and educational activities.

The post-Famine decades saw a remarkable change in religious practices in Ireland. Perhaps the most striking feature of this 'devotional revolution' was the rise in churchgoing, specifically mass attendance. Prior to the Famine, Sunday-mass attendance in Irish-speaking counties was between 20 and 40 per cent. By the end of the century, church attendance had become the social norm. The number of priests and nuns also rose significantly. In 1840 there was one priest for every 3,000 people, and one nun for every 6,500. By 1871 these figures had changed to one priest for every 1,560 people and one nun for every 1,100 (Foster, 1988; Larkin, 1984).

One of the most striking features of the cultural Anglicisation of Ireland in the nineteenth century was the crucial role played by the Catholic Church in the process. It was not only that cultural Anglicisation coincided with the consolidation of Irish Catholicism, but that the Church itself played a crucial mediating role in the process. Could this explain why Ireland, unlike Scotland, was propelled towards separation from the United Kingdom?

Scotland, however, had its own confessional quarrels with England. Only a small minority of Scots ever adhered to the Episcopalian tradition; from the Reformation to the present day, Presbyterianism has been closely associated with Scottish national identity. Yet this confessional difference did not drive Scotland towards separatism. If Scotland was to be a Presbyterian-coloured region of Britain, why should Ireland not have become a Catholic-coloured one? For the strength of Catholicism in Ireland to provide an explanation for the rise of national separatism, it would need to be shown that the Church itself played a proactive role in promoting independence. In fact, it did nothing of the sort.

The Catholic Church and National Independence

The hostility of the English to the Catholic Church in Ireland in the seventeenth and eighteenth centuries was in large measure driven by concern regarding its international connections. They were always fearful that Irish Catholicism could be used as a Trojan horse by their continental rivals. The presence of large numbers of Irish *émigrés* in the armies of France and Spain did little to reassure them. However, these very same international connections provided some protection for the Catholic Church in Ireland. England's most consistent ally in the various struggles for supremacy in Europe was Austria, heart of Catholic Habsburg power. These connections put a brake on any projects for a more severe repression of Irish Catholicism, even during the Penal era (Wall, 1976).

The French Revolution strengthened the connection between England and the Vatican, giving it an ideological component it had previously lacked – a shared hostility to the rise of radicalism. Westminster came to see the Catholic Church as a potential bulwark against the Jacobin threat. As well as rescinding most of the Penal Laws against Catholics, they funded the building of St. Patrick's College, Maynooth, for the education of Catholic priests. This was designed in part to reduce the flow of young Irish people travelling to the continent for an education, thus limiting the contagion. The Catholic bishops in Ireland shared the Vatican's loathing of radical politics, 'the French disease', and denounced the United Irish rebellion in 1798. When London pressed for the dissolution of the Irish Parliament, and the passing of an Act of Union, in 1801, they did so with the support of the Catholic hierarchy, who were promised in return that full Catholic Emancipation would be introduced in the newly unified kingdom. The Catholic hierarchy clearly conceived of their project as being not the establishment of a separate state, but rather the consolidation of Ireland as a Catholic region within Britain, a parallel project indeed to that of the Scottish elite (Keogh, 1993).

In the event a change of administration at Westminster put an end to that plan, and it took the development of a mass campaign in the 1820s, and the election of Daniel O'Connell to a parliamentary seat in Clare, before Catholics were permitted to become members of the Houses of Parliament. The same Act which conceded Catholic Emancipation in 1829 also reduced the Irish electorate from 100,000 to 10,000. This deep reluctance to permit Irish Catholics into the circles of power did little to strengthen support for a Catholic Unionist project (Ó Tuathaigh, 1990).

In the 1840s O'Connell led a campaign for the re-establishment of an Irish parliament: the Repeal movement. In both the Emancipation and Repeal movements, the Catholic clergy played a central organising role. Clerical involvement in the Repeal movement did not signify Catholic Church support for independence from Britain; the movement's demands were much more modest than that. The Repeal movement though had a dynamic of its own, and an articulate separatist current, the Young Ireland group, emerged within it, which threatened to push Repeal further than its original goals. The defeat of the Repeal movement alongside the bitter experience of witnessing the Great Famine had the effect of radicalising much of the younger generation (Lee, 1973; Ó Tuathaigh, 1990).

A group of Irish émigrés in Paris, some of whom had been associated with the Young Irelanders, founded a new organisation, the Irish Republican Brotherhood (IRB), which provided a more formidable challenge both to British power and to clerical influence in Ireland. Mid-nineteenth-century Paris was a seedbed of revolutionary ideas, and the IRB carried the marks of its origins. While it represented a rejuvenation of the radical politics of the 1790s, in key respects it went further. The IRB sought the establishment of a democratic republic, the liquidation of landed property and the elimination of all forms of colonialism. To achieve its goals, it sought to build a clandestine organisation dedicated to insurrection (Comerford, 1985; Lyons, 1973).

Neither its goals nor its methods endeared the IRB to the Catholic hierarchy, who from the very beginning approached the Fenians – as the IRB became known – with unrelenting hostility. Yet clerical enmity could not prevent the IRB establishing an underground organisation in Ireland with a membership numbering tens of thousands, with substantial sister bodies in Britain and the United States. The IRB's efforts at insurrection were not particularly successful, but what they did achieve was to politicise the lower classes, and to contribute crucially to the formation of a mass peasant movement – the Land League – in the 1870s. The 'Land War' launched by the League and its successor bodies, established a level of popular mobilisation that broke the back of landlord power in Ireland, forcing the British Government to introduce what Terry Eagleton has described as a 'revolution from above', which instituted peasant proprietorship of the land (Eagleton, 1995). This was achieved with very limited involvement from the Catholic Church, indeed in the face of hostility from most of the Catholic hierarchy and much of the clergy.

One feature distinguished Irish Catholicism from virtually every other Catholic Church in Europe: not only its cadre, but its leadership came from predominantly peasant stock. Nor was the Catholic Church a major landowner; that role was occupied by the Church of Ireland. There were of course significant, and growing, differences within the Irish peasantry in the nineteenth century, and Catholic priests mostly came from more prosperous farming backgrounds. Nonetheless, these social differences between the Catholic clergy and the poorer rural population remained as tensions within the peasantry; it did not place them in the ranks of the landowning class.

Antonio Gramsci has written about Catholicism:

Every religion, even the Catholic one (or rather, especially the Catholic one, precisely because of its efforts to remain 'superficially' unitary in order not to break up into national churches and social stratifications), is in reality a multiplicity of distinct and often contradictory religions. (Gramsci, 1967, p. 91)

Some features of Catholicism were of course common to all adherents. One characteristic of the Catholic tradition was the sharp distinction made between the office of the cleric, and the person. It was accepted in Catholic teaching that there were many bad priests, bishops and even popes. However, these human failings did not detract from the sacred functions of the office. It was not uncommon in Ireland in the late nineteenth and early twentieth centuries for people to be simultaneously committed Catholics and fierce anti-clerics, an attitude captured in the Christmas dinner scene in Joyce's *Portrait of the Artist as a Young Man*.

It is not being suggested here that confessional difference played no role at all in the development of the Irish national independence movement, merely that it cannot take the primary role so often accorded it.

The Parameters of Collective Identity

The discussion so far has taken for granted the existence of an Irish nation. Yet if nations are not natural species, neither are they timeless entities. How and why an Irish nation emerged in the first place needs some explanation.

There is no consensus among Irish historians as to when an Irish national identity emerged. Some see it already present in the era of Elizabethan conquest, others see it as a product of nineteenth century Romanticism. Nineteenth century historians tended to project the idea of an Irish nation back in time. It is certainly the case that distinctive ethnic identities existed in the medieval period and earlier, but these were not necessarily understood as grounds for political allegiance.

Throughout the medieval era, the Scottish and Irish Gael shared a language and cultural identity. This facilitated communication between the two regions, but at no time did they constitute a single political community. Political alliances tended to be localised, with the Scottish Gael giving fealty to the king of Scotland. Ethnic identities within Ireland were hardened by the creation of 'English' and 'Irish' as legal identities within the English colony. Gaelic literature likewise made a clear distinction between Gael and Gaill that lasted at least into the Tudor era. However, as noted in earlier chapters, these identities were beginning to erode too in the late medieval period, with many of the Gaill becoming thoroughly gaelicised (Caball, 1998; McLeod, 2004).

The Tudor State Papers distinguish between 'English-Irish' and 'Irish'; though the former were often referred to as 'degenerate English' and the latter as 'wild Irish' or 'mere Irish'. It seems clear, however, that an 'Old English' identity continued to exist within sections of the elite into the seventeenth century, though it is not clear how far down the social scale this identity went. The end of a legal distinction between 'English' and 'Irish' would surely have gone a long way towards eroding these older identities. Language difference would no doubt continue to be a major point of distinction, but in a context where bilingualism was common, even this demarcation would have become somewhat blurred.

From the beginning of the Stuart era, there are references to 'British' migrants in Ireland in the State Papers, but the term 'British' does not seem to have been widely used in Ireland before the nineteenth century. The terms 'Scotch' and 'English' seemed to have been more widely used to refer to the settler communities in the seventeenth century, though by the eighteenth century confessional references had become commonplace to distinguish communities within Ireland. The eighteenth century also saw a shift in the use of the word 'Irish' (Foster, 1988).

As early as the 1730s, there were expressions of discontent among Irish Protestants about London's role in Irish politics. For one thing, London had a policy of excluding anyone born in Ireland from achieving high positions in the government's administration of the country. This was the very same policy that did so much to estrange the Old English community from the Tudor monarchy in the sixteenth century, and it was introduced for similar reasons. The English Government was afraid that an administration in Dublin run by Irish-born people, whatever their origins, might develop policies inimical to London's interests. Moreover, members of the local elite could concentrate their power in Ireland in a way that would make them difficult to dislodge in the event of a conflict of interests.

Added to their resentment at exclusion from high office in Dublin, Irish Protestants had to live with many government policies that they strongly objected to. The imposition of a debased currency – Wood's halfpence – that provoked a riposte from Jonathan Swift, was only one of the more famous sources of resentment. Throughout the eighteenth-century, Protestants in Ireland became more conscious of themselves as being 'Irish'. This is evident enough in the case of two of the best known of them, Dean Swift and Bishop Berkeley. Berkeley, as a student in Trinity College, referred to the Irish as 'natives'; some years later he had come to describe himself as Irish. Swift, though Dublin born, was resentful at being 'exiled' in Ireland, but came to write vitriolic denunciations of what he saw as English misgovernment of the country (Barnard, 2003; Foster, 1988).

In the 1770s opposition to commercial restrictions on Ireland led many Irish Protestants to espouse a 'Patriotic' politics, a move sharpened by sympathy for the colonists in North America. The 'Patriots' identification with the North American rebellious colonists was understandable. They were both part of the expansion of an Atlantic community and economy. They were English-speaking and Protestant (of one denomination or another) and felt unrepresented, and discriminated against, by Westminster. There were crucial differences though. The colonists in North America had overwhelmed the indigenous population; the colonists in Ireland had not. In many respects, Irish Protestants were in a situation more analogous to that of the colonists of South America, whose descendants remained a minority throughout most of the continent and who likewise felt excluded from power, and increasingly alienated from their Iberian overlords. The long-term consequences of their challenge to the Iberian monarchies would prove very different to that launched by the North Americans (Barnard, 2003; Foster, 1988).

In the late eighteenth century the radical 'United Irish' movement consciously sought to develop a national discourse which would replace the communalist one that had dominated the discussion in the previous century. The events of the 1790s showed both their achievements and their limitations.

Most discussion on identity formation tends to focus on the opinions of the elites. This is understandable, in part, because the elites were more literate and left more records of their opinions. However, it would be unwarranted to assume that popular opinion was simply a reflection of elite views; likewise, elite interpretations of popular opinion need to be treated with caution. However, even where popular literacy is very limited, one can begin to gauge the opinions of the broader population by examining the actions of popular movements and the kind of demands they raised.

Literisation and Popular Consciousness

The 'long peace' of the early eighteenth century was broken in the 1760s by the rise of agrarian popular movements across much of Ireland. Though geographically dispersed and diffuse in their demands and activities, they had some crucial features in common. They emerged in the more prosperous lowland agricultural regions, both Irish and English speaking, of the south, east and north of Ireland, but not in the less fertile upland areas or the west. They arose in response to changes being introduced by the landlords or other elite groups, like the Established Church. While their grievances appeared localised, they were all reacting to the changed international context occasioned by the rise of industrial capitalism (Beames, 1983).

The previous chapter explored the contrasting responses to attempts to introduce agrarian capitalism in Ireland and Scotland. In both the Scottish Highlands and the Scottish Lowlands the landowners succeeded in imposing a capitalist agrarian order in the countryside, though it took very different forms in both regions. In Ireland the landowners did attempt to reorganise the lowland regions, though with limited success. In the upland areas or the west, older patterns persisted.

While some of the agrarian opposition began as public protest movements they were suppressed easily enough, and most forms of agrarian resistance survived and grew as clandestine bodies operating at night. Their demands were defensive, upholding customary tenure and other elements of 'moral economy'. Landowners or even their agents were rarely targeted: to do so would have provoked a state response. Instead the agrarian movements concentrated their activities within the peasantry, ensuring that the rules of custom were not transgressed. Ostracism was the most common weapon, but exemplary punishment could be meted out if considered necessary (Beames, 1983, Donnelly, 1978).

The 'Whiteboys', as the agrarian resistance in the south came to be known, did not have a centralised organisation, nor did they attempt to build one. They did maintain a loose network with bands from neighbouring villages helping each other out. They produced no newspapers or pamphlets outlining a programme or justifying their cause. The United Irish movement did make some efforts to organise the Whiteboys in the 1790s but met with very limited success (Beames, 1983; Whelan, 1996).

The early decades of the nineteenth century saw the continuing spread of literacy and a gradual change in the forms and goals of popular struggles. Alongside the political agitation for Emancipation and Repeal, the pre-Famine decades saw changes in the character of peasant agitation. Whiteboy-type networks persisted and probably spread, but they were now accompanied by more overtly political agitation, the most significant of which was the anti-tithe campaign. The payment of tithes – theoretically one tenth of one's produce – to the Established Church had long been a source of popular discontent. However, in the eighteenth century opposition had focused on the form and amount of payment, not on the principle itself. The switch from payment-in-kind to money payments had been particularly onerous for the poorer peasants who had only a marginal relationship to the commercial economy. Likewise, the introduction of tithe-farmers who sought to precisely calculate the amount due, rather than accept the customary donation, had become a source of acrimony. Only in the nineteenth century, however, did peasant agitation begin to challenge the principle of paying tithes to a Church they did not adhere to (Beames, 1983; O'Donoghue, 1965).

These decades also saw the increased use of literate forms of communication. The *Nation* newspaper, which was linked to the Repeal movement in the 1840s, came to have a readership larger than any of the established papers and became the focal point for political debate across the country. The Repeal reading rooms, along with the Temperance reading rooms, became focal points for political and cultural activity (Ó Tuathaigh, 1990).

The emergence of national separatism in Ireland seems to have been closely associated with the process of literisation. This linkage needs explaining. One possible explanation, that the newly literate population were responding to the general direction of written opinion, is untenable because most of the communicative system was controlled by the overwhelmingly Unionist elite. The content of the educational curriculum was thoroughly conformist and pro-imperial, while the Catholic Church showed little in the way of political defiance. Yet defiant is what much of the population became. A section of the intelligentsia certainly began to articulate and propagate a separatist programme, but why was it they to whom the populace listened?

The Social Consequences of Uneven Development

To what extent did the divergent socioeconomic path of Ireland vis à vis England, Scotland and Wales play a significant role in influencing the rise of an Irish national independence movement?

The absence of a social agency in the Irish countryside for carrying through the capitalist reorganisation of agriculture left the landowners with little option, given their need to maintain English-orientated standards, but to press for the highest possible rent. These rents were actually much lower than they might have been had the owners been able to improve the productivity of agriculture through investment and close cooperation with a sector of the peasantry. But for the reasons discussed in the previous chapter, this had not happened. Unable to maximise output, the Irish landowners settled for maximising the surplus.

The Great Famine, which led to an estimated one million people dying and another million emigrating, was a crucial moment in modern Irish history. The exact numbers of deaths through hunger or hunger-related disease are not known: the resources of the state were too overwhelmed to keep track. It was not the first large-scale famine in Ireland. A century earlier famine took another million lives. The circumstances surrounding the 1741 famine are less well known, though it would appear to follow a long-standing pattern for Ireland and similar subsistence economies. An exceptionally bad winter killed off much of the livestock and crops, and the population did not have enough to live on. The Famine of the 1840s was different in a number of respects. It was not a bad winter that killed off the animals or crops, but a humid summer that encouraged a fungus which destroyed one crop, the potato. The dependence of a substantial section of the population on a single crop distinguished the 1840s famine. Our information on this famine is also vastly greater than on earlier ones; the expanded systems of communications and state bureaucracy ensured that contemporaries in Europe and North America were also aware of it (Dickson, 1995).

Much of the generation that followed the Famine would see it as caused by 'landlordism' and British rule, with some seeing it as deliberate genocide. Westminster did in fact provide some financial aid for famine relief, though not enough, and too circumscribed. Government tardiness was partially dictated by the belief that Ireland was overpopulated anyway and that it was unhelpful to interfere with the workings of the free market. Some landlords helped those starving; others took advantage of the Famine to clear their estates. An amendment to the Famine Relief Act of 1846 – Gregory's clause – prohibited those holding over a quarter acre of land from receiving relief aid. Many landowners used the Famine to drive the poorer cottiers off the land. Over 100,000 families were evicted in 1847 alone (Donnelly, 1995; Kinealy, 1995, 2002; Newsinger, 1996).

Despite the catastrophic population loss in the Famine years, small farms continued to dominate the Irish countryside: the great majority were under 30 acres. The Famine would certainly have increased a sense of insecurity among tenants. One consequence was a sharp reduction in the practice of sub-division of holdings. Denied access to land, the rural population increasingly opted for emigration as a mechanism of survival. Emigration in turn encouraged the process of centralisation of farm holdings. It was, however, a very gradual process, and the Irish countryside never became dominated by large labour-employing farms (Clark, 1979).

In the decade after the Famine, some of the more prosperous farmers established an association, the Tenants League, designed to strengthen their position and give them greater security of tenure. The landowners responded by having Parliament enact a statute, the Deasy Act, in 1860 which sought to protect landlords from any customary rights tenants might claim. It explicitly denied any legal status to non-contractual agreements between landlord and tenant, and granted landowners full power over their estates. The 1860 Act shows clearly enough the political difficulties facing the large tenant farmers in Ireland. The landowners showed little inclination to establish a long-term social alliance with them. On their own, without the backing of the state, the large tenant farmers were in a weak position. In the 1860s tenant farmers with holdings of over 100 acres constituted no more than 5 per cent of the total number of tenant farmers in Ireland. Tenants with between 50 and 100 acre holdings represented another 10 per cent. If they were to consolidate their social position, they could not afford to put too much distance between themselves and the greater mass of the peasantry. While Gladstone's Liberal Government did introduce a Land Act in 1870 that sought to give legal status to customary practice, landowners were able to circumvent many of its provisions (Clark, 1979).

Urban life in Ireland, with the exception of Belfast and surrounding towns, mirrored the economic stagnation of the countryside. Industrial employment actually fell in Ireland over the course of the nineteenth century. Such employment as did exist tended to be in service sectors: transport, commercial activity or domestic labour. A lot of employment tended to be on a casual basis, with unemployment and underemployment ubiquitous (Cullen, 1972; Ó Gráda, 1994).

Poverty was endemic with much of the population of Dublin living in slums. According to historian Emmet Larkin, Victorian Dublin was unique among all the

> slumdoms produced in the western world in the nineteenth century ... (because) its slums were not the product of the industrial revolution. Dublin in fact suffered more from the problems of de-industrialisation than industrialisation. (Quoted in Davis, 2004)

The contrast with Victorian Britain could hardly have been more striking. There the second half of the nineteenth century was a period of unparalleled prosperity. Not only was Britain the 'workshop of the world', it had come to dominate global trade and finance while acquiring the largest empire the world had ever known. The chronic instability of the early industrial age had given way to a more mature phase of industrialisation which saw standards of living rise across the board. In this context a powerful labour movement emerged which was able to achieve significant gains for the working class without engaging in any frontal assault on the existing social hierarchy, and without engaging in any sustained challenge to the political order (Anderson, 1992).

The pioneering role of Britain in the industrialisation process had a marked effect on perceptions of economic and social change. Because the great transformations of the eighteenth century seemed to have occurred spontaneously, there was little pressure from any sector of British society to push the state into playing an active role in the economy. The Victorian state was tiny compared to that of France or Germany and was noticeable for its reluctance to engage in the type of developmental strategies pursued by its Continental rivals, not least in the field of communications or education. Likewise, even after the US, Germany, France and other states had introduced tariffs and British industries had lost their global pre-eminence, free trade remained the order of the day. The propertied classes in Britain could afford to be sangfroid about this turn of events because they were increasingly reliant on investments abroad. 'After 1870, (British) capital exports regularly surpassed capital formation at home; by the last years before the First World War, their volume was twice as large' (Anderson, 1992, p. 149).

The point here is not to suggest that national separatism emerged as a result of differences over economic strategy, rather that the strategy pursued by London had the effect of intensifying the social differences between Ireland and Britain.

Emigration and the spread of literacy combined to increase awareness of the world outside of Ireland. The post-Famine emigration wave was not a one-off phenomenon; instead it started a chain movement, with the emigrants sending back money so that other family members could join them. They also sent letters describing the new worlds they were encountering. Emigrants rarely wrote accounts of their difficulties, only of their achievements. And so modernity became something of a mirage for nineteenth-century Ireland: a marvel, always visible in the distance, but never within reach.

Class Conflict in the Countryside

It took the global agricultural recession in the late 1870s and a series of bad harvests to ignite a major social upheaval in the Irish countryside. Once again the spectre of famine seemed to haunt the land but the popular response this time round was very different from the 1840s. Public meetings were held which created a mass organisation – the Land League – with a programme of 'obtaining the soil of Ireland for the people who cultivate it' (Curtis & McDowell, 1968, p. 256). Significantly, the locus of this revolt was not the more prosperous agricultural regions of the south or east, but Mayo, which was probably the poorest county in Ireland with the greatest number of smallholdings. The League went on to launch the 'land war' that broke the power of the landlord class in Ireland and laid the foundations for the establishment of a mass movement for independence.

The Land League was not a pre-planned movement, devised by some central committee or 'supreme council', though key organisers and strategists were Fenians or ex-Fenians who had become disillusioned with the IRB's seemingly futile insurrectionary strategy. Neither, however, was it a purely spontaneous movement. Its founding programme, and the broad popular response to it, reveals decades of political organisation, education and debate. While the agrarian crisis itself took everyone by surprise, it did not find a population unprepared. A year after its formation the Land League had over 1,000 branches and 200,000 members. A leading government official, William Forster, wrote: 'The Land League is supreme ... I am forced to acknowledge that to a great extent the ordinary law is powerless' (quoted in Foner, 1978, p. 16). That the impoverished peasantry of Connaught were capable of launching a national popular organisation, that challenged and ultimately defeated the British Government and the dominant class in Ireland, was an indication of how much had changed since the 1840s.

An important feature of the new movement was, paradoxically, a strong international perspective. This external component is most evident in the case of Michael Davitt, the Land League's main leader. Though born in Mayo, he had grown up in a working-class Irish community in Lancashire, where he had been imprisoned as a result of his involvement in the clandestine IRB. On his release from prison he returned to Mayo to find the county on the verge of famine. The American connection was no less important. The American Fenian organisation, *Clan na Gael*, threw its weight and influence behind the League at a time when the Paris-based leadership of the IRB was reluctant to divert its energies from insurrectionary planning. The presence of substantial Irish communities in Britain and North America, instead of weakening any drive towards national independence, had strengthened a sense of national consciousness within Ireland. Marx had predicted as much as a decade earlier when discussing the effects of land consolidation and emigration:

> Like all good things in the world, this profitable mode of proceedings has its drawbacks. The accumulation of the Irish in America keeps pace with the accumulation of rents in Ireland. The Irishman banished by the sheep and the ox, re-appears on the other side of the ocean as a Fenian. And there a young but gigantic republic arises more and more threateningly to face the old queen of the waves. (Marx, 1976, p. 870)

In both cases these emigrant communities were heavily influenced by the context of their host nations. Eric Hobsbawm has described the Irish in Britain in the post-Famine era:

> Their wages were lower than anyone else's, they lived in the worst slums, and the English and Scots despised them as semi-barbarians, distrusted them as Catholics, and hated them as under cutters of their wages. (Hobsbawm, 1968, p. 310)

A generation earlier Irish activists had played a significant role in the Chartist movement, but in the second half of the nineteenth century there was no mass movement for political and social change that they could identify with. A political culture of imperial self satisfaction held little appeal for these immigrants; thus their social disaffection deepened their sense of national oppression.

Irish emigrants to the United States in the Famine-era encountered every bit as much hostility as did those to England or Scotland. The 'know-nothing' current who opposed their arrival became a national political force for a brief period. The growth of American capitalism, however, was so rapid that the 'nativists' were overwhelmed, and Irish immigrants were able to consolidate their position in the northern cities. The American notion of a democratic republic, a land without kings or aristocrats, where everyone was born equal, had an obvious attraction. So the Irish immigrant communities in the American cities could simultaneously identify with both their new homeland and their old, and the two became linked in a myriad of ways (Foner, 1978).

Samuel Clark has summarised the changes in collective action by Irish peasants before and after the Famine: there was a switch from local to national, from reactive to proactive and from communal to associational. However, the crucial shift here was not just temporal. The United Irish movement of the 1790s was proactive, associational and national, at least in aspiration. As noted earlier, it only succeeded in organising in areas where literacy was widespread. It was the post-Famine decades which saw literacy become generalised across Ireland. Within each of the shifts outlined by Clark, the advent of literacy played a critical role. For each of the crisis decades – the 1790s, the 1840s and the 1880s – movements for political change were accompanied by an outpouring of printed material, spearheaded by newspapers which had huge readerships and even larger audiences. One commentator remarked:

> The Irish peasantry still live in hovels often in the same room with animals, they have very few modern comforts; and yet they are in close communication with those who live at ease in the cities and farms in the US. They are also imbued with all the advanced political notions of the American Republic and are sufficiently educated to read the latest political doctrines in the press which circulates among them. Their social condition at home is a hundred years behind their state of political and mental culture. (Quoted in Bew, 1978, p. 31)

If we contrast political developments in nineteenth-century Ireland with Scotland, the general picture seems clear enough. There was a huge socioeconomic chasm between them, and this gap created a very different context for political action. There is, however, one difficulty with this presentation. Socioeconomic cleavages between regions do not in and of themselves induce national separatism. For example Languedoc, a region in France, despite experiencing many of the features of 'underdevelopment', including mass emigration, never showed much sign of throwing up an independence movement.

Emmanuel Le Roy Ladurie explicitly contrasted the process whereby the French took control of Occitania in the thirteenth and fourteenth centuries and the later colonisation of Algeria. For Le Roy Ladurie, a crucial difference was the 'massive land spoliation' that occurred in Algeria, but which had not been part of the medieval incorporation of Occitania into the kingdom of France (Le Roy Ladurie, 1977).

The social memory of conquest provided the Land League with a powerful argument with which to challenge the power of the landowners. They were able to use the mobilisation around the land question to construct a mass movement for national independence. Broadening out the movement also brought to the fore crucial social and political tensions within Irish nationalism. While the majority of tenant farmers were smallholders, the course of the nineteenth century had seen more and more land concentrated in the hands of 'graziers' with larger holdings, whose social instincts were considerably more conservative than those of the original base of the Land League. For one, they had a lot more to lose than the Mayo smallholders, and they were wary of the more 'extreme' demands being pushed by radical elements, in particular any suggestion of a more equitable land distribution. Politically they were more conservative too, and were more naturally inclined to a federal solution to the national question than a separatist one. They did, however, feel seriously threatened by the depression of agricultural prices, and were pushed into more radical positions because of it (Bew, 1978).

Key to broadening out the movement was the establishment of an alliance, the 'new departure', with the charismatic leader of the constitutional nationalists Charles Stuart Parnell. The conditions of the agreement included support of peasant proprietorship, full self-government, and complete political independence from Westminster (Bew, 1978).

The Ulster Exception

In Ulster, the Land War produced a mixed response. The landlords were of course implacably hostile to the Land League, and its links to the Home Rule movement confirmed their suspicions about the social implications of the national independence movement. The relationship of other social classes to the Land League was more complicated. The Orange Order, which had grown in membership and support over the century, actively aided landlords fighting the League. However, a significant number of Protestants, including some members of the Orange Order, did join the Land League (Bew, 1978).

In Antrim and Down, where Presbyterians were most numerous (and Catholics fewer) the tenant farmers supported many of the League's objectives, without endorsing Home Rule. Politically they aligned themselves with Liberalism. Elsewhere, the Land War tended to stoke up the old communal divide, with Land League protests being interpreted as nationalist demonstrations, and provoking Orange counter-demonstrations. Landlord hegemony over the Protestant, even the Anglican, peasantry was shaken by the Land War, but never decisively broken (Bew, 1978).

The Liberal Prime Minister, Gladstone, had seen his role in resisting the Land League as 'the deadly fight with social revolution' and introduced a series of land reform measures, as well as acceding to home rule, in order to reduce the danger (quoted in Bew, 1978, p. 205). Even the Tory leader, Lord Salisbury, came to recognise that there was a real danger of Protestant Ulster going nationalist if concessions were not made to the tenant farmers. The set of concessions which were made, resulting in a policy of state aid to tenants to buy out the landlords, proved sufficient to block this development (Bew, 1978).

In determining Ulster's overall direction, the Belfast region was the decisive factor. The population of Belfast grew from around 20,000 in 1800 to over 250,000 by the 1880s. Belfast was the only Irish city to experience significant industrial growth in the nineteenth century. Initially its industrial expansion was linked to the cotton industry, but this collapsed in the 1830s, unable to compete with the mechanisation of the Lancashire industry. After this period industrial growth was focused on linen, later consolidated by shipbuilding. Linen had been slower to mechanise than cotton, and the time gap involved had enabled Belfast, with its lower wages, to compete successfully. Despite these achievements Belfast's industrial base remained fragile. Linen was something of a luxury product, and while it enjoyed a great boom during the American Civil War period, it fell back thereafter. The growth of the shipbuilding industry helped to give greater stability to the economy, but even here a similar situation existed. The Belfast shipbuilding industry was centred on the manufacturing of passenger boats, which provided a more limited potential for growth than freight shipping (Budge & O'Leary, 1973; Cullen, 1972; Ó Gráda, 1994).

The limited character of industrial growth in Belfast had important social consequences. Most importantly, it was unable to provide employment for the surplus population of the Ulster region, let alone for Ireland as a whole. Between 1841 and 1911, the population of Ireland halved; that of Ulster fell by a third. So even though the northeast was able to escape the worst excesses of underdevelopment, it remained shaped by this wider context. One of the effects of these high levels of unemployment and emigration was to establish conditions where communal divisions could be recreated in an urban context. Belfast, like many of the cities of England, Scotland and North America saw a huge population influx in the Famine years. Not all the refugees from famine were Catholics, but most of them were, and the settled population in Belfast felt threatened by this influx of impoverished refugees. The Anglican labourers from mid Ulster had brought the Orange Order with them to Belfast in the early nineteenth century. From the Famine period onwards, Orangism began to broaden its support, socially and denominationally. Significantly, after the mid-nineteenth century the Catholic proportion of Belfast's population, which had grown considerably from very small numbers in 1800, stabilised and even fell (Budge & O'Leary, 1973; Cullen, 1972; Ó Gráda, 1994; Patterson, 1980; Rowthorn & Wayne, 1988).

The Belfast middle classes, especially the merchants, had been traditionally liberal in their politics, but under the impact of the Land War and the rise of the Home Rule movement they began to shift ground. They worried about the social radicalism evident in the Land War and clearly visible in sectors of the Fenian movement, and about the economic implications that might follow moves towards national independence. The key Ulster industries were reliant on international markets, including imperial ones. However, it seems unlikely that opposition to Home Rule was motivated solely by narrow socioeconomic considerations. Populations of prosperous regions tend to see their good fortune as a product of their own special qualities, rather than the result of some objective set of circumstances. The fact that the northeast was the most economically advanced part of Ireland was a product of the industrious character of its inhabitants, in contrast to the rest of the population. Increasingly, they came to identify with British industrial advance, and with its empire, which was likewise understood as a symbol of their collective character and achievements. Once the Gladstonian Liberals opted for Home Rule as the best hope of preventing social revolution, the Belfast liberal bourgeoisie threw their lot in with their traditional Conservative rivals to establish Unionism. The shift was facilitated by the earlier disestablishment of the Church of Ireland in 1869, which removed the Presbyterians' remaining bone of contention with the Anglican establishment (Miller, 1978; Patterson, 1980).

David Miller has put forward an influential theory of Ulster Unionism that helps explain its exaggerated – by English, Scottish or Welsh standards – insistence on Britishness and loyalty to the Crown, alongside its threats of rebellion in the event of 'disloyalty' by the British Government. Ulster Unionism, although it had many characteristics of nationalism, never conceived of itself as such. For Miller, Ulster Unionism is better understood in terms of a pre-modern sense of contract between rulers and ruled. He sees the roots of Unionism's 'contractarian' beliefs in the practices designated as 'Ulster custom', whereby landowners gave preferential treatment to Protestant tenants. This older ideology was reborn, initially in Mid-Ulster, in the late eighteenth century as a response to the stresses of modernisation and proto-industrialisation, before migrating to the Belfast region, where its reanimation encouraged a new system of preferential treatment for working class Protestants, especially in relation to employment (Miller, 1978).

While this stress on the importance of a sense of continuity with the pre-modern past – or more precisely the early modern past – is undoubtedly justified, it is only part of the picture. The insistence on imperial identity might be better understood if one considers the historical context of Ulster Unionism's formation. It emerged not as a movement seeking greater autonomy for Ulster but as part of a wider current seeking to block Irish nationalism, specifically campaigning against Home Rule for Ireland. It was unlike the Scottish or Welsh sense of nationality in that it was not focused around a *spatially defined* collective identity. Insofar as Ulster had a spatial identity it was based on nine counties, not on six. Ulster Unionism began to differentiate itself from Irish Unionism once it became clear that it could not prevent Home Rule being introduced. It settled for six counties because the demographic balance within a nine-county Ulster was too precarious to risk. Ulster Unionists were always intensely conscious of their historical roots as settlers, which furthered their identification with the imperial order. Historians have noted that while the Scots had a clearly utilitarian approach to Empire – as a context for social advancement – Ulster Unionists tended to view it as a heritage (Walker, 1994).

The other problematic aspect of Ulster Unionist British identity flowed from the peculiar multinational character of British identity, a question made more complex in that Ulster Unionism was itself a merging of two older identities, one Scottish and predominantly Presbyterian, the other English and predominantly Anglican. It has been argued that the development of a British identity was primarily the work of Scottish rather than English opinion makers or statesmen. While this may well be the case, it is also true that the Scots asserted (or reasserted) a Scottish identity in the modern era. Moreover, the Scots were insistent that theirs was no mere regional identity: Scotland was a nation. This paradoxical situation, of 'inventing' Britishness while insisting on Scottish identity, would seem to find its source outside of Scotland, in the deep-rooted attachment of the population of England to an English national identity. It was not to 'freeborn Britons' that the pamphleteers appealed, but to 'freeborn Englishmen' (Colley, 1992; Smout, 1989).

The point about English identity was that it was much older than the British one and that it emerged in a period when literacy was beginning to become more widespread in England, roughly speaking in the age of Shakespeare. Indeed, it could reasonably be argued that much of Shakespeare's drama was both an expression of this newly emerging patriotic sentiment, and an active contribution towards it. Moreover, while the state encouraged such patriotism, it did not create it. English nationality emerged more or less spontaneously and did so at a time when English society was becoming increasingly commercialised. In England, a British identity came to be grafted, largely from above, onto the older one, but never replaced it. While the two terms were often used interchangeably, an important distinction remained: British referred to institutions, English to population. It was this persistent English popular identification that made a Scottish national identity so necessary.

This background ambivalence made British identity both uniquely accessible to Unionists in Ireland and singularly problematic. A British identity could both be shared and permit difference. It had, moreover, its own hierarchy. One of Gladstone's officials commented in a memo during the Land War period: 'The active support of Orangemen and Protestants is the ultimate resource of English rule in Ireland, but ought to be kept until every other card has been played' (quoted in Bew, 1978, p. 214). So while the official national identity of the state was 'British', the deeper collective identities were different and, in the case of 'English' at least, much older. This was certainly one of the reasons why socioeconomic tensions and differences could, unlike in France, so easily slip into national conflicts.

National Identity and the Transition to Mass Literacy

Why was the 'cultural Anglicisation' of Ireland not accompanied by political assimilation? Ireland's uneven development was clearly a crucial factor. However, the case of Languedoc in France shows that uneven development, in and of itself, does not necessarily lead to the development of national separatism. Religious difference was certainly another factor, but once again it did not drive Scotland out of the Union. More fundamentally, the country in Europe which had been most plagued by religious difference and religious war in the sixteenth and seventeenth centuries, Germany, set these differences aside to establish national unification in the nineteenth century. Class conflict in the countryside certainly played a role, however, this cannot fully explain why national separatism should arise. In the nineteenth century, the landlords in Ireland tended to refer to themselves as 'Irish'; the term 'Anglo-Irish' only came to be widely used in the twentieth century. While the Land League might have condemned 'landlordism' as alien, it did not describe Irish-born landlords as outsiders. The fact that Charles Stuart Parnell, the leader of the Home Rule movement, was himself a landlord, a Protestant, and an Irish patriot, is itself an index of the complexity of national identity in nineteenth-century Ireland. Nonetheless, it seems likely that the class struggle in the countryside would never have been so intense without the presence of nationalism. Which came first: class conflict or national separatism? While defensive struggles by the peasantry had been widespread in many regions in the eighteenth century, the rise of a more assertive approach seems to have coincided with the emergence of a national consciousness.

It has often been noted that while nationalities are a fairly modern phenomena, they tend to envisage themselves as being timeless, or at least as stretching far back into the past. This in itself provides a valuable clue to the nature of nationality. The creation of a new sense of collective identity clearly needs to locate itself in time, and establish a collective narrative that can accomplish this. The educational system attempted to create one such collective narrative, one that saw the incorporation of Ireland into the British Empire not as conquest, but as an emancipation from backwardness.

Why did this narrative prove unacceptable to most of the Irish population? A couple of points are worth noting here. Firstly, it was an attempted imposition of a collective British identity *from above*. English and Scottish national identities were not superimposed from above, rather they evolved slowly through the interaction of state institutions and society, both from above and below. People *felt* English or Scottish, whereas Britishness has always been associated with state institutions, monarchy and empire. Another difficulty that faced the promoters of a British identity in Ireland was that the collective narrative they proposed was at variance with the mainstream of 'social memory'.

Some historians speak of 'social memory', referring to a type of collective memory that is found primarily in oral societies, but can also be found in literate ones (Fentress, 1992). In the case of Ireland in the eighteenth and nineteenth centuries, there is a huge amount of (admittedly impressionistic) evidence to suggest that a social memory of the conquest was widespread. Given the scale of death and destruction involved – historians have estimated that around a third of the population lost their lives in the Cromwellian era alone – it would be surprising if an oral memory of the period had not survived. Social memories, like individual ones, can be selective, but they are more likely to be preserved if they retain a social relevance. Historical events leave their impact not only on memory but also on social organisation. In the case of Ireland, the specific patterns of agrarian relations and the persistence of communalism were both legacies of conquest. Because the conquest of Ireland was itself uneven, oral-based memories would no doubt have been likewise. What mass literacy did was to encourage the articulation of a collective past, in which the incorporation of Ireland into the British state system appeared in a rather different light to the official version.

Identities necessarily involve distinctions – the creation of boundaries. In the case of modern national identities it is not only communities which are imagined, but these communities are felt to be spatially bounded. The uneven development of capitalism encouraged this, as people came to identify their way of life with a particular territory. By the same token the emergence of collective identities, based upon a sense of exclusion, can come to be associated with the exclusion of a particular space from developments elsewhere. A sense of Irish national identity seems to have emerged in large measure as a product of a sense of exclusion. The character of this exclusion varied greatly, and so did the sense of national identity. National identity meant different things to different people. The process whereby the excluded came to identify themselves with a place seems to have been closely linked to the process whereby the place itself became a source of exclusion. Both spatial and temporal elements are involved in the creation of national identities, with one reinforcing the other.

Unlike in England, Scotland and Wales, the spread of mass literacy in Ireland was accompanied by agrarian revolt, political defiance and the emergence of a movement for national independence. While these developments cannot be attributed to the spread of literacy – they had their roots in the chronic underdevelopment of the Irish economy and in a perception of political exclusion and national difference – the literisation of Irish society impacted on the forms that these protest movements took. As the populace became more literate, so popular movements became better organised and more ambitious in their projects. Local networks upholding tradition gave way to national organisations challenging the agrarian social order and seeking political independence.

Inspired by the French Revolution, a major radicalisation occurred in Ireland in the 1790s culminating in the 1798 rebellion. The fact that the 1798 rebellion was essentially confined to the country's east coast, which had fairly high rates of literacy, very little impact in western regions and where the Irish language predominated and literacy levels were low, would suggest that written forms of agitation, and thus literacy, played an important role in radicalising the population.

Mass literacy emerged in Ireland in the late eighteenth and nineteenth centuries. It was driven primarily by socioeconomic factors linked to the rise of a money economy. The push for acquiring literacy came from below, and until the third or fourth decade of the nineteenth century the demand for learning was largely met by 'unofficial' hedge schools. Prior to the 1830s neither the state nor the various Churches played a central role in establishing a system of mass education. The development of a state-funded and state-controlled system of education – the National Schools – was in direct response to elite fears that the growing system of popular education would encourage sedition within the populace.

The introduction of state schools was accompanied by linguistic Anglicisation. However, while the new state-controlled educational system was successful in spreading the English language – which was perceived as the language of power and, especially after the Famine experience, as the language of survival – it did not succeed in winning the political allegiance of the population. While the language in which the message was delivered was adopted, the message itself did not get through: the incorporation of Ireland into the British political order was not perceived as advantageous and beneficial. The 'official message' was at odds with social memory and collective experience.

However, the introduction of a state-controlled education system contributed to the advance of literacy, which was accompanied by political radicalisation. While popular oppositional movements had preceded the emergence of mass literacy, these had tended to be localised and defensive in character. The spread of mass literacy, however, brought with it new forms of communications. Radical newspapers, books and pamphlets were widely circulated and, unlike the 'official message', the 'revolutionary message' struck a chord with broad sections of the population because it reflected their experience and corresponded with their social memory.

In practice, the processes of literisation and monetisation were closely linked. The rise of capitalism was not just about mechanisation. More fundamentally it involved the transition from a social order based upon relations of personal dependence to one where social relations are mediated through symbolic objects: money and writing. This transition involved the erosion of older senses of time and place, based upon direct personal encounters, where the known consisted of what had been seen and heard. In these tradition-bound worlds the past and the present were at one; there was no sense of the new being qualitatively different from what had gone before. The disruption of these traditional communities by the generalised use of writing and money to regulate human relations created a need for a new sense of community. And though the process of the commercialisation of societies was highly uneven, it resulted in the creation of what Benedict Anderson has described as 'imagined communities' (nationalities) spread across the globe (Anderson, 1983).

In the second half of the nineteenth century, industrial capital in Britain created its own legitimacy by being seen to raise popular standards of living (or at least permit them to be raised). This long social peace that characterised the mid- and late Victorian era helped consolidate a sense of British identity and a pride in Empire that became linked to it. The same period in Ireland saw a protracted social war between the peasantry (especially the poorer strata) and the landed elite, while the cities saw more emigrants passing through on their way to the boats than they saw industrial jobs being created. Economically, nineteenth-century Ireland displayed what would become the classic features of underdevelopment: rural over population and urban stagnation and regression, setting the scene for widespread social and political discontent and intense class struggle in the countryside. Culturally, Ireland acquired mass literacy while retaining a sense of distinctiveness. In this context neither Empire nor British identity had a great deal of appeal (outside of the northeast).

The rise of an independence movement coincided paradoxically with Ireland's cultural and linguistic incorporation into the British social formation. Despite the success of the state-controlled schooling system in advancing linguistic homogeneity, it failed to win the political allegiance of the newly literate population. This shift occurred alongside the diffusion of market relations. The erosion of customary relations and the inrush of a stronger sense of the outside world entailed the emergence of a more abstract sense of identity – personal and collective. In and of itself, the development of national identity need not have led to a mass independence movement (as the Scottish case demonstrates). However, the huge socioeconomic gap between the two islands, the scale of discontent in Ireland, and the degree of social peace prevalent in Britain in the second half of the nineteenth century, made this outcome more likely.

3
Legacies of Uneven Development

In the weeks following the assassination of Archduke Ferdinand in Sarajevo, the major headline in the London *Times* was not the threat of an impending European war but the continuing Home Rule crisis in Ireland. It is easy to dismiss this retrospectively as parochial, but there are arguably deeper connections between the two stories. The same centrifugal forces threatening to tear apart the Habsburg and Tsarist empires were also at work on Europe's western periphery. This is not to suggest that the British Empire was essentially similar to the Habsburg or Tsarist ones; but the differences between them shaped Ireland's distinctive trajectory.

Imperial Power and Uneven Development

Within Irish historical studies, the question of whether Ireland's relationship with Britain was a colonial one has been a source of debate in recent decades. Some historians have suggested that it makes more sense to see eighteenth-century Ireland as a typical *ancien regime* rather than as a colony. The term 'colony' was not widely used to refer to Ireland prior to the twentieth century; it referred rather to British settlements overseas, in the manner that US historians still write about the 'colonial' period. Others have argued that because Ireland was, from the nineteenth century, constitutionally part of the United Kingdom, with elected representatives in Westminster, it is mistaken to see it as a colony. Moreover, many Irish people were involved in British imperial structures, in the army or administration, and could be seen as benefiting from empire.

Some of this discussion is semantic, and as words do change their meaning, it is best to clarify terms. Aijaz Ahmad suggests a precise meaning for the word 'colonial' in its modern sense:

> the fundamental fact [is] that the ruling class of a colony is located outside that colony, and the colonial state is the instrument of that externally based ruling class; with decolonisation, this structural feature of the dominated formation no longer applies and the

formation ceases to be colonial, regardless of any other kind of dependence.' (Ahmad, 1992, p. 204)

Eighteenth-century Ireland, from this perspective, was a social formation with deeply contradictory features. While a significant number of landowners in Ireland lived in England, the majority would seem to have lived in Ireland, and this dominant class had its own parliament. However, and this is the rub, this parliament did not have executive power in Ireland. The Irish executive – with control over the key organs of government – was chosen by Westminster. Moreover, legally the Irish Parliament was subordinate to the Westminster Parliament. This legal subordination was no mere constitutional technicality but was consistently used to ensure that neither Irish merchants nor Irish produce could compete with their English counterparts (O'Hearn, 2005). Underlying this subordinate role of the dominant classes in Ireland to their British counterparts was not so much the coercive power of the British state over the Irish elite, but that this elite, precisely because it lacked internal hegemony, needed the external coercive power of the British state to ensure its own survival. While comparisons with other European societies' *ancien regimes* can usefully be made, it is best not to lose sight of this central sociopolitical fact.

The 1801 Act of Union (which closed down the Irish parliament and unified the two kingdoms) was not the action of a confident Irish ruling class integrating with a successful fraternal class in Britain. On the contrary, the Act of Union was more or less imposed by Westminster upon an Irish elite which had been traumatised by the rebellion against British rule in 1798. While the Irish elite had access to the British Houses of Parliament, the civil service and the army, they were never equal partners in the affair (Eagleton, 1995).

The presence of large numbers of Irish soldiers in the British Army is taken by some as evidence that Ireland was not a colony. In fact, most of the soldiers in Britain's 'Indian Army' were themselves Indian. What distinguished Ireland was that a significant percentage of British Army officers were also from Ireland, albeit almost exclusively from Anglo-Irish (Protestant landed elite) backgrounds. The introduction in 1857 of a system of recruitment through public examination opened up the imperial civil administration, especially the Indian, to large numbers of Irish applicants. While many of the senior administrative officers were from Anglo-Irish landed backgrounds, most of their Irish recruits were Catholics (Campbell, 2009).

Comparisons between Ireland and Asian colonies, especially India, were not unusual in the Victorian era. British officials tended to justify colonial rule, at least by the nineteenth century, by insisting that they were bringing civilised values and 'improvement' to the backward regions they ruled. John Stuart Mill believed that 'Englishmen who know India are the men who can best understand and interpret the social ideas and economic relations of Ireland' (quoted in Boylan, 2007, p. 168). For Marx, India was from a 'social point of view ... the Ireland of the East' (Marx, 1969). From Marx's perspective, the crucial similarity was that both Ireland and India had been transformed by British rule into agricultural provinces of England.

In a recent historical survey of empire, John Darwin sums up the global divide which had arisen by the late nineteenth century: 'a global division of labour in which the manufactures, capital and credit of the industrial-imperial countries were exchanged for the raw products and commodities of the rest of the world' (Darwin, 2008, p. 311). From this economic perspective Ireland, excepting the northeast, was clearly in the global camp of the colonised. Darwin continues:

> Of course, this new global market was not just the result of purely commercial activity. Nor could it have been. In several crucial ways it depended upon the assertion of power, an expansion of empire, both direct and indirect. (Darwin, 2008, p. 311)

A comparison between Ireland and India reveals some striking similarities in the way the two societies came to be located on the same side of this global division of labour.

Contrary to received wisdom, the largest centres of manufacturing in the world prior to the nineteenth century were in India and China. Not only did India produce a quarter of global manufacturing goods, but the living standards of textile workers were higher than in England. For most of the eighteenth century, Indian textiles dominated the English home market. By the late Victorian era this situation had been reversed. Not only had British textile manufacturers recovered their home market, they had captured the Indian market too. The British share of world manufacturing output was 1.9 per cent in 1750; by 1880 it had risen to 22.9 per cent. In the same period India's share of world manufacturing output fell from 24.5 per cent to 2.8 per cent (Davis, 2001, p. 294). This was the age of the Industrial Revolution, with mechanisation transforming

Lancashire's textile industry and initiating a much wider process of capitalist industrialisation. This shift to mechanisation and a factory system occurred, at least in part, in response to competition from Indian goods. Duties on Indian textile imports were raised threefold in the 1790s and ninefold in the early decades of the nineteenth century. Once Britain had successfully mechanised and acquired a global competitive edge, protective tariffs were abandoned and the age of 'free trade' commenced (Arrighi, 2008; Davis, 2001; Darwin, 2008; Pomeranz, 2000).

While Ireland never possessed a manufacturing base comparable to India, it also experienced a process of 'de-industrialisation' in the nineteenth century (Cullen, 1972; O'Malley, 1989). While trade restrictions played a significant role in undermining the industrial base of both societies, the main damage was done by 'free trade'. Mechanisation had opened up a huge competitive gap. Britain's colonies were not the only countries who had to confront the consequences of Britain's industrial 'blitzkrieg', but they were in the weakest position to defend their societies against it. In Europe and in the US, governments took action to withstand competition from Britain and to build up their own industrial structures, whether through the imposition of tariffs, state aid to industry, the promotion of scientific and technical education or the restructuring of the state bureaucracy to enable it to play a more directive role in economic organisation. Japan, the Asian society which most successfully resisted European domination, pushed through a radical social reorganisation in order to maintain its autonomy. Such adaptive strategies presupposed political independence (Chang, 2003).

The economic impact of British rule in India was not confined to the manufacturing sector, it also impacted on agriculture. Both the parallels and the differences with Ireland are striking. In both societies, the British rulers moved to abolish collective ownership of land and replace it with a private property regime. In Ireland, in the sixteenth and seventeenth centuries, this transformation produced a deep social crisis and a widespread political revolt. In response, Britain eliminated the native elite and replaced them with a class of English landowners. In India, the introduction of a system of private land-ownership was less dramatic; the social crisis came later. In the 1790s the East India Company, having gained control of Bengal, imposed the main principles of English law on the region. Complex systems of tribute payment, corporate responsibilities and group rights were replaced by a system of individual ownership and a land tax. The older stratum of tribute collectors, the *zamindars*, became a landowning class and were supplemented by a stratum of moneylenders, civil servants and merchants to become a new rural oligarchy. Over the course of the nineteenth century, British rule – and law – extended across the Indian subcontinent (Wolf, 1982).

Ranajit Guha speaks about British rule in India as 'dominance without hegemony'. On the face of it, this might seem to contradict Mahatma Gandhi's claim that the Indians had 'allowed' the British to rule. It is certainly the case that the British never established a modern system of hegemony in India to secure their power. What they did attempt was to rule through intermediary strata: the merchants, the agrarian elites and the partially anglicised professional stratum – the *bhadrolok*. To a considerable degree, the agrarian elites could rely upon the traditional authority of customary law. As long as these forms of traditional authority remained, the British were 'allowed' to rule. However, over the course of the nineteenth century, the subjugation of Indian agriculture to the dictates of the global market – and British interests in particular – led to the erosion of customary rights, and in its wake, of traditional authority. Peasant access to forest and commonage was curtailed, pastoralists were prevented from moving cattle and were more or less criminalised, and the number of landless labourers soared. Most important of all perhaps was the elimination of the traditional system of grain reserves, to be replaced by commercial systems and calculations. The full implications of these changes only became apparent in the famines of the 1870s and again in the years 1899–1900 (Davis, 2001).

It was in its response to outbreaks of famine that British rule in India was most strikingly reminiscent of its rule in Ireland. In both cases, poor harvests were linked to weather patterns and were cyclical by nature. The poor harvests were greatly exacerbated by the commercialisation of agriculture which imposed systemic pressure to produce cash crops and reduce crop diversity. In both countries, food was exported to cover rent and taxes while peasants starved. The central government and the colonial administrations were very reluctant to admit that there was a serious famine, or to spend state money to ameliorate it. Famine relief was hampered by concern not to distort the working of the free market; both countries were believed to be overpopulated, and the rigours of the market were necessary to give the poor the discipline of character which they clearly lacked. The governments were slow to 'give away' food, instead it had to be worked for. In Ireland in the 1840s, the destitute had the option of workhouses (if there was space) where families were broken up; husbands were separated from their wives and children from their parents. In India in the 1870s, labour camps were established, again separating everyone by age and gender. The daily food ration in the Madras camp in 1877 was lower than that in Buchenwald. Disease spread easily among the weakened inhabitants of both workhouses and labour camps, resulting in high mortality rates. By contrast, in pre-colonial India, local elites maintained food reserves and took responsibility to feed the peasantry in the event of harvest failure (Davis, 2001). Ireland and India were of course vastly different, not least in population and size. The fact that societies so dissimilar should have had such parallel experiences suggests that the role of imperial domination in both cases needs to be explored to make sense of their entry into 'modernity'.

Empire and Class

The British Empire differed from the empires of central and eastern Europe in that it was an overseas one and its territory was primarily extra-European, similar in this respect to the French, Dutch and Portuguese empires. In terms of scale, the British dwarfed all others. Moreover, for most of the nineteenth century Britain had been the primary industrial power and the global hegemon. It established the ground rules which other states followed. It was able to do so because of its wealth and its maritime power. With the world's largest navy, Britannia literally ruled the waves. Even after its loss of industrial primacy in the last decades of the nineteenth century (to the US and Germany), Britain continued to dominate global trade and finance. This loss of industrial primacy arguably made the survival of empire even more important.

The issue of empire was closely tied up with class. With the exception of France, all the European empires were monarchies. While the power of monarchs varied, all shared a certain political culture. Authority was hierarchical and hereditary. Acceptance of this hereditary authority and respect for one's superiors was crucially important for securing social peace in pre-war Europe. The hereditary principle, though, had been fatally undermined by the rise of capitalism, and linked to it, the pernicious doctrines of liberty and equality that emanated from the French Revolution.

Industry, commerce and urban dwelling had broken the older patterns of wealth, settlement and power. The millions migrating to the cities were far removed from the supervision of local aristocratic elites, while the newly prosperous middle classes sought access to power as a natural corollary to their wealth. In the pre-industrial age, the number of wealthy merchants was limited and they could be ennobled without disruption to the social hierarchy. But the social disruption occasioned by the rise of capitalism was so great that the piecemeal approach of old no longer worked. Not only did the nobility resent sharing power with commoners, but once political representation broke with the hereditary principle, it became difficult to know where to draw the line. The spectre of democracy haunted Europe.

Britain had handled the transition to urban capitalism with a smoothness that the rest of Europe marvelled at. While scholars can debate the relative role that the earlier development of agrarian capitalism played in the rise of industrial capitalism, there can be no doubt that these agrarian changes *facilitated* the process. A class of capitalist landowners was much less threatened by the ascent of merchants, industrialists and financiers. Not only did they share a commercial cast of mind, the political arrangements that had been made in the seventeenth century ensured that new wealth could secure an entry to the corridors of power. In the nineteenth century, the 'public school' system helped bind landed and commercial elites into a common upper-class culture. In Britain, as in most of Europe, the nascent bourgeoisie was less concerned with challenging the power of aristocracy than with winning their acceptance. For much of the century, Britain had been a model for others. What particularly impressed the European elites was how Britain had managed to extend the system of representation while maintaining an aristocratic aura to the exercise of power. Nor was it merely an aura. The landed elite continued to dominate the upper echelons of the British state at least up to the Great War (Anderson, 1992; Hobsbawm, 1968; Mayer, 1981).

This transition to a well-ordered liberal parliamentary state was less successful in Ireland. Neither agrarian nor industrial capitalism had been successfully implanted there. The Irish landed aristocracy could rely not on deferential reserve, but on a reservoir of loathing. For Westminster, this meant that Ireland could not be ruled in the same way as England, Scotland or Wales. Throughout the nineteenth century, the Irish landowning class was the key agency through which Britain ruled Ireland. By the beginning of the First World War, the power of this class had been greatly weakened in Ireland. The Church of Ireland, to which the great majority of the landowners owed allegiance, was disestablished as the state church in 1869. The introduction of the secret ballot in 1872 made it much more difficult to control elections, while the 1880 Land Act established the dual ownership of land between landlord and tenant. The land purchase acts went further, initiating a process whereby the peasant occupiers bought the land with loans from the British exchequer. While the land purchase scheme rescued the landlords financially, it finished off their social power at a local level. The change in land ownership occurred over decades – by 1914 landlords still owned nearly half the land – and brought its own conflicts.

Landowners and their progeny continued to play a central role in political life. The largest landowners had seats in the House of Lords and carried considerable weight, especially in the Conservative and Unionist Party. Most of the senior posts in the Irish civil service and the Royal Irish Constabulary – the police force – were held by men from landed backgrounds. Irish landowners or their progeny were also a significant element in the British Army officer corps (Anderson, 1992; Campbell, 2009).

In Ireland, as elsewhere, there were some signs of a convergence between landed and commercial elites. Some successful businessmen bought up landed estates in the post-Famine era and more landlords became involved in the world of commerce. Almost half the directors of the major Irish business enterprises in this period were from landlord backgrounds, and many former landlords invested their gains from the government land purchase scheme in commerce, not least in imperial enterprises. What made the Irish situation more complicated was the scale of communal divide within the middle classes. It wasn't only landholding which was dominated by Protestants, so too were the higher professions and the upper echelons of business. Catholics were not only largely excluded from the higher ranks of commercial life, in many enterprises they were even kept out of clerical work. A telling statistic of the time is that there were more Catholics in state employment, following the introduction of competitive examination for entry into the civil service, than there were in the private sector (Campbell, 2009; Cullen, 1972).

Fergus Campbell concludes from a detailed study of the Irish elite in the period leading up to the Great War:

> The British state in Ireland since the Act of Union (1801) had been largely based on its alliance with the landlords and the Irish Protestant middle class. Indeed, the Protestant middle class regarded themselves as a privileged governing minority who were intent on maintaining their position in Irish society. (Campbell, 2009, p. 81)

This divide compounded the difficulties facing the state and the propertied classes in creating a viable system of hegemony in twentieth-century Ireland.

There were Catholics in the business elite (Campbell suggests a figure of around 10 per cent) and they would play an important role in the politics of the period. Catholics were also increasingly involved in the professions, but here too they occupied a subordinate position. The virtual exclusion of Catholics from many elite circles had the effect of cementing relations between the Catholic professional classes and the Catholic clergy. Schools, colleges and hospitals run by clerics all provided employment for Catholic professionals in a context where opportunity for social mobility was limited (Campbell, 2009; Pašeta, 1999).

By the first decades of the twentieth century a distinctive Catholic upper middle class had emerged, which was positioned socially and culturally between the Protestant upper middle class and the wider Catholic middle-class population. They had their own schools – the Jesuits were especially favoured – which the much more numerous Catholic petit bourgeoisie could only aspire to, or resent. Like the Protestant schools, they played rugby, cricket and hockey and displayed little interest in the revived Gaelic sports and language movements. They were particularly influential in the Home Rule movement (the Irish Parliamentary Part) and they used their influence to steer the nationalist movement in a conservative direction. While the Catholic bourgeois were resentful at what they perceived as exclusionary practices by the Protestant elite they looked favourably upon the empire, and many sought advancement in the imperial services. In these circles, support for Home Rule was increasingly accompanied by enthusiasm for empire. Thomas Kettle, a Home Rule MP and an articulate representative of this new elite, argued that the 'inevitableness of Home Rule resides in the fact that it is, as one might say, a biped among ideas. It marches to triumph on two feet, an Irish and Imperial foot' (quoted in Pašeta, 1999, p. 128).

The question of empire had been central to the debate on Home Rule from the beginning. Gladstone, in his speech on the first Home Rule Bill, emphasised that Home Rule would strengthen the Empire, not weaken it. While imperial ideologues like to stress the grandeur of empire and the onerous responsibilities it placed on them to civilise the backward races, imperial statesmen had a very clear grasp of its economic significance. Winston Churchill, with characteristic lucidity, told his cabinet colleagues in 1914:

We are not a young people with an innocent record and a scanty inheritance. We have engrossed to ourselves an altogether disproportionate share of the wealth and traffic of the world. We have got all we want in territory, and our claim to be left in the unmolested enjoyment of vast and splendid possessions, mainly acquired by violence, largely maintained by force, often seems less reasonable to others than to us. (Quoted in Darwin, 2011, p. 268)

While the 1886 Home Rule Bill kept custom and excise powers with Westminster, the *Economist* magazine opposed the measure because of the risk that protectionist measures by an Irish parliament would, at some future point, damage the empire. Their concerns were well founded. The last quarter of the nineteenth century had witnessed the relative decline of British industry, with Germany and the US in particular taking the lead in the more advanced areas like chemicals. Protectionist policies – and state intervention in the case of Germany – had played an important role in this turnaround. In his more radical moments Parnell advocated similar measures for Ireland: 'Without a parliament with full powers for Ireland, we can do nothing in the way of reviving her industries' (quoted in Strauss, 1951, p. 176). Despite the refusal by all sections of ruling opinion in Britain to permit Ireland to control its own trade, Westminster did sanction the introduction of tariffs in both Canada and Australia, having clearly concluded that they were in no position to prevent them (Darwin, 2011).

A generation later, very little of Parnell's radicalism remained in the upper echelons of the Home Rule movement. While maintaining homage to Parnell's memory, the Parliamentary Party leadership had made their peace with the British establishment. John Redmond, the party leader, declared in 1912: 'Our demand for Home Rule does not mean that we want to break with the British Empire. We are entirely loyal to the British Empire as such' (quoted in McMahon, 2004, p. 196). The 1912 Home Rule Bill contained only the most modest elements of autonomy. Responsibility for customs and excise, relations with the crown, defence and foreign policy, as well as land purchase, were all reserved for Westminster.

Not everyone accepted John Redmond's distinction between the 'domestic' and the 'imperial'. The Tory leader Lord Salisbury referred to the Irish Home Rule MPs as 'eighty foreigners'. Sir George Campbell, the former governor of Bengal, wrote in *Fortnightly Review* that Ireland:

is a colony which we have only partly colonised, and in which the natives have neither been exterminated nor thoroughly assimilated and we have the race difficulties in the way of self-governing institutions with which we are familiar in other colonies, but in a more aggravated form. (Quoted in McMahon, 2004, p. 185)

In the original Home Rule debates, Gladstone had attempted to develop an analogy between Ireland and Canada, and was dismayed that the issue of India kept coming up.

The Catholic bourgeois elite's project of becoming Ireland's new ruling class within the British Empire faced a number of obstacles. First and foremost was their numerical and structural weakness. The Catholic elite were thin on the ground and lacked economic clout. Ireland remained a predominantly rural country, and within rural Ireland the economic and political power of the landlords was being replaced by that of large farmers and shopkeepers. It was this middle or petit bourgeois layer who had come to dominate local government in the new century. Even within the cities, most of the large employers were Protestants. The ability of the Catholic bourgeois elite to achieve a hegemonic position depended upon their acceptance by this larger middle-class stratum.

If the rise of the Land League was a turning point in the long conflict between landed elite and peasantry in Ireland, it was not the end of that conflict. While the Land Act of 1881 stabilised rents and made evictions more difficult, it only applied to land which was tenanted. Non-tenanted land, which accounted for 13 per cent nationally (and 18 per cent in Connaught) was not subject to these laws. Landowners rented most of this land out to 'graziers' – mostly shopkeepers or big farmers – who grazed cattle on it for eleven-month periods. From 1900 onwards, serious land agitation developed in Connaught that changed the map of class relations in rural Ireland, pitting smallholders and landless peasants against a combination of landlords and (Catholic) graziers. The formation of the United Irish League, in support of the smallholders and the landless, revealed the incomplete character of the earlier land settlement. The United Irish League soon became a national movement and the Irish Party in Westminster had to formally endorse its charter for continued land reform (Campbell, 2005).

The dependence of the Catholic bourgeois elite on the Catholic clergy went beyond issues of educational and social advancement. In the conflict between the smallholders and the graziers in Connaught, the bulk of the Catholic clergy had sided with the graziers, understandably enough in that most priests came from prosperous farming backgrounds. The structural weakness of the Catholic bourgeois elite (their very limited leverage over the population) accentuated this dependency. Their increased absorption into British imperial culture did not help. The more they distanced themselves from the rest of the population, the greater their need to stress their identity as Catholics. Fostering Catholic communalism became a substitute for leading a movement for national independence (Campbell, 2009; Pašeta, 1999).

The social tensions threatening the Home Rule leadership were not confined to the conflict over land. Discontent with the Home Rule project was also found in the lower middle classes and the intelligentsia. Many became involved in the project of attempting to establish a national culture clearly distinct from Britain's. The Gaelic League, committed to reviving the Irish language, became a mass organisation while the Gaelic Athletic Association was the largest civil society organisation in Ireland. Sinn Féin with a programme for developing an independent economy, though smaller in membership, had a growing influence (Lyons, 1973).

Limited industrialisation and persistent under-employment hampered labour organisation in Ireland. Trade-union membership was largely confined to craft workers, and was strongest in the northeast. In Belfast, divisions between skilled and unskilled workers overlapped with the confessional divide: skilled workers were overwhelmingly Protestants and the craft unions had little interest in organising unskilled labour. When a labour movement organising unskilled workers did emerge, it was led by radicals. James Larkin and James Connolly, the key figures in the movement, were both products of the Irish diaspora, from Liverpool and Edinburgh respectively, and were influenced by revolutionary syndicalism. The Irish Transport Workers Union which they founded was at the centre of a major confrontation with capital, the 1913 Dublin Lockout. The employers' leader, William Martin Murphy, was a Home Rule supporter, and owner of the influential *Irish Independent* newspaper. While the employers were successful in the short run, it proved to be a pyrrhic victory, and many of the forces drawn to support the workers were at the heart of the 1916 Easter Rising (Lyons, 1973; O'Connor, 1992).

From the time of Gladstone, the Irish Parliamentary Party had maintained a close alliance with the Liberal Party. For the most part this was a dormant alliance as the British party did not need their support. Lloyd-George's attempt to bring in a 'Peoples Budget' in 1911 brought about a full-scale confrontation with the House of Lords and, following a general election, the Liberals found themselves dependent upon the Irish Party and were forced to reintroduce a Home Rule Bill for Ireland in 1912. Ulster Unionists responded by establishing a mass paramilitary body, the Ulster Volunteer Force, and with the tacit support of the Tories, threatened to forcibly resist Home Rule. When the Ulster Volunteer Force landed arms from Germany, the British Army – whose officers came disproportionally from Anglo-Irish backgrounds – refused to move against them. Radical Irish nationalists responded by establishing the Irish Volunteers, which the Home Rule Party felt compelled to participate in so as not to lose control of the nationalist movement (Lyons, 1973; Strauss, 1951).

The Impact of the Great War

The years preceding the Great War saw, across Europe and beyond, an extraordinary coming together of technological dynamism, cultural efflorescence and social revolt. Social Democracy, syndicalism and feminism challenged class and gender hierarchies while nationalist movements challenged the integrity of empires.

The First World War was decisive in breaking London's attempt to establish a system of controlled autonomy in Ireland. Both the Ulster Unionists and the Home Rule Party declared their support for the British Empire and offered the services of their respective volunteer forces. For the Home Rulers it was an opportunity to show that autonomy did not mean disloyalty. For the Unionists, the war was a chance to demonstrate their enduring allegiance to crown and empire. The Ulster Volunteer Force was permitted to join the British armed forces as a regiment under their own officers, and huge numbers of them joined up. The Irish Volunteers were not permitted to join collectively, though encouraged individually. The organisation split, with a few thousand joining the British ranks, and most drifting away. A radical minority, led by Fenians, maintained their own force and determined to use the war as an opportunity to stage an insurrection. Joseph Lee notes that 'enthusiasm for the war was never as widespread in nationalist Ireland as the media, dominated by pro-war elements, suggested.' The numbers enlisting in Ireland were significantly lower than in Scotland, England or Wales, and almost half of those came from Ulster (Lee, 1989, pp. 23–4).

The war greatly weakened rulers' authority throughout Europe and beyond: the slaughter in the trenches gave legitimacy to revolutionary violence. In Ireland many of the forces involved in supporting the workers during the 1913 Lockout came together to stage an insurrection in Dublin at Easter 1916. The rebellion was suppressed within a week and its leaders executed, but it sparked a spirit of revolt that spread across the country.

A few months later, tens of thousands of Irish soldiers in the British Army, including many Ulster Unionist volunteers, died in the battle of the Somme, fighting to gain six miles of German territory. The contrast between the two events would play an important role in Ulster Unionist consciousness. The background of the European war was also central to the republican view, as a line from a popular ballad of the time had it: 'better to die under an Irish sky, than on the battlefields of Flanders.'

Conscription had been introduced in England, Scotland and Wales in 1916, but it was considered too risky to introduce in Ireland. By 1918, after the Bolshevik Revolution ended the war in the East, the Allies found themselves facing defeat on the Western Front. British cabinet papers showed that while 17 per cent of the adult male population of Great Britain has enlisted, only 5 per cent of those in Ireland had. London determined to impose conscription on Ireland. The British move faced massive opposition in Ireland and was deeply damaging to the Home Rule Party, which found itself in the unenviable position of supporting the war but opposing conscription (Kostick, 2009; Lee, 1989).

The popular movement against conscription was the deepest and widest mass movement in Ireland since the Land War, including in its ranks the Catholic Church, the labour movement, and virtually every shade of nationalism. For the first time, the labour movement played a central role in Irish politics. A general strike was hugely successful throughout the country, except paradoxically in Belfast, where labour was most organised (Kostick, 2009).

The new Sinn Féin which emerged to contest the 1918 elections – winning 73 out of 100 seats – was a coalition of disparate forces from constitutional nationalists to radical republicans. Veterans of the Easter Rising played a crucial role in it, but so too did many who had been closer to the Home Rule Party and were looking for a new formation to succeed it. Many of its candidates were still in prison. The 'moderate' element was considerable but the radicals were strong enough to ensure that the Dáil declared an oath of allegiance to the Republic and to pass the Democratic Programme which declared 'the right of the people of Ireland to the ownership of Ireland' and insisted that 'all right to private property must be subordinated to the public right and welfare.' Critics have often dismissed these provisions as empty rhetoric but they did provide an impetus for the struggles – armed and otherwise – which followed (Lyons, 1973; Strauss, 1951).

The War of Independence developed more or less spontaneously, with the Sinn Féin leadership initially condemning armed attacks by Volunteers on the Royal Irish Constabulary and only later being pushed into supporting the guerrilla campaign. Though the Irish Republican Army (IRA) – as the Volunteers came to call themselves – was poorly armed and equipped, they succeeded in paralysing the workings of the state, and in particular the police and courts. By 1920 a system of dual power had developed, encouraging a wave of labour and agrarian struggles (Kostick, 2009; Rumpf & Hepburn, 1977).

A government-imposed wage freeze and wartime price inflation had greatly reduced workers' incomes. The resulting discontent encouraged a wave of strikes in the postwar period. Even in Belfast there was a huge general strike in 1919 demanding wage increases that paralysed the city. Throughout Ireland, trade-union membership soared. In 1914 there were 110,000 workers affiliated to the Trade Union Congress, most of whom were members of skilled unions. By 1920 a quarter of a million workers were affiliated, of which 130,000 were members of the radical Transport Union. Union membership peaked in 1921 with 300,000 workers organised in unions. The rise of labour struggles was closely linked with the independence movement. Many of the organisers were former political prisoners. The Royal Irish Constabulary and the Dublin Metropolitan Police had long been vigilant in suppressing workers' struggles; they now found themselves vulnerable to retaliation (Mitchell, 1974).

There was also an upsurge of agrarian battles, with land seizures and other actions by smallholders and landless labourers spreading from Connaught to affect 16 counties by 1920. The Sinn Féin leadership was opposed to the land agitation, arguing that this represented 'sectional' interests and that there was a need to maintain the unity of all classes in the national struggle. The Dáil established its own Court system, using British law, and passed judgements, often siding with landlords. In some cases the local IRA was used by the Sinn Féin leadership to uphold the rights of landlords. Elsewhere, IRA units were actively involved in supporting the land agitation (Campbell, 2005; Fitzpatrick, 1977; Strauss, 1951).

The dual power situation left Westminster little option but to negotiate with the rebel forces. All sections of the British governing class were agreed that Ireland must be kept within the Empire, which ruled out a republic. For Lloyd George, the British premier, capitulating to the Republicans was inconceivable:

> It will lower the prestige and dignity of this country and reduce British authority to a low point in Ireland itself. It will give the impression that we have lost grip, that the Empire has no further force and will have an effect in India and throughout Europe. (Quoted in Jones, 1971, p. 109)

Westminster formally partitioned the country in 1920, establishing a Northern Ireland parliament which controlled most of Ulster. Despite the 1919 general strike in Belfast, radical forces never succeeded in dislodging the great majority of Protestant workers from their allegiance to Unionism. The Belfast shipyards had the greatest concentration of industrial workers anywhere in Ireland. In 1920 there was a wave of expulsions of Catholic workers, and socialist activists, from the yards. The Northern Ireland government established its own armed police force, in effect a Unionist militia, to suppress the republican insurgency. By 1922 there was one armed policeman for every two Catholic families in Northern Ireland. The imposition of partition had the benefit not only of satisfying Ulster Unionist opinion, but also of giving London added leverage over the whole island (Farrell, 1983; Lee, 1989; Strauss, 1951).

Aside from confirming partition, the Treaty agreed in 1921 between the British government and Sinn Féin delegates established the Irish Free State as a dominion within the British Empire, with all public representatives compelled to swear allegiance to the British monarch. The British also maintained a number of naval bases and extracted various other concessions from the newly 'independent' state. The Treaty was carried by a small majority in the Dáil, but opposed by a majority of Sinn Féin members, by virtually the entire Cumann na mBan (the women's independence organisation) and crucially by a majority of the IRA.

The conventional interpretation among Irish historians has it that the civil war was fought between extreme Irish nationalists who favoured a militarist solution and a moderate nationalist current who upheld democracy (Lee, 1989). What this explanation does not consider is that the Treaty itself was not freely chosen by the Irish delegates or by the Dáil, but was imposed by Britain using the threat of full scale war (Regan, 1999). For most Irish historians, democracy is considered as synonymous with the liberal constitutional order. If 'democracy' is understood in its older meaning as representing the wishes of the 'demos', the lower strata of society, the civil war appears in a different light. The Treaty was supported by virtually the entire social elite in Irish society – by the professional and commercial classes (both urban and rural), by most of the prosperous farmers, as well as by the Catholic (and Protestant) Churches. Opposition to the Treaty was concentrated among the urban and rural working class, the small farmers and among sections of the lower middle class. The connections between these social divisions, and the political issues raised by the Treaty, eludes most historians.

The Dáil debates on the Treaty, along with biographies of key republican fighters like Tom Barry, Dan Breen and Ernie O'Malley, make it clear that the Oath of Allegiance to the British monarch and the denial of the Republic – not partition – were the key stumbling blocks to acceptance of the Treaty. Superficially, this would seem to have little connection with issues of social class, yet within a few months a civil war had broken out that divided the national independence movement – and southern Ireland – largely along lines of social class.

Conor Kostick has argued that the struggles of these years could have transformed Ireland into a socialist republic had a different leadership existed. Francis Mulhern suggests a very different reading of Irish social politics in this period:

> Southern Ireland in its formative decades, was shaped by its articulation of two compatible but nonetheless distinct modes of production. A modest capitalism led the urban economy, at a low level of industrialisation, and an important section of agriculture. But the greater part of Irish rural space was dominated by a class of smallholding farmers, who indeed, were only partly (and indeed sometimes not at all) involved in commodity production. Thus, most Irish economic property was not capitalist, and the salient labouring class was not proletarian: the social dominant was a free peasantry. (Mulhern, 1998, p. 24)

A couple of qualifications are needed here. While the small-farming class was *numerically* dominant, in terms of modes of production it was capitalism which was *structurally* dominant. Not merely was the capitalist sector wealthier, the system of simple commodity production – small farming and artisanate production – faced constant erosion. This structural weakness of the smallholding economy was expressed most vividly in the huge rates of emigration, the 'flight from the land'. Despite these qualifications, Mulhern's argument about the centrality of the small-farming stratum is an important one. Moreover, it is one which the Irish labour movement singularly failed to address. The debates in the eastern and southern European left about alliances between social classes – especially between the working class and the peasantry – found little echo in the Irish left.

In their classic study of a small-farming community in Clare in the 1930s, *Family and Community in Ireland*, American anthropologists Arensberg and Kimball describe a world in which agricultural labour is still largely collective and cooperative. If these smallholders were culturally conservative – religious belief and seasonal patterns rhymed – they were not politically conservative, and their social outlook included a strong egalitarian streak. Nicos Poulantzas' description of the Jacobin mentality has close parallels to this:

> in its 'social' content it is basically the ideology of the *smallholders*. Jacobinism projected as its social ideal a society made up of small-scale independent producers (both peasants and artisans), a society in which each man owns his field, his own shop or stall and is able to support his own family without recourse to wage-labour and without being exploited by the 'very rich'. (Poulantzas, 1978, p. 179)

Their relationship to landless labourers was very different to that found in regions dominated by large farming. The children of the smallholders would, for the most part, take the same boats to Britain or America as the children of the landless labourers and once there, do the same jobs (Newman, 1964).

The civil war also revealed significant tensions within the middle classes. These were not identical to a divide between 'upper' and 'lower' strata, though they overlapped with that divide. While the upper middle classes were overwhelmingly conservative, and pro-Treaty, the much more numerous lower middle classes contained a substantial socially radical element, which had imbibed an egalitarian republican philosophy and an equally substantial conservative layer that deferred to authority. The opposition to the Treaty among subaltern strata, urban and rural, was deeply rooted in people's social experience. The notion of an independent Republic was not simply about constitutional niceties, but expressed a radically different social ideal to that being proposed by the Treaty's advocates (Andrews, 1979; Greaves, 1971).

Writing shortly before his execution in 1922, the republican leader Liam Mellows noted the failure of the anti-Treaty forces to develop a clear social programme, but did not address its source (Greaves, 1971). Arguably, the political vagueness of Irish radicalism was in part a consequence of the lopsided development of Irish intellectual life. An Irish intelligentsia emerged in an intellectual context dominated by the dual forces of Catholicism and English empiricism, both deeply hostile to theoretical investigation. Intellectual discontent in Ireland sought to turn the English traditions on their head, but operated largely within their boundaries. Romanticism, the most radical current in English intellectual life, had an obvious attraction but it directed the intellectual radicals to seek a social alternative in the sphere of culture and to emphasise (or create if necessary) cultural differences from the ruling nation, rather than investigate the workings of social power.

Whether a different type of Labour leadership could, as Conor Kostick suggests, have brought about an egalitarian transformation of Irish society is an unanswerable question. What is worth noting though is that the state which did emerge was not a product of the victory of these forces, but of their defeat.

From an international perspective however, the picture is somewhat different. The crucial significance of Irish independence, for all its limitations and hesitations, is that it began the breakup of the British Empire, and was seen to do so. In India in particular – the jewel in the imperial crown – the Irish situation was closely watched, and Indian nationalists drew the conclusion that if imperial power could be broken in Ireland, it could also, with adequate organisation, be broken in India. The end of British rule in India in turn signalled the collapse of European colonialism.

THE LIMITS OF INDEPENDENCE

In the first decade of the Irish Free State, social and economic policy differed little from the era of British rule. The new government placed its main emphasis on stability and the maintenance of institutional continuity. The civil state institutions and the legal system were taken over intact from the British. In practice, institutional continuity meant continued subordination to the British market and the British state. Over 90 per cent of Irish exports went to the British market. The Irish currency was tied to sterling and Irish interest rates were determined by the Bank of England and the Treasury in London. The Irish banks were structured along the British joint-stock model rather than the continental investment-banking system and kept most of their deposits in the City of London (Fanning, 1978; Lee, 1989; Ó Gráda, 1997).

The Free State government was dominated by ministers from the Catholic upper middle class, mostly from big farming backgrounds. They followed the British model of minimal public expenditure, low income tax and a conviction that prosperity would follow from fiscal rectitude. The government explicitly rejected any programme of attempting to industrialise through import substitution and state-led initiatives, and argued that national prosperity would arrive from focusing on agricultural exports, which in practice meant aiding the wealthy minority of big farmers and exporters. The best way of reducing farmers' costs was through reducing farm labourers' wages, which fell by more than 20 per cent during their stay in office. Kevin O'Higgins, the key figure in the Cumann na nGaedheal government, dismissed the Democratic Programme as 'poetry', and denounced its claims on national resources as 'communistic'. In Lee's words they waged a 'coherent campaign against the weaker elements of the community' (Lee, 1989, p. 87).

Old-age pensions and pensions for the blind were reduced. Little effort was made to improve education or housing: as late as 1932 only 9 per cent of children received a post-primary education. Dublin remained one of the worst cities for slums in Europe (Lee, 1989; Ó Gráda, 1997).

The Cumann na nGaedheal government was already unpopular before the global depression that followed the Wall Street Crash, but this became accentuated afterwards. Unemployment rose and the emigration routes closed. The depression also led to falling agricultural prices. In the west, smallholders, led by republicans, began a campaign against the debt payment owed to Westminster over land purchase: the annuities campaign. Fianna Fáil – formed by anti-Treatyites in 1926 – came to office in 1932 with the conviction that national independence and socio-economic development were closely linked. They also began the process of dismantling the formal connections with Empire, beginning with the Oath of Allegiance (Rumpf & Hepburn, 1977).

The key to social development was the promotion of industrialisation, employment and self-sufficiency. Industrialisation was to be achieved through import-substitution. The introduction of protectionist tariffs did result in a significant rise in employment in manufacturing industry that continued up until the early 1950s (though falling off during the war). Fianna Fáil also sought to shift agricultural production from export-orientated pastoral production to more labour-intensive tillage. The aim here was not merely to increase rural employment, but to make sure that the country was self-sufficient in food. Manufacturing industry was focused primarily on food and clothing, with little development of a capital goods industry. The most important structural advances occurred through the development of semi-state bodies in the infrastructural area, especially the gradual spread of electrification (Ó Gráda, 1997; O'Malley, 1989).

If the results of Fianna Fáil's industrialisation drive were modest, so too was the drive itself. In nineteenth-century continental Europe the rise of manufacturing industry was facilitated by the development of new systems of credit directly established by, or closely linked to, public authorities. Many European states made a concerted effort to generate a comprehensive industrialising programme. The development of an advanced system of technical and scientific education played a crucial role in the rise of industry, most notably in Germany. Transformations in these three spheres – credit, planning and education – were critical for continental Europe's efforts to catch up with and in many cases surpass Britain in the second half of the nineteenth century. In each of these areas, independent Ireland failed to make much headway (Chang, 2003; Gerschenkron, 1962).

Sean Lemass – Fianna Fáil's key economics minister – was aware of the need to transform the credit system and break the Irish banks' dependency on the City of London, and at one stage envisaged the development of a state bank to push economic development, but the idea never came to fruition. Opposition by Department of Finance officials partially explains the inaction. Finance officials also blocked moves towards planning which they thought smacked of communism. It seems likely that Fianna Fáil was divided on the adoption of radical measures. In the event, not only did Ireland not possess a publicly directed credit system to finance development, it retained its currency link with an overvalued sterling (Fanning, 1978). The currency link facilitated trade with Britain, but it acted as a significant obstacle to industrial advance because the Irish state deprived itself of the monetary tools crucial for a serious development strategy.

The protectionist programme, and Fianna Fáil's support for withholding 'annuities', led to an 'economic war' with Britain. The British responded with retaliatory measures aimed at Irish imports which were particularly painful to the more prosperous farmers who dominated the export trade. This stratum provided a mass support base for the Blueshirt movement, led by veterans of the Free State Army and modelled on European fascist movements. The political life of the early and mid-1930s was dominated by battles between the Blueshirts and a popular coalition of Fianna Fáil, Labour and Republican activists, with the Blueshirts losing most of the street battles and the wider political contest (Strauss, 1951; Regan, 1999).

The Fianna Fáil government did introduce a series of measures to improve the living conditions of the working class and the poorer sections of the population. Their housing programme was especially important: 12,000 houses a year were built, on average, in their first decade in office. Some elements of a welfare state were gradually put in place. Trade unions were given greater legal protection and union membership rose throughout the 1930s and 1940s (O'Connell & Rottman, 1992; Smith, 2005).

The prospect of a European war concentrated minds at Westminster and in 1938 a settlement was made ending the 'economic war', which included the British abandoning three naval bases around the Irish coast that had been retained under the terms of the 1921 Treaty. Ireland adopted a policy of neutrality in the ensuing war, which also witnessed a huge exodus of emigrants seeking work in the cities of Britain.

Opening Ireland

Prolonged stagnation in the Irish economy in the 1950s stood in marked contrast to the 'economic miracle' occurring in Germany and most West European states. While the civil servants worried about a balance of payments crisis and a fiscal deficit, it was the scale of mass emigration that brought home to most people the extent of the state's failure to develop the economy. This situation encouraged a radical reassessment of the development strategy pursued by the Irish state since the 1930s. Officials of the Department of Finance, in close consultation with World Bank advisors, drew up a strategic programme advocating the abandonment of protectionism and the introduction of a system of economic planning; Ireland joined the World Bank and the International Monetary Fund (IMF) in 1957. The involvement of the World Bank was crucial in a number of respects. It overcame the resistance of the more conservative elements in the civil service who viewed planning as suspiciously close to Communism. More importantly perhaps, World Bank endorsement for the Irish programme for economic development opened up credit lines from the international banking system. For the first time the Irish state could engage in a significant level of borrowing to fund growth (Fanning, 1978; Smith, 2005).

The shift in economic policy adopted by the Irish Republic in the late 1950s did not involve a wholesale endorsement of economic liberalism. The state remained committed to a development policy. Trade liberalisation, and encouraging an inflow of outside capital, was combined with a stress on developing infrastructure, both physical and cultural. The public sector – in particular the semi-state companies – remained an important part of the economy. While industry increased its share of the labour force from 26 per cent to 31 per cent between 1956 and 1971, the share of the services sector rose from 34 per cent to 43 per cent (McCarthy, 1990). Throughout the 1960s and into the 1970s, the Irish Republic experienced reasonably high growth levels. Some of this was a consequence of the setting up of foreign-owned manufacturing industries, but it was mainly a result of the growth of services, in particular the development of the public sector. Post-primary, and later tertiary, education expanded hugely over the following decades (Lee, 1989; Ó Gráda, 1997; Share & Tovey, 2003).

Agriculture's share of output and employment fell throughout the twentieth century. Farm sizes increased, though gradually. Mechanisation also occurred slowly. Agricultural productivity and farm incomes were among the lowest in northern Europe. Prior to Irish entry to the European Economic Community, virtually all agricultural exports went to the British market. While Irish economic history in the second half of the twentieth century is generally told in a narrative of a movement from 'protectionism to liberalisation', for agriculture, the key sector of the economy, the opposite was the case. The British market drew on global suppliers (mostly ex-colonies) and prices were low. The European Economic Community (EEC) operated a protectionist system and prices were high. In the first decade of Ireland's entry into Europe, real incomes in agriculture doubled. This new wealth was not all evenly shared; while the Irish countryside became a good deal more prosperous, a substantial degree of poverty persisted. Over a period of decades a huge number of small farms disappeared. While agriculture accounted for 53 per cent of the work force in 1926, by 2004 this figure had dropped to 6 per cent (Curtis et al, 1996; Lee, 1989; Ó Gráda, 1997).

Culture and Politics

The old alliance between the Catholic middle classes and the clergy had been given a new institutional grounding by the

Cumann na nGaedheal government following the Treaty. Divorce and contraception were banned, and a strict code of censorship introduced. This re-enforcement of clerical power represented more a continuity than a breach with previous British policy. Throughout the eighteenth and nineteenth centuries, Westminster had been happy to farm out education, health and social provision to religious and other voluntary bodies in both Britain and Ireland rather than have the state accept public responsibility for them. Practical and ideological elements were combined here. The state avoided the costs incurred, while social discipline of the population, especially the lower classes, was considered best left to religious bodies. Victorian liberalism and Catholic corporatism concurred (Ferritor, 2004; Lee, 1989).

This symbiotic relationship between Church and State was continued by the Fianna Fáil government, though in a modified way. De Valera was careful not to estrange the Protestant community. Protestant schools were subsidised, and Trinity College came back into favour (partially as a balance against the National University colleges, where Blueshirt elements were entrenched). The government resisted clerical pressure to support Franco in the Spanish Civil War. Clerical invective against 'Godless' communism was useful, however, for keeping socialist forces marginalised, and the state continued to enforce Catholic 'moral' codes in the sexual field (Lee, 1989).

The Vatican's Ecumenical Council in the 1960s opened up debate within the Irish Catholic Church, seeming to herald a less authoritarian relationship between clergy and laity. By 1968, with the publication of the papal encyclical against contraception, it became clear that conservative elements had regained the leadership of the Church. In Ireland it was the opening fusillade of a long battle between secular and clericalist forces across a range of issues including abortion, contraception, censorship, divorce and homosexual rights, in which the clericalist forces have been increasingly on the losing side. While urbanisation weakened the power of the Church, it is arguable that their greatest setback was the decline of clerical influence over women. The issues that these battles have been fought on have been precisely those questions associated with demands for sexual autonomy and gender equality. By the end of the twentieth century, female participation in the labour force increased hugely to the point that they outnumbered males (Inglis, 1998; Share & Tovey, 2003).

The religious shift in Ireland has largely been a generational one, stretching across classes. Mass attendance has become very much a minority affair among younger people, and even those who still attend are mostly sceptical towards Church institutions, and selective as regards Church teachings. Aside from loss of influence, the Catholic Church has suffered from a massive loss of cadre. The numbers entering the priesthood have declined precipitously and many religious orders are facing extinction. The revelations that the Church (along with the state) has been involved in the systematic cover up of child abuse extending over decades, has further diminished an already gravely weakened organisation. Nonetheless the Church retains a significant institutional power, especially in the educational sphere, despite the fact that few members of religious orders are still involved in teaching.

Generations of Irish writers imagined that once the power of the Catholic Church was broken, a great intellectual awakening would occur. In the event, secularism coincided with the rise of new communicative forms, especially television, and a trend towards the diminution of literature. In its first phase, the publicly-owned Irish television station was a challenging institution, but this changed in the 1970s. Its board was dismissed in 1972 for permitting interviews with Republican leaders, and subsequently the public broadcasting organisation came to embrace censorship with enthusiasm. The formal restrictions on republicans mutated across the media into a blanket censorship prohibiting discussion on the roots of the northern conflict and questions related to national independence more broadly. To question such practices was to court 'terrorism'. Journalist Mary Holland described the atmosphere in the state broadcaster Radio Telefis Eireann (RTE): 'Self-censorship has been raised to the level of an art. Caution lay thick on the ground over everything' (quoted in Purcell, 1996, p. 257). In the conventional interpretation, the changes occurring in Ireland in these decades, urbanisation and secularisation, entering the European Union and becoming integrated into the circuits of North Atlantic capital, were all part of a single process of 'modernisation'. The wall of self censorship that traversed the media – and much of the academy – inhibited critical engagement with the conventional verities. For the most part, the influence of Catholicism has been replaced by a deeply conformist consumerism: the 'liberalism' of the new elites rarely extends beyond issues of sexual mores.

The conflicts of the 1920s and 1930s shaped the later structure of Irish party politics. In subsequent decades Fianna Fáil retained the support – in most elections – of a majority of small farmers and urban workers, while Fíne Gael, for the most part, retained a majority support among larger farmers and the professional middle classes. Since the Second World War there were huge demographic shifts and structural changes, yet there persisted a remarkable continuity of electoral support for these parties, especially for Fianna Fáil. The poorest areas were those – roughly speaking – where Fianna Fáil polled highest. This needs some explanation, not least because Fianna Fáil has become closely associated, especially in recent decades, not with poverty but with wealth (Rumpf & Hepburn, 1977).

The most obvious explanation is that these votes are based on loyalty to electoral machines operating effective 'clientelist' systems. This is partially the case, but only partially. All the successful politicians, in all the parties, develop such machines, 'persecuting civil servants' in support of their constituents. Moreover, 'clientelism' is most important at the level of local government, whereas the continuity of party support is pronounced in national elections.

Fianna Fáil has won the largest number of votes, of any party, in every general election between 1932 and 2007. This electoral hegemony is a result of their success in projecting themselves as the party of 'national development'. In the 1930s, national development and national independence were seen as more or less synonymous. Through achieving greater political independence, Ireland could advance, socially and economically. This was often painfully slow, but it was real. Social conditions did improve, not least housing and welfare. The scale of Fianna Fáil's success here can be gauged from the extent to which other parties adopted their discourse. Labour supported most of the Fianna Fáil initiatives in the 1930s. Apart from some mavericks, all the key political forces supported Fianna Fáil's policy of neutrality in the Second World War. Fíne Gael became increasingly marginalised in the 1930s and 1940s and only recovered by distancing themselves from more reactionary forms of discourse. New political forces that arose after the war, like Clann na Poblachta (a left republican current) or Clann na Talmhún (a small farmers party), did not break with the dominant discourse, but rather complained that Fianna Fáil had moved too far from its roots (Lee, 1989; Rumpf & Hepburn, 1977).

The shift from a protectionist to an export-orientated economic strategy might have created a political rupture if it had occurred in a different socioeconomic context or been directed by other political forces. The fiscal crisis of the mid-1950s though was accompanied by high unemployment and massive emigration, and a sense of national failure. The Whitaker report did not only advocate a switch to an exporting strategy, it also argued for national planning for development. The political figure guiding this strategic change was the same one who had directed the protectionist strategy in the first place: Sean Lemass. The changed direction was accompanied by an upsurge of economic growth and social spending (made possible by the World Bank's green light for private banks to lend to Ireland). The 1960s saw an unparalleled expansion of education and housing programmes. Once again, the other main political parties followed Fianna Fáil's shift without demur. Within Fianna Fáil itself, this changed orientation was greatly facilitated by the rise of a new generation of political figures closely linked to business (Lee, 1989; McCarthy, 1990).

Irish entry into what was then called the European Economic Community (EEC) was again led by Fianna Fáil, though a key argument in favour of entry was that membership would not only be economically beneficial but it would also diminish Ireland's dependence on Britain. Fíne Gael supported Irish entry into the EEC, though it was opposed by the Irish Labour Party and most of the trade unions. The referendum to join was won overwhelmingly: the only areas registering significant opposition were the Dublin working-class constituencies, and even there most voted in favour. A subtle shift in political discourse had occurred. National development would now occur through a dilution of sovereignty but national development remained the central thread (Lee, 1989).

The most serious test for Fianna Fáil governance since the 1930s was their handling of the Northern Ireland crisis. Earlier campaigns against partition in the 1940s and 1950s had been suppressed easily enough. The Troubles of the late 1960s were different. This was a mass revolt and had a wide resonance throughout the island. A key objective – arguably *the* key objective – of all sections of the Irish elite in these decades was to insulate the southern state from the northern conflict. The IRA did have a significant degree of support in the south and in crisis situations, like the aftermath of Bloody Sunday or during the hunger strikes, these levels of support rose sharply. While the state always had the measure of the Republican underground, its strategic aim was to prevent any mass radicalisation which linked social discontent with support for the northern revolt. This necessitated ensuring that elements of a welfare system be maintained, and even expanded (at a time when the welfare state was being eroded in Britain). It also placed certain limits on the coercive capacity of the state. In both areas Fianna Fáil proved more adept than their political rivals.

While Fíne Gael never succeeded in gaining a majority or even a plurality of votes or seats, they remained the second largest party, and have maintained a substantial influence in the professions, the universities and in the media. In office, their instinctive response is one of fiscal rectitude and the promotion of stern measures against subversion. Labour, with whom Fíne Gael has always had to share office, has generally acted as a foil to Fíne Gael's conservatism, encouraging more generous social provision and moderating their authoritarian instincts (Lee, 1989).

The historical weakness of the Irish Labour Party and the social democratic tradition was related to Ireland's social structure but not reducible to it. High levels of unemployment and underemployment placed Irish labour in a position of objective weakness, but workers compensated with a tradition of militancy: the picket was sacrosanct. The Civil War revealed tensions within the Irish working class which were present for most of the twentieth century: a tradition of spontaneous rebellion existed alongside a leadership committed to political moderation, in actions if not in words. While the Free State victory in the Civil War was the occasion for breaking strikes, ending factory occupations and driving down workers' wages, the Labour Party had accepted the Treaty, and strove for neutrality in the Civil War, and the government could not risk pushing its advantage too far. The relationship between the Labour Party and the unions was tenuous with the largest union, the Irish Transport and General Workers Union, only affiliating with the Party in 1959 (Mitchell, 1974; O'Connor, 1992; Regan, 1999).

From the 1930s onwards, the trade union movement and Fianna Fáil maintained a *de facto* social pact. Fianna Fáil governments permitted high levels of unionisation and were slow to use state forces against the unions. This social compact, alongside a strong tradition of solidarity, enabled Irish workers to achieve a degree of employment security (O'Connor, 1992).

In the late 1960s the Labour Party briefly embraced the left, declaring the 'seventies will be socialist', and rejecting any coalition with 'right-wing' parties. A few years later, they were in coalition with Fíne Gael, where Conor Cruise O'Brien, at that time the dominant figure in the Labour Party, surpassed his coalition partners in his zeal to curb sedition and impose censorship. The government introduced a range of measures restricting civil liberties. Fíne Gael responded to the global crisis of the 1970s with policies of fiscal austerity which the Labour Party somewhat reluctantly endorsed, while the Fianna Fáil opposition advocated a Keynesian expansionary approach. The trade unions distanced themselves from the Labour Party and in the 1977 elections working-class voters overwhelmingly deserted them (Lee, 1989). The fate of the 1973–77 Coalition government illustrates the limits of representing Irish party politics in terms of a left-right divide. All the major political parties in the Republic were conservative on fundamental political and socio-economic issues; the major differences between them flow from their degree of reliance on working-class votes. For their part, trade-union leaders sought to play Labour and Fianna Fáil off against each other.

Union membership increased more or less continuously from the 1930s until the 1980s' recession/depression. Membership rose with the expansion of services and industry, but this period also saw the arrival of new employers resistant to labour representation. The 1960s and 1970s were the high point of labour militancy which became a source of concern not only to government and employers but also to much of trade-union officialdom (McCarthy, 1971).

Inflation in the 1970s resulted in large sections of workers paying very high rates of income tax and in the late 1970s and early 1980s this led to deep unrest expressed in huge demonstrations throughout the state. The trade-union leadership sought to direct these protests against farmers and the self employed while emphasising the unity of all employed taxpayers. This approach disregarded huge income differences among farmers and self employed while minimising those among employed groups. It also chimed with the emerging neoliberal discourse against the welfare state.

In 1987, the government introduced the first of a series of 'social partnership agreements' between employers, unions and government. The Irish partnership agreements had distinctive features:

> in most corporatist wage deals, union moderation on wage increases was usually reciprocated by government increasing public expenditure or launching a new social programme. But in Ireland the *quid pro quo* was a sustained reduction in personal income taxes. (Donaghey & Teague, 2007, p. 21)

The social partnership agreements certainly led to a significant reduction in strikes. With the upturn in the 1990s union membership rose, but much less steeply than employment. Union density, the share of the Irish labour force which was unionised, fell throughout the social partnership period despite the disappearance of unemployment. This pattern was particularly marked among industrial workers. The agreements provided little added institutional protection for workers; employers could easily disregard the mild penalties which the Labour Court might impose. Nor did the agreements attempt to create a Nordic style 'solidaristic' wage. The partnerships also weakened trade-union organisation at the shop-floor level, leading to a shift of power to the centre. Academic studies suggest that despite the agreements, a strong 'us' and 'them' polarity remained in the Irish workplace (D'Art & Turner, 2002; Donaghey & Teague, 2007).

While economists speak about the macroeconomic stability which the social partnerships provided, it is arguable that their greater significance lay in ensuring that the labour movement became part of a political consensus that accepted without question the beneficence of North Atlantic capitalism. The Labour movement's acceptance of the social partnership agreements followed a paradigm shift within the unions (and the Labour Party) in the 1970s. Historical experience had closely associated struggles for workers' rights and national independence. Trade-union opposition to the EEC was partially motivated by a belief that sovereignty was linked to the social advancement of labour. Once in government the Labour Party came to accept membership of the 'Common Market'. Support for Irish involvement in Europe quickly morphed into an uncritical endorsement of all its institutions and all its new ventures. The Labour Party had limited influence on the politics of the unions. More significant was the broader 'turn' against nationalism. Added to this, rising unemployment from the mid-1970s onwards shook the unions' confidence in the traditional culture of worker solidarity, and (especially after the collapse of the Soviet Union) the European project seemed to offer the only alternative avenue for social advance. From an uncritical endorsement of 'Europe', it was only a small step to accepting the mantras of neoliberalism. By the 1990s, the Irish Congress of Trade Unions was arguing that 'improved competitiveness is crucial for economic growth and job creation and must be protected from upward pressure on pay and inflation' (quoted in Derwin, 1995).

While the aggressive variant of neoliberalism espoused by the Progressive Democrats made little headway with the electorate, a milder version came to dominate virtually all political, social and economic discourse in Ireland. In this worldview, states have lost most of their salience and global markets are paramount. Societies, firms, communities or individuals who wish to survive have to adjust to the rules of these markets and make themselves competitive and flexible. This outlook became codified by the European Union (EU) with its adoption of the 'Lisbon Strategy' in the 1990s. This intellectual environment contributed to the depoliticisation of Irish society that characterised the Celtic Tiger era. Party membership and voter participation both declined. If politics could not affect significant change, political involvement could only be useful for career advancement. One consequence of this has been that political parties, especially Fianna Fáil, have become easy prey to special interest groups, of whom property developers were the most active and influential (Cafruny & Ryner, 2003; Mair, 2000).

The End of Neutrality

The adoption of neoliberalism coincided with the effective abandonment of an independent foreign policy. The Irish state had distinguished itself in the early decades of the United Nations by its opposition to colonialism and its refusal to participate in military alliances. Little of this spirit remains. The US has been permitted to establish a de facto air force base in Shannon which has been used to facilitate the invasion and occupation of Iraq and Afghanistan (Browne, 2008).

Irish compliance towards Washington in this area is closely connected to its increased subordination to Brussels' foreign policy which, like so much of the workings of the EU, is not subject to public scrutiny or democratic accountability (Storey, 2008). The EU has been portrayed as a paragon of virtue, an inspiration for the rest of humanity. Even before the North Atlantic financial crisis, this picture was increasingly at variance with popular opinion. Ireland is one of the few countries where its constitution guaranteed its citizens the right to vote on changes in the EU. In referenda on the Nice and Lisbon treaties, they voted down the proposed changes. The Irish elite were traumatised; the Brussels functionaries were incandescent with rage at the 'ingratitude' of the Irish. In both cases, the elite's response was identical. The popular decision was rejected and the referendum was held again. In the second Lisbon referendum, it was made quite clear that unless Brussels got the result it wanted, the country would be severely penalised.

The Wikileaks documents are revealing about the relationship between Washington and the Irish political elite, not least the Labour Party leader, Eamon Gilmore.

Gilmore, who has led calls against a second referendum, has told the embassy separately that he fully expects, and would support, holding a second referendum in 2009. He explained his public posture of opposition to a second referendum as 'politically necessary' for the time being, the Ambassador said in a 'confidential' dispatch sent to his colleagues in Washington and across the EU. (Irish Independent, 2011)

The US embassy is routinely notified of important government decisions before the Dáil gets informed. Aside from the deferential attitude of the Irish political elite towards Washington and Brussels, the Wikileaks documents also make clear that there is a significant disjunction between elite and popular opinion. The US ambassador noted that Shannon airport is 'a symbol of Irish complicity in perceived U.S. wrongdoing in the Gulf/Middle East' and that 'popular sentiment was manifest in the July 25 jury decision to acquit the "Shannon Five," a group of anti-war protesters who damaged a U.S. naval aircraft at the airport in 2003' (quoted in Browne, 2011). In recent years, the Irish elite has also made a valiant effort to relegitimate the British imperial militarist tradition through celebrating the role of Irish soldiers in the First World War – in the name of inclusiveness – though this too has had little popular resonance.

Miracles and Mirages in a Bridge Economy

After a decade of persistently high unemployment and mass emigration, the wave of growth that came in the 1990s appeared miraculous, with a huge expansion in the labour force that was unprecedented in modern Ireland. Unemployment fell from an official figure of 17 per cent – the actual rate was a good deal higher – to around 4 per cent. Not only did emigration cease, but emigrants returned in huge numbers and Ireland experienced a significant level of immigration. While the great majority of the new jobs were created in the service sector, few disputed that the decisive turn occurred in the manufacturing sector, with Ireland becoming a major hub of the information technology and pharmaceutical industries (Smith, 2005).

From being seen as an economic basket case, Ireland came to be portrayed in the financial media as a great success story, a model for 'emerging' economies to emulate. The Celtic Tiger arose at the high point of 'globalisation' discourse – between the fall of the Berlin Wall and the invasion of Iraq – and the Irish example provided an instructive parable for other states, especially East European ones, of the benefits of pursuing neoliberal prescriptions. Ireland was successful because it had adjusted to become competitive in the global market. Corporations were free to transfer their profits home. Not only did Ireland have a low corporate-tax to attract transnational corporations, it also had a policy of low income-taxation which greatly benefited high earning professionals and executives. Moreover, its tax system was sufficiently flexible to ensure that many of its wealthiest citizens paid no tax at all. Meanwhile, the Irish trade unions had voluntarily accepted a code of wage restraint which ensured an environment of social and economic stability. Within the Irish media, neoliberal doctrine acquired canonical status (Allen, 2000; Smith, 2005).

In fact, foreign investment in Ireland rose *after* corporate taxation was increased from zero to 10 per cent. Wages within the transnational capital sectors of the Irish economy were, on average, *higher* than in the domestic sectors. This would suggest that neither Ireland's low corporate-taxation policy nor its (relatively) low wages were of primary importance in attracting foreign capital. In earlier decades, Ireland had attracted inward investment in textiles and other sectors as a consequence of its relatively low wages, but these firms had mostly moved on to greener pastures. Most of the foreign corporations investing in Ireland are from the US, and most of their products are sold to the EU. Rather than viewing the Celtic Tiger as a model of globalisation, it makes more sense to see it in the context of North Atlantic capitalism, with Ireland establishing itself as a bridge between the US and the European economies. The fact that Ireland was an English speaking member of the EU was probably at least as important a factor for attracting US capital as its tax or wage regime (O'Riain, 2004; Smith, 2005).

Some critics have suggested that the Celtic Tiger boom was a mirage, pointing to the divergence between the GDP figures and the GNP figures for Ireland, with growth in the 1990s looking much higher in the former than the latter. The discrepancy between the two figures can be explained by the huge amounts of profits repatriated by transnational corporations from Ireland alongside the more clandestine practice of 'transfer pricing', whereby companies can choose which country to pay taxes in by manipulating internal pricing (O'Hearn, 1998).

Nonetheless, even if one focused solely on GNP figures, it is clear that there was a very significant level of growth in Ireland in the 1990s. The increase in productivity was real as was the increase in employment, but the actual growth rates were lower than the more widely advertised figures. O'Riain sums up:

> Clearly, a boom in foreign investment did drive the rapid expansion in growth and exports in the late 1990s. But many of the best-known foreign firms were simply moving goods through their Irish operations to take advantage of low tax rates, creating an entrepôt economy that provided the illusion of growth and development. Significant elements of the Celtic Tiger were a mirage. (O'Riain, 2004, p. 36)

The notion that Celtic Tiger growth was a natural outcome of the workings of the free market is even less plausible when the expansion of manufacturing is scrutinised more closely. The key industries attracted to Ireland (IT and pharmaceuticals) were targeted by Irish development agencies like the IDA because they were 'high value-added': not only did they promise high wages but, by cultivating a programme of technical and scientific education, the Irish state could train a labour force that was 'fit for purpose' (O'Riain, 2004; Smith, 2005).

The downturn in the global computer industry after the crash of the 'dot com' bubble in 2000 had its impact on the Irish economy. Investment fell dramatically, unemployment grew, and it appeared that Ireland was heading back into economic stagnation. In Ireland, as in the United States, the situation was saved by a boom in the construction industry, facilitated by exceptionally low interest rates.

Finance and the Building Boom: The Celtic Bubble

The share of the Irish national income in house building in the 1990s was about 5 per cent. A decade later, at the peak of the boom, this share had trebled while other construction accounted for a further 6 per cent. The surge in house building was accompanied by a spectacular increase in house prices. Up until the mid-1990s, the banks were slow to lend to house buyers and the very gradual rise in house prices kept in tandem with incomes. While wages did increase in the later 1990s, house prices accelerated far more rapidly. Between 1995 and 2007 house prices increased five times faster than average earnings (Punch, 2009).

Morgan Kelly, one of the very few economists to predict the Irish financial crash, summarises:

In 1995, the average first time buyer took out a mortgage equal to three years' average earnings and the average house (new or second hand, in Dublin or elsewhere) cost four years' average earnings. By late 2006 (bubble peak) the average first time buyer mortgage had risen to 8 times average earnings, and the average new house cost 10 times average earnings, while the average Dublin second hand house cost 17 times average earnings. (Kelly, 2009, p. 2)

The bubble in house prices was partially driven by the state's withdrawal from the provision of public housing. In 1975 one third of all housing was built by local authorities; during the boom years this had been reduced to around 6 per cent. A rising population, especially of young adults, increased demand for houses. At the other end of the scale, the state introduced a series of tax avoidance schemes for builders and for others financing construction. It was the banks though, who were the major element driving the housing – and credit – bubble (Cooper, 2009; Punch, 2009).

The Irish banks had been notable for their conservatism, if not parsimony. In the 1990s, at the height of the manufacturing boom, the Irish banks were lending considerably less than their European or British counterparts: 60 per cent of GNP as opposed to an average of around 80 per cent. This shot up to over 200 per cent of GNP by 2008. By the time the credit bubble peaked, Ireland was building half as many houses as Britain, which had a population 14 times larger. There is a very clear correlation between the inflation of housing prices and the credit explosion. The domestic property boom was already ebbing by 2006; it was the international financial crisis of 2007/8 that turned into a full scale crash, and brought down the Irish banking system with it (Kelly, 2010a).

Throughout the credit bubble the government, aided and abetted by the Central Bank and the Financial Regulator, insisted that there were no difficulties with finance. The media maintained a helpful silence. Novelist Anne Enright summarises it well:

From 2001 to 2007 it was not possible to be off-message about the Irish economy or, especially, about the housing market. You would barely be published. Your article would end up in the middle of the supplement, unflagged. (Enright, 2010)

The property boom did not only involve banks and major developers. The 2006 Census showed that 15 per cent of Irish houses were vacant (less than a fifth of which were holiday homes). Many, probably most, of these buy-to-rent houses were owned by middle-class professionals, ensuring a wider constituency for pushing the property bubble to its limits.

With 13 per cent of the Irish labour force and around 20 per cent of output, involved in construction, the collapse of the building boom was always going to cause major difficulties for the Irish economy. However, the government's handling of the crash hugely magnified the problems. After an extended period of denial, the government finally acted in the wake of the Wall Street crisis, providing a state guarantee not only for all Irish bank deposits, but for all the bondholders of the Irish banks. This action appears to have been taken at the behest of the European Central Bank (ECB). The Irish government poured huge sums into the banks, and a few weeks later, nationalised Anglo-Irish Bank, an investment bank which had close links with the political elite, especially with a network of property 'developers' around Fianna Fáil. Media reports suggest that over half of all Anglo-Irish loans were to ten individuals. When it became apparent that the Irish banks were, in effect, insolvent the government decided to create a 'bad bank', NAMA (National Assets Management Agency), to which the banks' bad loans would be transferred (Cooper, 2009; Kelly, 2010a & 2010b).

The credit bubble, in effect, operated as a state-backed scheme for the redistribution of resources from the general public to the propertied stratum. The Irish case gives us a vivid illustration of how the scheme operated. The banks and the property speculators made huge profits from inflating asset prices but once the bubble burst, the state stepped in to ensure that the financiers and the propertied elite kept as much of their wealth as possible. Someone has to pay of course. Sean Fitzpatrick, the chairman of Anglo-Irish Bank, grasped this principle well when, one week after the Irish state stepped in to rescue his collapsed bank, he proposed that old age pensions and children allowances be reduced to pay for the costs of the bank bail-out (Cooper, 2009; O'Toole, 2009).

Aside from bailing out the banks, the government introduced a series of measures cutting public sector pay, welfare benefits and public services. The effect of these pro-cyclical measures was to deepen the recession brought about by the construction and credit crash. The banks remain dysfunctional. National income has contracted by almost a fifth: the most extreme contraction of any west European country since the Second World War. By the summer of 2010, Ireland had the second highest rate of unemployment in the

EU, with nearly half a million people out of work. Mass emigration had returned by the autumn. The continuing fall in property prices ensured that banks' bad loans increased, and with them the public debt. The collapsing economy led financial investors to conclude that Irish state bonds were a risky bet, pushing up bond rates. In December, the ECB and the EU pressurised the Irish government into accepting what is in effect a takeover of the Irish state by the ECB and the IMF. In return for accepting a forced loan by the ECB and the IMF, the Irish state agreed to a programme of structural adjustment, involving massive cuts in social spending, privatisation of much of the public sector and a reduction in the minimum wage. The terms of the ECB/IMF takeover – its architects and the media prefer to designate it a 'bailout' – cemented the Irish government's commitment to ensuring that the Irish citizenry pay to protect the banks.

In discussing Ireland's spectacular boom and bust, most commentators distinguish between two booms, the 'real' Celtic Tiger boom of the 1990s and the bubble of the following decade. The first boom occurred in manufacturing industry, notably in electronic engineering and chemicals, based upon the import of foreign, mainly US, capital and was an integral part of the wider process of the globalisation of production that has been a feature of recent decades. The second boom was based on construction; it was a homegrown affair and was at least in part fraudulent, with the Irish state colluding in sharp practices. This narrative obscures as much as it clarifies.

If we look at Irish growth patterns over the two decades they are remarkably similar to those of the US, with a strong wave of growth in the later 1990s, led by the information technology (IT) sector, followed by a sharp contraction (the 'dot-com' boom and bust). This was followed by a construction boom, facilitated by low interest rates and 'easy money', which by the middle of the decade led to an over-supply of housing. The fall of house prices led to a banking crisis, which in turn resulted in a deep recession. This is not to suggest that Ireland is simply an 'offshore' part of the US economy – though it is partially that – or that its dynamics are overwhelmingly determined by developments in the US. The key to understanding Ireland's development over recent decades is to recognise its character as a *bridge economy* between the US and Western Europe. The conventional interpretation of the Irish Tiger economy as a product of 'globalisation' fails to grasp this, or its implications.

Irish membership of the EU was arguably a precondition for both booms. One of the articles of the Treaty of Rome – the founding treaty of European integration – authorised US corporations based in any of the member states to enjoy the same access to trade across European community borders as any indigenous firms (Gowan, 1999). Ireland's small domestic market would not have attracted very many of the US corporations that located there in the 1980s and 1990s. The most important attraction of Ireland for US corporations was that it permitted unfettered access to the European market. In the case of the pharmaceutical industry, a 'business-friendly' legal environment facilitated the arrival of US companies orientated towards the European market (O'Donovan & Glavanis-Grantham, 2008).

The huge surplus of money in the international money markets looking for investment was one factor inflating the property bubble. Another key determinant was the low interest-rates that flowed from membership of the European currency union. Research in Ireland shows that even though house prices rose enormously compared to income, the actual monthly payments to the banks, relative to income, remained in line with earlier periods. People took out higher mortgages because they could afford the interest payments. They assumed of course that the interest rates would remain constant, or that their income would rise (Kelly, 2010a; O'Toole, 2009).

Quite apart from low interest rates, the ECB played a critical role in encouraging the Irish credit bubble. The ECB has a central policy objective of preventing inflation, and a key part of its remit is to ensure that the national economies of the Eurozone do not adopt inflationary policies. Yet when it came to assessing what constituted inflation, the ECB did not include asset inflation in its calculations. Shares and property prices were free to rise without hindrance from central bankers, but wages and consumer prices had to be checked. The consequence of this approach – which followed the direction of the Fed (the US central bank) – was that instead of seeking to contain the banking bubble, the ECB encouraged it. The IMF was equally nonchalant about the build up of debt. The IMF report for Ireland published in July 2006 – the month before the global financial system began to implode – concluded that 'the [Irish] financial system seems well placed to absorb the impact of a downturn in either house prices or growth more generally' (quoted in IMF, 2006, p. 5). The regulatory bodies in Ireland – the Central Bank and the Financial Regulator – could use the imperator of the

ECB and the IMF to justify their inaction in the face of the starkly evident credit and property bubbles.

Both booms flourished under the banner of free market economics. If neoliberal ideas do not provide an adequate explanation for the Celtic Tiger boom, they certainly contributed to shaping some of the social consequences of that boom. The notion that a society worked best if the state played only a minimal role helped legitimise the government's reluctance to develop public services. While the Celtic Tiger era saw a significant increase in the average standard of living in Ireland, it also witnessed a deepening level of social inequality. The incomes of higher earners rose much more rapidly than those of lower earners. Across Ireland, gentry-style mansions were built while there was a virtual halt to the construction of public housing. The health system bifurcated into a modernised private system and an understaffed overstretched public one. The numbers attending fee-paying schools climbed. Sales of luxury cars trebled. Car ownership in general increased, and a motorway system was greatly amplified while, with a few exceptions, public transport stagnated. By almost every index of inequality, Ireland was located near the bottom rung for OECD countries, slightly above the US, slightly below the UK. Celtic Tiger Ireland had become a land of private wealth and public squalor (Allen, 2000; Kirby, 2002; Wickham, 2004).

To argue that there exists a continuity between the two booms is not to suggest that one was the inevitable consequence of the other. The Irish state could, in principle, have used the taxation system to redistribute wealth to the poorer sections of Irish society and to expand public services. In practice, during the boom era, the government actively restructured the taxation system to redistribute wealth towards the rich. The highest rate of income tax was reduced from 48 per cent to 42 per cent and was extended to over half the labour force. Capital gains tax was halved. A raft of measures was introduced which enabled the wealthy to evade tax altogether. A significant section of the country's top earners paid less than 5 per cent of their income in tax. The government sought to raise most state revenue through high consumption taxes, which hit the poor disproportionally (Cooper, 2009).

Though officially Ireland paid fealty to notions of free markets and global competition many, if not most, of the state's economic policies had little to do with making Ireland more competitive in the global market. Inflated property prices clearly made the country less competitive. The same applied to the privatisation programme. Ostensibly it was to make the companies concerned, and the economy as a whole, more efficient. In practice it often had the opposite effect. The privatisation of the Irish telecom company, Eircom, was a major setback to the state's declared aim of providing Ireland with an effective nationwide broadband network. Likewise, notions of Ireland as a developmental state need to be treated with caution. If the state was seriously concerned about national development it would seek to maximise public returns from potential natural resources. The case of Corrib Gas, where the government handed over a huge area of gas resources for free to a consortium led by Shell, illustrates the extent of the Irish state's commitment to national development. The minister responsible, Ray Burke, had private meetings with energy companies against the advice of civil servants. Despite the fact that Ray Burke was later found by a public tribunal to have received corrupt payments, neither the Fianna Fail/Green government nor the Fine Gael/Labour coalition have moved to revoke this decision. Instead the new coalition government has handed over more maritime areas for gas and oil exploration – for free – to corporate investors (Connolly & Lynch, 2005; Siggins, 2010).

The rise in inequality in Ireland during the boom years led many to contrast the 'American social model' to the 'European' or 'EU social model', with the former stressing individual social mobility and the latter social cohesion. While there is some validity in this contrast, the notion of an EU social model is seriously misleading. Neither the EU, nor its predecessor bodies ever sought to design a social model. The 'social models' in Europe are all *national* models, created by Christian Democratic or Social Democratic governments at the level of individual nation-states, not at a pan-European level. Agriculture is probably the only area where the EU sought to establish a common social model, and even this has been greatly diminished as the EU has expanded eastwards. Conversely, US social practices have not simply been based upon economic liberalism; the Social Security system remains an important vehicle of social protection, despite attacks from economic liberals.

No less importantly, the EU as an institution has, since the 1980s at least, acted as a spearhead for neoliberal policies across the continent. The EU has quite explicitly focused on *markets* rather than on *societies*. The formation of a currency union has accentuated this trend, with the creation of a set of tight rules prohibiting individual states running budget deficits beyond very narrow limits. No such parsimony applied to the expansion of private debt. This point needs stressing because the fiscal crisis in Ireland and Spain is precisely not a product of these states running high public debt. The fiscal crisis of these states is a direct consequence of the private debt – accumulated under the auspices of the ECB – being taken over by the individual states (Cafruny & Ryner, 2003; Storey, 2006).

If the ECB followed the US Federal Reserve in facilitating the buildup of private debt, once the financial crisis broke in 2008 the ECB's response was similar to the Fed's – to pour in public money to protect the private banks: profits get privatised, losses get socialised. One cannot explain this behaviour by reference to free market ideology. The money markets were clearly broken, and the public institutions were intervening to rescue them. Private debt was turned into public debt. In both the US and the EU, it seems clear that the financial regulators service the financiers.

A crucial difference between the two central banks is that the Fed represents a unified federal state, the ECB does not. The euro created a currency union, and not a fiscal union: the European nation-states raise their own finances. This discrepancy was always likely to cause difficulties for the Union, but these problems have been greatly magnified by the ECB's monetary policies. These monetary policies were driven by the needs of the core European states, but the rules applied to the whole Eurozone. Artificially low interest rates helped the German economy recover – it was still struggling to incorporate East Germany – but resulted in wild property booms in the Union's peripheral states. The ECB did nothing to prevent this property bubble, or even to warn of its dangers. Once the property bubble crashed, the ECB has sought to impose extreme austerity measures on the EU's periphery.

Ireland's *nominal* income would need to grow at a rate higher than the interest being charged by the ECB and the IMF if it is to escape the current debt trap. (The relevant index here is GNP not GDP for reasons discussed earlier.) This can only happen if there is a huge increase in foreign direct investment in Ireland or if the rate of inflation in the EU is higher than the interest being charged. In the context of a protracted downturn in the North Atlantic economies, where investment has effectively collapsed, it seems most unlikely that Ireland will experience a major influx of foreign investment. Reducing the debt through inflationary measures is also unlikely. Preventing inflation is the ECB's central policy. They will not permit a high rate of inflation, and if inflation increases interest rates will be raised, effectively blocking any further economic growth. While the Greek popular upsurge against austerity (with the implicit threat of default) forced the EU into lowering the interest rate being demanded from over 6 per cent to 3.5 per cent, the scale of the austerity measures is such that the real economy in Ireland continues to shrink, while the ratio between debt and national income (GNP) continues to grow. Added to this, the state continues to pour money into the banks and which remain insolvent with overvalued assets. If the debts of NAMA are added to those of the banks, Ireland is facing a debt ratio of 140 per cent to GNP by 2012, a figure comparable to Greece. Such an amount will be impossible to service (Kelly, 2010b).

The widespread media reports of an Irish recovery are so much wishful thinking, based upon the same erroneous GDP figures that we used over the last couple of decades to exaggerate Irish growth rates and prosperity. Any fall in unemployment rates is due to rising emigration. The Central Statistics Office figures show that total *employment* has continued to fall while the numbers of companies going bankrupt continues to rise (Slattery, 2010).

Ireland is being, in effect, driven into a debt–deflation spiral where the national debt keeps rising, the productive economy keeps declining and the government keeps cutting public spending. The consequence will most likely be further economic regression and the corrosion of the social fabric. The only viable alternative to the destruction of public services is the repudiation of the bankers' debt.

The Troubled State of Northern Ireland

The state of Northern Ireland occupied, from its inception, an anomalous role within the United Kingdom. Prior to 1998 it was the only region of the United Kingdom to possess devolved government – 'home rule'. Ironically it was the one region of the United Kingdom where a mass movement had mobilised *against* home rule. This peculiarity shaped the state from the beginning. It owed its existence not to a desire for self government, but from its opposition to being part of a self-governed Ireland.

The boundaries of the state had been problematic even before its foundation. Insofar as Ulster had a spatial identity it included nine counties, not six; the population of the other three, Donegal, Cavan and Monaghan, retain a strong sense of an Ulster regional identity. Two of the six counties in Northern Ireland, Fermanagh and Tyrone, had small 'nationalist' majorities (Lee, 1989).

Politically Northern Ireland was dominated by the Ulster Unionist Party, the regional branch of the Tory Party (officially titled the Conservative and Unionist Party) from its inception to its demise. The party enjoyed the support of all classes in the Protestant community:

landed aristocrats; industrialists and financiers; professionals, higher and lower; workers, skilled and unskilled; farmers, big and small. The great majority of Unionist MPs were members of the Orange Order, an exclusively Protestant mass organisation which facilitated communication across classes in the Unionist community. Northern Ireland's rulers saw their state as a centre of advancement; not only was it the most industrialised part of Ireland, but it was an integral part of the United Kingdom and the British Empire, the heart of industrial progress and global civilisation. In separating from the rest of the island they had escaped not only the threat of Roman domination, but also economic backwardness. Westminster for its part expected Northern Ireland to contribute to the upkeep of empire (Bew, 1979; Farrell, 1976).

From the very beginning though, Northern Ireland faced economic decline. Unemployment remained high throughout the 1920s and was higher in the 1930s: 19 per cent of the insured workforce was unemployed between 1923 and 1930; 27 per cent between 1931 and 1939. After the First World War, the North's shipbuilding industry faced competition from the US, Scandinavia and Japan, all of which used the opportunity of the war to develop their own shipbuilding industries, and had benefited from state subsidies. Linen too was in decline. While linen had always been more expensive than cotton, in the twentieth century it became less fashionable, and suffered as well from the overvaluation of sterling (Johnson, 1985).

The North's industrial decline was consistent with the wider British pattern in the twentieth century, though more extreme. Britain's industrial decline over the course of the century has occasioned a great deal of commentary. Geoffrey Ingram has argued in *Capitalism Divided* that the source is to be found in the divide within British capitalism between the 'City' and industry. The commercial and financial interests based in the City of London carried greater weight within the political order, and successive governments in Westminster were willing to allow industry to stagnate because they were unwilling to adopt policies which, though necessary for industrial resurgence, might damage the interests of this commercial and financial bloc (Ingram, 1984).

Industrial decline and the accompanying high levels of unemployment and emigration did not have the effect of significantly eroding Protestant working-class support for Unionism. The scarcity of employment seems to have made Unionism's patronage system more important. Unemployment rates were always higher among Catholics than among Protestants. Most skilled work was monopolised by Protestants. Catholics were also massively under-represented in large areas of the public sector, especially in higher and technical grades. Emigration rates among Catholics were more than twice those of Protestants (Farrell, 1976; Lee, 1989; O'Dowd et al, 1980; Rowthorn & Wayne, 1988).

In the post-war period, the reforms initiated by the Labour government at Westminster did have a positive effect on Northern Ireland. The public sector was expanded – especially health and education – and an effort was made to attract industrial firms from outside the region. Though Unionist MPs had voted against these measures at Westminster, it was the Unionist government at Stormont that implemented them, which had consequences of its own. Inward investment and public-sector expansion were refracted through the sectarian structures of the Northern Ireland state (O'Dowd et al, 1980; Rowthorn & Wayne, 1988).

Most new inward investment was located in the predominantly Protestant areas of Antrim, Down and North Armagh. Very little investment went to Belfast and even less to southern and western regions. Coleraine, rather than the larger town of Derry, was chosen as the location for Northern Ireland's second university. The Belfast-Derry railway line was closed. 'As late as 1971, male unemployment among Catholics was 17.3 per cent compared to 6.6 per cent among Protestants' (Lee, 1989, p. 413). Public housing was allocated through the local councils. These councils were virtually all controlled by Unionists, even in areas with Catholic majorities, through a system of creative electoral organisation known as 'gerrymandering'. Many of the councils were resistant to housing Catholics, which compounded the inequalities created by discriminatory employment practices (Farrell, 1976; Rowthorn & Wayne, 1988).

Historians debate the origins and causes of the Northern revolt. A more puzzling question is why Northern Ireland took so long to explode. The size of the repressive apparatus of the Northern Ireland state was one factor. The distinctive character of the Northern Irish Catholic community was another. Whereas elsewhere in Ireland the national struggle overlapped with class conflict, in the North it also took place *within* the popular classes. The Catholic Church also played a significant role in dampening down resistance to the Northern state. The traditional Catholic teaching that the appropriate response to oppression is resignation, because this world is a vale of tears, carried some weight, especially among the Catholic middle-classes. Catholic schools and hospitals were one of the few areas where educated Catholics could find employment and as result middle-class Catholics had a particularly close, not to say dependent, relationship to the Church.

The major political party in the Catholic community was the Nationalist Party, the direct heir to the Home Rule Party. Even during the War of Independence, the West Belfast constituency returned a Home Rule MP. Republicanism remained a minority current within the Catholic community. The IRA's 'border campaign' in the 1950s was ineffective and they made no attempt to build a mass resistance. The trade union movement did little or nothing to end discriminatory practices in the workplace. A Northern Ireland Labour Party was formed and won a good deal of support in the 1950s and 1960s, but it was not willing to engage with the issue of communal discrimination and rapidly became marginalised once a civil rights movement emerged in the late 1960s (Farrell, 1983; O'Connor, 1992; O'Dowd et al, 1980).

If Northern Ireland by the late 1960s appeared a static polity, the world which had formed it was less immutable. The Northern Ireland civil rights movement itself was directly inspired by the US example – this was the age of television – and images of police repression could no longer be contained. Britain itself had been greatly changed by the two world wars, the egalitarian impact of the welfare state, its relative economic decline and not least by the loss of empire.

The state violence (and state-backed loyalist violence) which greeted the civil rights movement had the predictable effect of radicalising civil rights supporters and encouraging a full-scale confrontation with the Northern State. The arrival of British troops on the streets of Derry and Belfast in 1969, and their increasingly antagonistic relationship with the nationalist community, led many to conclude that the Northern State was beyond reform, and that the abolition of partition and the ending of the Union was a precondition for democracy. This situation led to republicanism, which up until then had been a marginal force, acquiring a pivotal position among the radicalised youth (Bowyer Bell, 1993).

The killing of unarmed civil rights protestors in Derry on Bloody Sunday 1972 was a defining moment in the conflict. The killings radicalised a generation of activists who concluded that a sustained armed campaign against Britain was necessary. The massive protests both in Ireland and internationally taught Britain that there were significant limits to the use of military power in the Irish context. The decision by Britain to close down the Northern Ireland government had the effect of mollifying the Catholic middle class in the north and, perhaps more importantly, the Dublin government. The scale of the protests across Ireland also taught the southern elite a lesson about their own potential vulnerability. The closure of Stormont created a rift between the Unionist population of Northern Ireland and London (and England more generally) while encouraging the growth of loyalist paramilitary organisations. The British attempt in 1974 to establish a power-sharing agreement between 'moderate' Unionist and Nationalist parties fell before the combined forces of the republican insurgency and, in particular, opposition from the Unionist working class (Bowyer Bell, 1993).

The British state had considerable success in projecting itself through the world's media as a neutral force holding the peace between two rival atavistic communities, or in the British media's preferred term, 'tribes'. This framing glossed over the fact that the union with Britain (technically with 'Great Britain') was itself at the heart of the conflict, which made British 'neutrality' somewhat problematic. There was a significant disjunction between the formal grounds for British state action in Northern Ireland – the defence of British sovereignty – and the manner in which it sought to represent its actions, as a peacekeeping force between two conflicting communities. The British state's projection of itself as a peacekeeping force was, in part, designed to placate an international audience. Britain's imperial history was too well known for it to garner much support for a sovereign defence. London was concerned, as was Dublin, to emphasise the *discontinuity* between the earlier struggle for national independence and the later battles. However, Britain's representation of its role as a neutral force was also directed towards its domestic constituency. The presence of a substantial Irish 'nationalist' community within the island of Britain was one factor here. Sympathy for Irish independence and unity went far beyond those born in Ireland or of Irish descent, and included much of the labour movement, as well as many traditional liberals. More than that: the Northern Ireland conflict revealed all too clearly the multinational character of the British state. While Northern Irish Unionists might reasonably have expected a broad level of sympathy within Britain for their plight, little such empathy existed outside of Conservative heartlands. Opinion polls consistently showed that a majority of Britons favoured troop withdrawal from Ireland. All the evidence suggests that as far as most English people were concerned, the conflict was an Irish one, and it excited little passion. Unionists could rely on some sympathy in Scotland on the basis of traditional anti-Catholic prejudice, but given the size of the Catholic population there (mainly of Irish descent) this was far too dangerous a card for any sector of the political elite to play openly.

This representation of the Northern Ireland conflict had its own political consequences. It put pressure on Britain to behave – in relation to Northern Ireland's civil society – in a more 'neutral' manner. It also intensified the sense of estrangement of the North's Unionist community from the population of Britain. In practice, of course, the British state differentiated between republican and loyalist forces. There is a huge body of evidence documenting the links not only between the police, but also (perhaps especially) between British military intelligence services and the loyalist paramilitary forces. But the British military's fidelity to Loyalism was always conditional upon political circumstances and they could and did turn on their allies whenever reasons of state demanded (Bowyer Bell, 1993 & 1996).

As early as 1978 a British army document argued that a military stalemate existed in Northern Ireland, and a political solution was necessary. At what point the Belfast Republican leadership came to a similar view is unclear, but they certainly seem to have done so by the late 1980s. The events surrounding the peace process are well documented and do not need further elaboration here. If the calculation of political leaderships, whether republican, loyalist or British, was crucial, it occurred against a background of war-weariness on all sides. Important changes in Northern Irish society had also occurred which have helped shape the peace settlement (Bowyer Bell, 1993).

The protracted conflict in Northern Ireland had a curious impact on its social and economic structure. Northern Ireland had hoped, like the Republic, to attract industrial investment from outside, but this became increasingly difficult to do despite the fact that industrial subsidies were around double those of other depressed areas of the United Kingdom. Recession in the mid-1970s led many industries to fold or pull out. Northern Ireland, however, had acquired a political significance for Britain that other regions lacked and saw a significant rise in public spending and in public employment, even during the Thatcher era. Some of this was in defence or the security area, but most of it was in civil employment. Northern Ireland became the most heavily subsidised part of the United Kingdom, experiencing what one might call 'counter-insurgency Keynesianism'. For the average person in Northern Ireland, the standard of living significantly improved during the Troubles, and the gap in income and wages between Northern Ireland and the rest of the United Kingdom narrowed. The need to contain the insurgency – and legitimate their governance – induced London to institute fair employment practices, which resulted in increased employment opportunities for Catholics, especially university-educated ones (Rowthorn & Wayne, 1988).

The combined effects of industrial decline, the Troubles and the state's efforts to contain them, have led to significant changes in Northern Ireland's demographic and social structures. The decline of the North's (largely pre-Fordist) manufacturing base, especially the shipyards, undermined Protestant workers' privileged access to employment. For the Protestant working class, it has been an era of social decline. This has not led to any convergence with Catholic workers; if anything communal divisions are deeper than ever, especially in Belfast where there is a rigid spatial segregation. Catholic employment rates have significantly increased, especially in the public sector, and even though poverty levels remain higher among Catholics the socioeconomic gap between the two communities has greatly narrowed. A new Catholic middle class has emerged, centred in the public and service sectors, while there has been a considerable degree of emigration among middle-class Protestants. These changes have impacted on the demographic balance: while Protestants remain the majority community, they are now a much smaller majority and it may well be that if immigrants are taken into account, neither community has an overall majority (Shirlow, 2008; Smyth & Cebulla, 2008).

At the core of the peace settlement was an acceptance that neither community could dominate the other, and the creation of an institutional framework to ensure as much. While the agreement has brought a welcome decline in violence, many of its limitations are also plain. The most obvious weakness of the Belfast agreement is that it institutionalises communalism. The political system is structured so that parties represent communities, and this makes it more difficult for parties to break through communal boundaries. While the veto system deters either community oppressing the other, it also inhibits necessary changes. Reforms in educational and policing structures are easily blocked. The 'security state' is largely unreconstructed. Communal inequalities persist, though in a less extreme form, and deep socioeconomic problems are unaddressed. Northern Ireland's peace dividend has not broken the cycles of poverty. Social conditions have not significantly improved in the areas most affected by the violence (Smyth & Cebulla, 2008).

The stabilisation of the North's power-sharing government coincided with a shift in party support. The Ulster Unionist Party (UUP) and the Social Democratic and Labour Party (SDLP) have been replaced as the largest parties by the Democratic Unionist Party (DUP) and Sinn Féin. The shift was largely driven by the UUP's efforts to exclude Sinn Féin from government until the IRA disarmed. Sinn Féin for its part used the disarmament issue to leverage for state reform. While the UUP is classified by the media as 'moderate' in contrast to the DUP, the differences between the parties are slight. The UUP is the inheritor of the old Unionist Party machine, with professional and business interests dominating. The DUP has a more lower middle class membership (though increasingly upwardly mobile) and close ties to Protestant fundamentalist currents. The SDLP, despite its title and membership of the Socialist International, is very much a mainstream Christian Democratic party, dominated by Catholic professionals, and closely tied to the Catholic Church. Sinn Féin's membership and support base has been predominantly working class with an attachment to leftist politics, though this has begun to change with the peace process.

While the agreement accepts that British sovereignty remains – as long as a majority of the North's population wants it – some have argued that British sovereignty is diluted both in practice and in law by London's recognition that the Northern Irish communities have political primacy in deciding their own future. The full significance of the retention of British sovereignty over Northern Ireland remains to be determined. The most immediate impact of British sovereignty on the power-sharing government has been Westminster's response to the financial crisis.

Northern Ireland did have a property bubble earlier in the decade, though not as extreme as the Republic's – indeed much of it was driven by investors from the Republic. Being part of the British dominion, its banks were bailed out by London. As the sovereign state, the United Kingdom controls the finances of Northern Ireland, providing an annual allocation which the Northern Ireland government decides how to distribute. Under New Labour, this caused few problems for the power-sharing government; 'conflict-avoidance Keynesianism' was an obvious successor to 'counter-insurgency Keynesianism'. With the Conservative/Liberal Democratic coalition in London adopting an austerity programme, the picture has changed. While there is a definite logic to the British government's desire to bolster the financial sector, it is not at all obvious that the austerity measures proposed will strengthen rather than weaken British capitalism.

The austerity measures seem likely to stretch London's capacity to maintain its dominion over the United Kingdom's peripheries while in Northern Ireland any serious programme of cutbacks runs the risk of reigniting communal conflict. London's austerity programme has placed Sinn Féin in a particularly invidious position. As the leadership of a protracted rebellion against British rule, they now face the prospect of implementing cutbacks damaging their own popular base, at the behest of Westminster. The DUP will also be uncomfortable imposing austerity measures on its electorate.

Sinn Féin is, of course, an all-Ireland party which has a presence in working class communities, urban and rural, throughout the Republic. More recently, it has had a small representation in the Dáil. When the financial crisis broke in September 2008, Sinn Féin's response was faltering, with its Dáil representatives initially backing the bank bailout. Sinn Féin's uncertainty was in large measure due to their political orientation since the peace process. While some critics have argued that Sinn Féin has simply replaced the SDLP and abandoned all republican principles, the reality is more complicated. National unity remains Sinn Féin's key objective but this is understood very much as territorial unity. The creation of an island economy was seen as a crucial strategic move. During the period of the Celtic Tiger there was a certain logic to this: the south seemed to have a dynamic economy, the north a stagnant one. The Sinn Féin leadership believed that by having the same structural conditions across Ireland, an island economy would emerge in a 'natural' way, and political unity would follow. This led them to advocate a policy of low corporate tax, and to discard many of the party's radical policies. The collapse of the Celtic Tiger was as disorientating for the Sinn Féin leadership as it was for the trade unions. Since then, under pressure from its southern membership, Sinn Féin has adopted a more radical approach, though is not clear whether this is a tactical shift or a strategic one.

Structural Adjustment

The two Irish states find themselves imposing austerity programmes on their societies, largely at the dictate of external powers. This seems likely to create political turmoil in both states. In Northern Ireland it remains to be seen whether a resistance develops which crosses the communal divide, or whether cuts in public spending reignite communal conflict. One consequence of the peace settlement is that it will be much more difficult than in former times to land one community with the main social burden of economic stagnation.

The only viable resistance to the austerity programs will be one that unites the poor and working populations of both communities.

In the 2011 elections in the Irish Republic, the Fianna Fáil vote collapsed. The 17.4 per cent of the popular vote they received was their lowest percentage ever. In Dublin, they lost every seat bar one. Fine Gael, with 36.1 per cent of the vote, became the largest party and formed a coalition government with the Labour Party which had won 19.4 per cent of the vote. The election was also notable for the strong showing by Sinn Féin, who won 9.9 per cent of the vote. An assortment of left-wing candidates was also elected, most notably five deputies from the radical left bloc, the United Left Alliance.

The new coalition has endorsed a slightly modified EU/IMF programme of structural adjustment. Plans for sweeping reductions in public services and wholesale privatisations have been endorsed. They have also committed themselves to further reducing wages. All too predictably, Labour Party ministers have begun disparaging the public sector, calling for a 'leaner' more efficient service and expressing concern that social welfare was becoming a 'lifestyle choice' for school leavers. Government ministers boast of their success in cutting state expenditure at a rate agreed with the ECB/IMF/European Commission (EC) troika, or even exceeding these demands. The economy, also predictably, continues to contract. While there have been protests in many areas against cuts in services, especially in health and education, these remain fragmented and largely divorced from any sustained political challenge to debt programmes. There has been no equivalent in Ireland to the mass revolt of the 'indignant' which has done so much to undermine the political consensus in Greece and Spain; it remains to be seen how long Ireland will stay immune to these movements.

Yet these revolts in Greece and Spain have had a significant impact on the situation of Ireland. The risk that Greece might default led to concerns in European governing circles that a full-scale financial crisis would develop across the continent along the lines of that which followed the Lehman's crash, and for similar reasons. The buyers of Greek debt have insured it through the same kind of complex financial transactions as were used with US mortgages. No-one quite knows where this debt has spread to; as a consequence the whole financial system could go into paralysis. Moreover, if Greece or any other EU state defaulted, this would have a huge knock-on impact on the financial stability of the rest. To prevent a full scale financial collapse, the European authorities gave Greece a longer timeframe to repay the debt, and reduced the interest rate to 3.5 per cent. At the same time they reduced the interest rate applied to the debt of Ireland and Portugal to the same amount. Conventional opinion suggests that the global financial crisis that broke out in 2007/8 is a temporary interlude that will be superseded by the return of normal growth. There are grounds for doubting this. Modern Irish history shows that there is nothing especially normal about growth: phases of stagnation have been at least as common as phases of growth. It seems more plausible that it was the huge influx of US industrial capital into Ireland in the 1990s which was exceptional and not its absence. The concluding chapter will argue that there are good grounds for doubting that a new wave of growth is likely in the North Atlantic economies in the coming period, or at least as long as the neoliberal model remains dominant.

4
Conclusion:
Ireland in a Changing World Order

A central argument here has been that Ireland's historical trajectory can only be grasped if we take into account both 'internal' and 'external' factors and how they interact. This was the case in the late Middle Ages and it remains so today.

What most sharply distinguished Ireland from other parts of the Atlantic Isles in the transition from the late medieval era to the early modern one was the way in which it was incorporated into the newly centralised political order: the brute fact of conquest. The conquest had a critical long-term impact, not only on Irish politics, but also on its socioeconomic relations and culture. Elsewhere in Europe centralising monarchical states often came into conflict with the interests of local elites, but in Ireland it went far beyond this. The incorporation of Ireland into the extended English/British state took the form of a full-scale conquest, involving massive human and physical destruction.

The weight of evidence suggests that the conquest of Ireland was the consequence of a collision of social orders, but this collision took a particularly violent character because of crucial changes taking place across Europe at that time, which were especially marked in England.

The distinctive features of the Gaelic social order were discussed in the early chapters of this book. The difficulties involved in extracting social surplus placed significant limits on the centralisation of power within this social order and acted as obstacles to its incorporation into a centralised early modern state. In particular there was huge resistance to the emerging system of individual land ownership. Similar obstacles were overcome in Wales and Gaelic Scotland because their incorporation into a more centralised state system took place over an extended period – three or more centuries – and the indigenous elite groups could be assimilated into an extended ruling class. But it wasn't merely the resilience of the older social order in Ireland which drove the conquest. Equally crucial were the structural changes that emerged in English social organisation.

Both of these factors – the resurgence of the Gaelic order and the structural changes in England – were responses to the systemic crisis of feudalism in the fourteenth century. In both countries, the manorial system and serfdom effectively collapsed to be replaced by very different forms of social power.

The state which carried through the conquest of Ireland in the early modern period was a very different organisation from the early English monarchy which had first claimed authority over the island. Enhanced military capacity was perhaps the most obvious change; the use of firearms and tighter military organisation gave England a crucial edge in warfare against its Irish opponents, even though the latter were better organised and better armed than at earlier periods. Changes in the wider English social organisation were at least as important as these military advances.

The disintegration of serfdom in England was accompanied by the restructuring of social power involving the consolidation of the monarchical state and the emergence of a new system of communication based upon the spread of vernacular literacy. The centralisation of monarchical power under the Tudors, especially in the field of law, reduced the opportunity for compromise with local rulers. A social system premised upon control of population was transformed into one premised upon control of land. These social changes, in particular the spread of vernacular literacy, played a major role in fostering the English Reformation. They also greatly facilitated the related rise of a new collective identity, an English nationality, which deepened the divide between the new ruling bloc in Ireland and the rest of the population. Patricia Palmer has shown that an increased intolerance towards language difference on the part of the 'New English' elite contributed to the radical estrangement between rulers and ruled, creating further obstacles to the advance of the Reformed faith (Palmer, 2001).

These religious and proto-national barriers were given added force by the wider context within which the takeover of Ireland occurred: European domination of the world's oceans and the conquest of the Americas. The intensified rivalry between European states in the early modern era made the 'pacification' of Ireland all the more necessary. This inter-state rivalry was given an added edge by the religious confrontations of the age. The fact that Ireland came to share a confessional allegiance with England's major rivals, France and Spain, played a significant role in shaping English policy towards Ireland. Nor was the colonisation of the Americas a mere intellectual backdrop to the Irish conquest. The colonisation of Ireland was to a large extent carried out by the very same people who colonised the Atlantic coast of North America and the Caribbean islands (Brenner, 2003; Canny, 2001; Smyth, 2006).

The combination of these factors ensured that the incorporation of Ireland into the extended English/British state was massively destructive. It was not just a matter of disempowering a quarrelsome local elite, but of eradicating a whole social order, a way of life. In the process, a significant section of the population lost their lives, settlement patterns were disrupted and there was widespread social dislocation. Much of the country was ethnically cleansed and the old mercantile networks linking the Irish ports to the European continent were destroyed. Most crucially, the new social structures established were premised upon high levels of coercion and the systematic exclusion of the indigenous population from institutions of power.

The conquest was not merely an unpleasant interlude on the road to the civilisation of Ireland: it had long-term regressive consequences. The fact that the indigenous population was radically disempowered ensured that the agrarian order which emerged from the conquest was based upon surplus maximisation rather than output maximisation: extracting as much surplus as possible rather than seeking to systematically increase total produce. The agricultural surpluses which Ireland produced contributed little to its own wider economic development. The religious dimension to the conquest ensured that the confessional divide would play an exaggerated political role into the modern era, marking lines of social exclusion. The conquest also ensured that the new Anglo-Irish elite would be in a position of excessive dependence on the colonial power, unable to challenge London's dominance across wide areas of power, most notably in the commercial arena.

The conquest of Ireland was not just a political event: it had long-term socioeconomic consequences. It was not so much that Ireland developed more 'slowly' than England in the early modern era. Actually, Ireland developed very rapidly in the early modern era, as evidenced by the growth of markets, exports and population. It was rather that this growth was of a hugely destructive social character, resulting in extreme degrees of poverty, misery and ultimately famine, a phenomenon that would become known as 'underdevelopment'. Despite Ireland's close geographic proximity to the homeland of industrial capitalism, its social conditions were far removed.

The social experience of underdevelopment in turn contributed greatly to the rise of the national independence movement: independence was seen as essential to escape Ireland's social wreckage. The Irish revolt would be followed across the colonised world. This was not a question of India and other Asian or African states copying the Irish example. It was rather that, despite the huge differences between them, those societies which had been subjected to colonial domination shared common features and experiences which encouraged movements of revolt and the development of new – or the revitalisation of older – collective identities. One of the side-effects of the forced commercialisation of the conquered world was the spread of popular literacy, often using the language of the colonial powers. This transformed system of communications in turn altered people's perceptions of the world and contributed to the rise of independence movements.

Uneven Transitions to Capitalism

The Irish case, especially when contrasted with Scotland, throws some interesting light on the debates within radical scholarship on the origins of capitalism. The work of Immanuel Wallerstein and Robert Brenner, briefly outlined in the Introduction, has been particularly influential, with Wallerstein stressing the importance of West European states monopolising global trade, and Brenner arguing for the crucial role played by the earlier development of agrarian capitalism.

Why was it that agrarian capitalism emerged in England rather than elsewhere? Brenner argues that the key element here was the particular balance of class forces in the countryside that prevailed as a consequence of the fourteenth-century crisis. He distinguishes three routes: the East European, the French and the English. In Eastern Europe peasant resistance was crushed and a new system of coerced labour, the 'second serfdom', was instituted, which acted as an obstacle to long-term economic development. Popular resistance to the lords was strongest in France where the peasantry were able to consolidate their control of the land. This enabled them to maintain a system of subsistence agriculture and withstand being pressurised into wage labour. In England a middle route emerged. Neither peasants nor lords won decisively. Instead, a compromise emerged based upon the abolition of serfdom and demesne agriculture alongside the consolidation of aristocratic ownership of land. Landowners came to rely on free wage-labour or else rented out land to wealthier peasants who themselves hired labourers to farm the land. In a commercial environment where there existed a market for tenancies, farmers were forced to adopt improved agricultural techniques if they were to stay in business and so a capitalist system of agriculture emerged characterised by rising levels of productivity. Not only did agrarian capitalism create a food surplus in England, but it 'freed up' labour for work away from the land (Brenner, 1985, 1996).

How does the Irish case fit into this schema? Ireland in the epoch following the fourteenth-century crisis saw neither a return to serfdom nor the rise of peasant proprietorship nor the development of a commercial system of tenure. The decisive factor shaping Ireland in the period following the fourteenth-century crisis was the revitalisation of the Gaelic social order, which impacted not only on those areas recaptured from the Anglo-French but right across the island, even within the Pale. It was the sway and resilience of this social order throughout Ireland, into the Renaissance era, that precipitated the conquest.

The conquest ensured that there was no strong class of prosperous peasants who could collaborate with the landowners to establish capitalist social relations in the Irish countryside. The Penal Laws inhibited the process of social differentiation within the peasantry while rural poverty retarded the emergence of a mass market for manufactured goods and left little space for capital accumulation. Furthermore, the failure of the Irish elite to establish a wide measure of popular consent gravely weakened their position in the event of political or commercial conflict with Westminster. The Irish elite were in no position to develop either an English-style agrarian model or to muscle its way into the British imperial trading networks.

In Scotland a sufficient level of differentiation within the peasantry emerged, enabling an alliance between the landowners and the wealthier peasants to develop which implemented a capitalist reorganisation of agriculture; in Ireland, for reasons discussed, it did not. It has been suggested that a similar differentiation within the English peasantry played a crucial role in the earlier transition to agrarian capitalism. In both England and Lowland Scotland, a stratum of prosperous peasants emerged which had both an interest and a capacity to establish itself as an intermediary layer between the landowners and the mass of the peasantry, most of whom became landless labourers. This transition occurred over a period of centuries. Agrarian capitalism emerged not merely as response to the coercion of the marketplace as Brenner and Woods emphasise, but also because the new structure of social relations offered significant opportunities for advancement by a section of the peasantry. This rise of a prosperous 'middling' stratum was not merely of economic importance, but was of crucial political importance too. This emphasis on the importance of a rising middle stratum in fostering capitalism also engages with another criticism of Brenner's thesis. Jack Goody has pointed out that the development of capitalist plantations, worked by wage labour in Ceylon and elsewhere, did nothing to further industrialisation there. Clearly, something more than wage labour in agriculture was needed to encourage capitalist industrialisation (Byres, 2006; Goody, 2004; Harman, 1998).

Developments in the Atlantic Isles make clear that the manner in which territories were incorporated into more centralised political formations impacted hugely on subsequent patterns of social relations. In Ireland, the much more limited degree of differentiation within the peasantry resulted precisely from the conquest, from the very process of political and military expansion of the European Renaissance states that Wallerstein and the 'world systems' theorists emphasise in their work. This would suggest that both 'internal' and 'external' factors need to be taken into account when attempting to understand patterns of industrialisation and uneven development. The contrast between England and Spain certainly demonstrates that the acquisition of riches from the colonies is no guarantee of long-term economic prosperity for the ruling nation. If anything it seems that the precious metals stripped from its American colonies devastated the Iberian economy through the spread of hyperinflation. Moreover, given the overwhelming demographic predominance of the countryside in pre-modern societies, fundamental social changes would only catch on throughout a society if they were deeply rooted in the countryside. Otherwise, like the early flowering of urban capitalism in Renaissance Italy, they would be easily isolated and submerged. It also seems undeniable that in the early stages of the Industrial Revolution, and preceding decades, the British state did achieve global dominance in trade, and that profits from this trade did help finance many industries. British colonies, especially India, provided a captive market for British industrial goods, at the expense of the indigenous handicraft industry. Most telling of all, surely, is the role played by 'New World' slavery in supplying, at an attractive price, the primary product for the sector which led the capitalist breakthrough: the cotton industry (Arrighi, 1994; Darwin, 2008; Hobsbawm, 1968; Vilar, 1971).

Geopolitics certainly played a role in shaping English policy towards Ireland in the Elizabethan era, and in subsequent centuries. The sharpening of inter-state competition gave Ireland a strategic importance that it had never possessed in the medieval age. As England became a more significant player in the European and global political arena, Ireland offered potential opportunities for its continental rivals. However, here too it was precisely the failure of the English state to establish a solid system of hegemony that made its political control of Ireland so vulnerable. Military conquest followed on from the failure to incorporate the Gaelic (and gaelicised) elites into the English state system. The difficulties the English had in Ireland flowed from differences in the way in which society reproduced itself, and from the way in which the social surplus was extracted. The clannic-pastoralist system imposed obstacles in the extraction of the social surplus making it difficult to establish an English-type landowning class. The drive to control the social surplus was inseparable from the drive for territorial domination. Moreover, inter-state competition hardly originated in Renaissance Europe. Warfare has been accorded a central place in history from the earliest records. What was crucial about politics in the Renaissance and subsequent eras was the expansion of a money economy. It was this expansion which enabled European states to develop military organisations (and military technology) that would not have been possible previously. This would suggest that the military competition between states which Arrighi accords analytical primacy is best understood as part and parcel of a broader process wherein monetisation is a central feature.

The comparison between Scotland and Ireland also supports the notion that the Reformation played an important role in the transition to capitalism, but not quite in the manner that Weber envisaged. Its crucial importance was, as Gramsci suggested, its educational function by promoting mass literacy. The success of the Reformation ensured that Scotland, or at least the Scottish Lowlands, had a relatively high rate of literacy in the seventeenth and eighteenth centuries. This early spread of literacy facilitated the rise of agrarian capitalism in the Scottish Lowlands. It meant that not only were Scottish farmers able to understand clearly their lease agreements, but they entered into a framework of social relations where writing – and money – would play a key mediating role. Most likely, literacy also contributed to the development of a more commercial frame of mind, which made it easier for the upper echelons of the Lowlands peasantry to abandon customary obligations and enter into a strategic alliance with the Scottish landowning class. This solid system of hegemony that the Scottish elite established over the countryside ensured that the transition to a monetary economy would be fairly peaceful and strengthened its hand in any potential conflict with Westminster.

The emergence of a system of hegemonic power based upon vernacular literate forms in Scotland and England was crucial for the emergence of capitalist social relations in the countryside, while its corresponding absence in Ireland hindered such a process. Changes in systems of communications were a key part of the broader transformation. Industrial capitalism was preceded not only by agrarian capitalism but also by print capitalism, while the capitalist makeover of the countryside was dependent upon the earlier spread of written forms to restructure social relations. To make sense of the transition to capitalism then, and the uneven way it has subsequently developed, one needs to take into account changes and their interaction in a range of social spheres including production, commerce, state organisation (and inter-state competition) as well as communications, to establish a more rounded picture of the process.

Why did the development of the British Empire in the early modern and modern eras not involve, as a general pattern, the extension of the British social organisation to its newly conquered regions? Or to put the question differently, why did the extension of British rule overseas lead, in the main, to destitution rather than prosperity? Only in North America and Australasia, where the British and other Europeans settled themselves, did the British model seem to take hold. Here, the predominant form of social organisation prior to conquest was hunting and gathering and populations densities were light. Options for tribute taking or commercial exploitation were correspondingly limited and the indigenous population was marginalised or exterminated. Yet even here, while the British brought laws and language, what did not happen was a reproduction of the English agrarian social model: the three tier class system of landowner, capitalist farmer and labourer, which seems to have played such a crucial role in the genesis of British industrial capitalism.

What developed instead in the US was a system of relatively small 'family farms' which, by the 1840s at the latest, were already engaged in commercial farming, producing goods for the market. This commercial farming sector in turn provided an expanding market for an emerging industrial sector, not least for agricultural machinery. This process was facilitated by high tariffs on imported goods. As the frontier moved westwards, and agriculture developed on a grander scale, the 'virtuous circle' between agriculture and industry intensified, and the US became the most dynamic centre of capitalism in the world. The major exception to this pattern of development was the southern states where a system of slaveholding emerged. While highly profitable for the plantation owners, slavery did little to encourage industrial growth, as slaves were never great consumers. A similar symbiotic relationship between farming and urban capitalism can be observed in the 'white dominions' of Canada and Australia. Despite being part of the British Empire, they were permitted by Westminster to introduce tariffs to protect their fledgling industries (Aglietta, 1979; Darwin, 2008 2011; Post, 1982).

What these cases suggest is that the transition to industrial capitalism necessarily involves a double movement: the transformation of agrarian society and the creation of a mechanised manufacturing base. Where societies successfully made this transition there was a dynamic interaction between city and countryside, and between agriculture and industry, to create a 'virtuous circle'. In regions where pre-capitalist agrarian systems existed, and where colonial power dominated in the age of industrialisation, the consequences were more or less catastrophic. The attempt by European colonial rulers to force-march these societies towards a commercial system of agriculture, created a huge population of 'surplus' labour, and brought ecological chaos in its wake. Whether the 'surplus' workers stayed in the countryside or migrated to the cities, they tended to depress wages, and in the process inhibit technical innovation. Alongside this, what manufacturing industries these societies possessed were first curtailed by mercantilist restrictions imposed by the colonial power, and then subjected to the blitzkrieg of 'free trade' by the newly mechanised industries of Britain and the other imperial powers. In the scissors of an agrarian 'surplus labour', and strangled industry, the other side of modernity emerged. In the words of Mike Davis: '"Modernisation" and commercialisation were accompanied by pauperisation' (Davis, 2001, p. 312). If the commercialisation of agrarian social structures was critically important for the development of industrial capitalism, it would seem to have been no less important for what would become known as 'underdevelopment', though the form of commercialisation involved was very different.

Drivers of Uneven Development

'Underdevelopment' is widely envisaged as the absence of development, not only by conservative and liberal thinkers, but by many on the left who view 'underdeveloped' societies as pre-capitalist formations which await capitalist development. The evidence from Ireland, supported by that from India, suggests otherwise: that 'underdevelopment is a process which is in large measure brought about by capitalist development. Underdevelopment is the collateral damage of capitalist expansion.

Capitalism has transformed all parts of the world, including those areas where capitalist production itself is not present, or where it is barely present. These older social forms are restructured in a variety of ways by the dominance of capitalist market relations to create social formations which are neither 'developed' nor 'traditional', but which are often characterised by pathological distortions. The hugely destructive impact of the slave trade on African societies and of the Iberian conquest on American societies is well documented (Wolf, 1982).

If colonialism played a crucial role in shaping uneven development around the world, the two phenomena are not reducible to one another. Patterns of uneven development are clearly evident in contexts where colonialism was absent and it has persisted long after the collapse of (direct) colonialism. Portugal for example was a colonial power itself, yet by the early twentieth century it had not only 'lagged behind' northwestern Europe, but had acquired a peripheral semi-dependent relationship to the core regions. Latin America retained most of the characteristic features of underdevelopment long after it achieved formal political independence. The collapse of European colonialism following the Second World War has not, for the most part, been accompanied by a significant wave of economic growth in the former colonial regions, much less by a general increase in global prosperity (Arrighi, 1991; Kiely, 2007).

All this would suggest that while colonial systems of domination had a hugely regressive impact on much of the world, uneven development is an intrinsic part of the capitalist order itself and not solely a function of colonialism. Technical innovation enables particular industries to produce goods using less labour than elsewhere and consequently more cheaply. This forces other firms out of business, unless they can afford to introduce similar innovations. Growth in one sector or one region is inevitably accompanied by decline and rising unemployment in another. High levels of unemployment restrict consumption levels, thus creating a vicious circle of retarded development. The negative social consequences of uneven growth require political intervention if a region or country is not to suffer extensive social deprivation.

In Latin America, the agrarian and commercial elites who have dominated power since independence are notoriously reluctant to contribute anything to social development, an attitude no doubt related to the colonial origins of these elites. This elite stance has contributed hugely to the social regression and mass poverty which has characterised most of Latin America since independence. In East Asia, by contrast, governments have sought to draw comprehensively on their societies' resources in order to bring about economic development, a stance perhaps based upon a realisation that failure to do so would lead to a much higher price than taxation being paid.

There is another important driver of uneven development which has become especially pronounced in recent decades, though it has a longer history: the phenomenon of national debt bondage. Debt bondage is the system whereby the governments and financial institutions of the core countries use the debt difficulties of peripheral states to restructure these economies and societies in their own interests. In the nineteenth century, Britain sent gunboats to threaten Latin American countries over payments of debt and in 1882 British troops occupied Egypt 'temporarily' to recover debts, and stayed there until 1956. In the 1970s, European and North American banks, awash with money from the oil price hikes, lent large sums at low interest rates to states across the Global South. These debts were denominated in dollars and when the interest rates on the dollar rose sharply in 1979 – the Volcker shock – most of these states were unable to pay back the interest, bringing about the so-called Third World Debt Crisis. The IMF entered the picture to resolve the crisis. The IMF's solution insisted that the banks be repaid in full, but restructured the debts so as to enable the peripheral states to pay. The debtor states were 'lent' money by the IMF on condition that they implement 'structural adjustment' programmes based on massive reductions in public spending – not least on welfare and educational provision – privatising public assets, eliminating food subsidies and 'opening-up' their economies to external competition. A comprehensive survey of urban settlement in the Global South by a United Nations team concluded that these structural adjustment programmes were directly responsible for the massive growth of slums which have come to characterise much of the Global South today (Davis, 2004). The prolonged phase of social regression which followed the structural adjustment programmes coincided with a huge outflow of money from the most indebted countries of the global South: 'Between 1982 and 1989 they had to transfer a net sum of $125bn to the creditor nations, and yet in the same period their combined debt rose from $433.5bn to $625bn (Altvater, 1993, p. 162).

The proliferation of structured debt bondage is closely associated with a huge increase in the power and sway of financial capital which has occurred over the last few decades, a process known as 'financialisation'. The process of financialisation has also been accompanied by a spate of severe financial crises. In the late twentieth century these financial crises were confined to the Global South, East Asia and Eastern Europe. With the crash of 2007/8, financial crisis has come home to the North Atlantic economies and with it the phenomenon of national debt bondage. So too have structural adjustment programmes – the currently preferred term is austerity programmes – and as is the way of the world, they have come to be implemented unevenly. The rise of financialisation is a crucial background to the structural crisis which has emerged within the EU, and which is threatening to ruin Ireland and other peripheral countries.

Legacies of Uneven Development

With the financial crash of 2008, Ireland came to be classified in the financial press as one of the EU's 'peripheral' states. This return to peripheral status was accompanied two years later by the formal ceding of national sovereignty and its replacement by a supervisory team of *troika* officials (from the ECB, EC and IMF). To what extent has this represented a structural continuity: a legacy of Ireland's earlier history of retarded development?

From the start of the twentieth century it had been commonplace to divide the world's nations into categories of 'advanced' and 'backward', a divide which overlapped with, but was not identical to 'imperial' and 'colonised'. After the Second World War, the preferred terms were 'underdeveloped' and 'developed'. Leading Irish government officials like Ken Whitaker, used the term 'underdeveloped' to characterise Ireland. In those post-war decades, the distinction between 'underdeveloped' and 'developed' was more or less synonymous with 'agricultural' and 'industrial'. In later decades this distinction became more problematic as many countries which had been considered underdeveloped began to industrialise, without significantly reducing their high levels of poverty. Moreover, some of the world's richest countries, like the US, were major exporters of agricultural goods. One of the problems with these categories is that capitalism itself is a moving target, constantly transforming itself, yet curiously managing, much of the time, to reproduce the same spatial disparities in global incomes.

Samir Amin has distinguished between core capitalist formations, which are characterised by a self-centred development, and peripheral formations, whose centre is external and which are characterised by an inherently unbalanced pattern of development. A feature of peripheral capitalist formations is that they lack a capital goods sector (Amin, 1976). Ernest Mandel made a similar point, noting that in what he described as the 'semi-colonies', the growth of industrial employment cannot keep pace with the flight from the land. While there is much room for debate about the structural dynamics of uneven development, the symptoms of 'underdevelopment' seem clear enough. In Ernest Mandel's words *underdevelopment is ultimately always underemployment, both quantitatively* (massive unemployment) *and qualitatively* (low productivity of labour)' (Mandel, 1978, p. 60, italics in original).

There can be little doubt that for most of the nineteenth and twentieth centuries, Ireland was characterised by many of these features of 'underdevelopment'. The agricultural sector was unable to provide employment for the population of rural Ireland and its industrial base was much too weak to compensate. With the exception of a small engineering base in the northeast, Irish industry lacked a capital goods sector. Virtually all parts of the Irish economy were 'ex-centric', wholly orientated towards and structured around the British economy. The perennial affliction of Irish society was its huge levels of unemployment and underemployment, with emigration acting as both running sore and safety valve.

These socioeconomic tensions underlay most political developments in twentieth-century Ireland. Chronic underemployment triggered the republican insurgency in the years following the First World War, and the northern revolt in the late twentieth century. Paradoxically, these same pressures generated the Unionist bloc, cementing an alliance between Protestant labour and Protestant capital in a context of general decline. The consolidation of communalist politics to maintain order in the north of Ireland ensured that social revolt there would be focused on breaking the system of communal domination. In the south, politics had been largely structured around the need to contain these social tensions. The differing developmental strategies pursued in the 1930s and later from the 1960s onwards were both directed to this end, with mixed results.

A central feature of capitalist social organisation is the tendency for production to become more centralised in successive historical eras. Economies of scale operate ensuring that greater capital investment is necessary if an industry is to be competitive. One consequence of this is that states have become increasingly central to ensuring economic development. Public investment is needed if private investors are unable or unwilling to raise the finance required to initiate productive projects. This was already the case in the late nineteenth century but has become more pronounced since then. The issue of economic development is inescapably a political question. Funding and organising public investment involves adopting policies – taxation on wealth, tariffs on imports, capital controls and so on – which are often at variance with the interests of existing elites. So while economic development policies might seem to advance the goals of capital, in practice such policies are, as often as not, opposed by many if not most capitalists (Gowan, 2010).

These conflicting interests become magnified where earlier patterns of uneven development have created structural obstacles to wider social development. In the case of early twentieth-century Ireland, most of the propertied strata benefited from Irish economic dependence on Britain, even though this dependency damaged the rest of Irish society. The effort to reduce Ireland's economic dependence on Britain faced considerable resistance from not only the Anglo-Irish elite, but also from the Catholic upper middle classes (including the more prosperous farmers).

The closer integration of North Atlantic capitalisms in the second half of the twentieth century seemed to offer the Irish elite an escape from the underdevelopment trap. Where earlier developmental strategies were premised on asserting greater national independence, further development was now to be achieved through subordinating Irish sovereignty to the requirements of North American and European capital. This approach not only healed divisions between government and propertied elites, it also opened up hitherto unimaginable enrichment opportunities for aspiring Irish capitalists. Unfortunately for the Irish population, this very process of subordinating Ireland to North Atlantic capital has hugely increased the country's vulnerability to shocks. Not only did the Irish state fail to establish an adequate safety net against financial collapse, it proceeded to demolish the few defensive systems which did exist. The willingness of the Irish state and the Irish elite to transfer the losses of British, German and French banks onto the Irish citizenry is a telling testimony to the Irish state's more general position of subordination to North Atlantic capital.

The details of how the Irish state came to convert private debt into public debt – or even to whom the debt is owed – has never been made public. Nonetheless, a few points seem clear enough. The loans made by the Irish banks were backed by bonds mostly owned by the major German, French and British financial institutions. These bonds in turn were insured, through various complex financial instruments, by other financial bodies, most likely by the major Wall Street banks (especially by Goldman Sachs which seems to have specialised in this type of operation). There was no reason in principle or in law why the Irish state should have taken on the responsibility of socialising this private debt. The ECB certainly encouraged them to do so. At a G7 meeting Tim Geithner, head of the Fed, apparently ruled out any suggestion that private banks pay part of the cost. The ECB's affinity towards the major German, British and French banks has become all too apparent over the last few years, as has the Fed's with Wall Street. While the motives of the ECB and the US Fed seem clear enough, the Irish government's compliance is harder to explain (Kelly, 2011).

Perry Anderson has written about a 'tacit hierarchy of states' within the EU (Anderson, 2007). A good example of this occurred in the run-up to monetary union. A very rigid 'Stability Pact' had been imposed on candidate members at the behest of the core states, especially Germany. Countries in breach of these tight budgetary rules were to be severely penalised. In the event it was Germany and France which broke the rules, but no penalties were imposed. Weaker states have less leverage and are more vulnerable to sanctions, of one sort or another. However, the crippling sanctions levelled against Ireland are a direct consequence of the Irish government's acquiescence in socialising the bankers' debt: this is a self-inflicted wound. To make sense of the Irish state's capitulation, one needs to see it in the context of a correspondence between class and culture which has emerged over the last half century.

Insofar as the state has had any development strategy, it involved inserting itself as intermediaries in the circuits of North Atlantic capital. The upper echelons of the Irish elite have become fabulously rich by establishing themselves as brokers in these circuits; many more have become moderately rich in the process. Any economic proposals or political stance which threatened this broker position was anathema to the Irish elite. This environment nurtured a similar culture, in which global markets were celebrated, and it was taken for granted that states no longer possessed much economic significance. Any serious debate about national development was implicitly prohibited, and history was rewritten to diminish, in so far as feasible, the quest for independence. The Irish elite seems to have imagined that joining the EU conferred on them a club membership, which would protect them from the harsh winds of the global economy and enable them to escape forever the experience of economic backwardness.

If we compare developments in Ireland to Latin America, it is clear that there are significant parallels. The debt crisis and the direct supervisory role being played by the *troika* have opened up a new phase in Irish history, establishing a relationship that can reasonably be described as 'neo-imperial'. This is not to suggest that the Irish elite are not wholly complicit in the process. On the contrary, there is every reason to believe that the Irish oligarchy will follow the lead of elites in Latin America and use the structural adjustment programmes to asset-strip the state, drawing on hoarded capital to buy up newly privatised resources at fire-sale prices (Medeiros, 2009).

The huge level of debt that has been imposed upon the Irish population makes it clear that Ireland is being driven into a debt–deflation spiral, from which the only likely escape is default. Labour and community bodies that have long operated in close harmony with the state are thoroughly disorientated as the social rights of their constituents are being eradicated. If the balance of political forces in contemporary Ireland seems to offer little hope of challenging the dictates of structural adjustment, one asset that Irish political culture does possess is a long tradition of rebellion against injustice. The land league, the anti-conscription campaign and the civil rights movement all provide valuable examples of movements of popular insubordination.

One of the ironies of the current situation is that sovereignty and national democracy – the key themes of the national independence movement that have long been considered to be antiquated and utterly irrelevant – have re-emerged as pressing claims in popular discourse. To say that the national question has been forcibly reasserted by the financial crisis is not to argue that there is a national answer to the crisis. Ireland's predicament of debt bondage is part of a wider pattern: resistance is only likely to be successful if it is part of a wider coalition.

Financial Ascendancy and European Disorder

The last few decades have seen a decline in productive investment and stagnation in real wages in the major North Atlantic economies (with the brief exception of computer-related growth during the Clinton era). They have also witnessed a remarkable expansion of the financial sector and a huge credit boom, known as 'financialisation'. The finance boom has been accompanied by a sweeping rise in social inequality, where the income of the wealthiest strata has risen hugely, while the income of most of the population has declined or stagnated. This is particularly striking in the US, but it is also true for the EU. Financialisation and a slowdown in the productive economy are connected. Credit expansion compensated for stagnant wages, averting a collapse of consumption but at the cost of ever rising debt. It is not a coincidence that the banking collapse should have been precipitated by a mortgage crisis. Wage earners could not afford higher interest rates. The credit expansion had reached it limits (Dumenil & Levy, 2004; Glynn, 2006; Harvey, 2005; Lapavitsas, 2009).

While the financialisation process was driven by developments in the US (and closely linked to it, the City of London), the EU adapted itself to these changes. This was not simply a matter of Europe subordinating itself to the new financial axis: European capital hoped to cash in on the new fountains of wealth (Sablowski, 2009). The so-called Lisbon agenda outlined by the EC had 'the integration and liberalisation of European finance as a key theme' (Grahl, 2010). This growing ascendancy of finance was the crucial structural background to European monetary union, and the transformation of the EU which occurred.

It was argued earlier that the EU never had a single social model; somewhat different social models coexisted in the various nation states. There was nonetheless a West European *social ideal*, which was shared across the EU core, namely a society characterised by the provision of full employment and the prospect of deepening social inclusion. This social ideal was largely achieved within the European core by the adoption of careful macroeconomic planning that ensured a close link between productivity rises and incomes, and which provided sufficient income support for the poorest sections of society to limit social exclusion and maintain economic demand. This social ideal was motivated not only by an aspiration to maintaining social cohesion, but also by the related goal of preventing a collapse of consumer demand and a return to prolonged depression, as occurred in the inter-war years. A crucial factor in ensuring effective macroeconomic planning was keeping a firm lid on finance. The promotion of this social ideal was partially driven by a determination that Europe would never again experience the kind of economic depression and political conflicts that led to the Second World War. It was also designed to provide an attractive alternative to the 'authoritarian–socialist' models that existed in Eastern Europe. For the populations of the EU's peripheral states, not least Ireland, this ideal arguably represented the primary appeal of closer European integration.

As early as 1943, the Polish economist Michael Kalecki had pointed out some of the more problematic aspects, for capital, of full employment, not least a decline in the fear of the sack. By the 1970s, faced with declining profitability, British and North American elites had come to the conclusion that full employment was too high a price to pay for social cohesion. The transformation of global finance began in the US with the ending of the dollar link to gold under Nixon was and was furthered by the policies of the Carter and Reagan administrations, helping to 'liberate' the financial sphere from political accountability. Capital could flow more easily across borders to make speculative gains. Governments led by Thatcher and Reagan began to systematically roll back labour rights and social entitlements, using rising unemployment to impose discipline on the working population (Glynn, 2006; Kalecki, 1943).

European governments followed suit in the 1980s, encouraged by the European Commission. The Maastricht Treaty and the Delors Plan made employment policy an indirect outcome of growth rather than an explicit policy objective. Brussels also pushed cost-cutting financialisation. By the close of the twentieth century, the conditions which had given rise to the EU's social ideal had faded. The social origins of the Second World War had largely been forgotten, and the Soviet Union and its satellite states belonged to the past (Bellofiore et al, 2011; Grahl, 2010).

This was the background to the restructuring of the EU that has taken place over the last couple of decades. Monetary union occurred in the context of liberalising the financial sphere. These were not separate processes; rather, monetary union was structured in such a way as to institutionalise a liberalised money market system. For the first time the EU has a single social model, and a deeply regressive one at that. Monetary union was premised upon making Europe more competitive globally, which was to be achieved by holding down popular living standards. The rules governing the currency union make this clear. Public debt was limited to 60 per cent of GDP and annual budget deficits restricted to 3 per cent of GDP, both figures ludicrously low for times of recession and high unemployment. Alongside this, an 'autonomous' central bank, the ECB, was permitted to control monetary policy in Europe. By establishing these structures, European governments effectively abandoned the crucial mechanisms for macroeconomic planning and pledged their economic fates to the whims of the global financial markets. They also ensured that macroeconomic policy in Europe would no longer be democratically accountable (Grahl, 2010; Scharpt, 2011).

The problems with the ascendancy of finance go further. By seeking to make Europe more competitive through holding down wages and repressing standards of living – the race to the bottom – Europe's rulers have placed themselves in a classic quandary: the problem of effective demand. Quite simply, if popular incomes are held down, and workers wages do not rise alongside productivity gains, capital is unable to sell the goods being produced because consumers cannot afford them.

This is a global problem, some would argue *the* central problem in the world's capitalist economy today. There are some similarities in the way the US and the EU have attempted to resolve this problem, but there are also crucial differences. While median wages in the US have been stagnant since the 1970s (with the exception of a brief period in the 1990s) the US avoided a full-scale slump by promoting domestic debt. As the home of the world's hegemonic currency, the US banking system was able to run up vast debts made possible by the global demand for dollars. These debts financed the huge gap between US exports and imports, especially with the East Asian economies. This mountain of debt was the reverse side of the financial explosion (Arrighi, 2005a, 2005b; Bellamy Foster, 2010).

The situation in the EU was somewhat different. The core economies, especially Germany, solved the problem of effective demand by building up trade surpluses. While wages and living standards stagnated, despite productivity gains, exports grew more rapidly than imports. Most of Germany's exports go to other EU states, 63 per cent in 2009. This imbalance was made possible by banks in the core states lending to banks (and in some cases states) in the peripheral regions, while holding down domestic debt. In both the US and the EU, the problem of effective demand was not resolved, it was merely displaced. It was only a matter of time before the enterprise collapsed (Bellofiore et al, 2011).

Once the bubble broke, the EC and the ECB moved not only to protect the banks but to use the crisis to promote a more long-standing agenda: in the words of a Commission document to make Europe '*the cheapest and easiest place to do business* in the world' (quoted in Grahl, 2010, italics in original). The austerity programmes prepared for the EU's peripheral regions fit the strategy. The impoverishment of the EU's periphery might also be expected to have a downward draw on wages and working conditions in the core states: 'there but for fortune (and prudence) go we'. Unfortunately for the EU, these very austerity measures exacerbate the economic crisis. As a consequence, the economies of the European periphery have entered a deflationary spiral similar to that which affected Latin America in the 1980s. There is no bottom to such downward spirals, at least not until sufficient popular resistance arises that forces governments to change course.

If European governments had hoped that liberalising financial markets would provide a useful tool for social discipline, they failed to note that this involved placing their own policy projects at the mercy of these same markets. The institutional structures established by the various treaties, which seem to have been designed to lock out all public scrutiny, much less popular sovereignty, act as obstacles to taking the political measures necessary to curtail the deepening economic malaise. A whole generation of planners and leaders in Europe appear to be unaware that high wages and social provision were not intended solely to appease an undeserving populace, but also, crucially, to prevent another prolonged slump.

The euro crisis is generally described as a sovereign debt crisis; this overlooks its more fundamental character as a *banking crisis*. It is the huge mountain of banking debts which threaten to bring down the whole financial order. The European authorities were able to use the weakness of the smaller states to impose the banks' debts on their citizenry, but the fact that this debt itself has been 'securitised' meant that no one quite knew where it had spread to, and it threatened to overwhelm the banking system if one or more of these states defaulted. 'Securitisation' is one of those wonderful inventions made by North American bankers, which were supposed to spread risk throughout the financial system but became so complex that even the financiers no longer understood them. As with the US, it was these very clever financial instruments, exalted by Brussels and Frankfurt, that are threatening to bring down the house of Finance. The EC and the ECB had no recourse but to pass on this debt to the citizenry of the EU as a whole, especially (inevitably) onto the taxpayers of the wealthier states, notably Germany. In doing so, they have exposed crucial structural flaws in the architecture of the EU (Lanchester, J. 2011).

While corporate Germany has benefited considerably from a single currency – their exports were cheaper than they would have been with a national currency – most German citizens have not. Wages in Germany have been stagnant for a couple of decades, social conditions have declined and poverty has grown. The German population, like most others, is increasingly sceptical of European integration, and estranged from its institutions. The German media and political leaders have complained about the burden of 'bailing out' the peripheral states, but keep quiet about the fact that it is the German (and other core state) banks that are being bailed out, not the public of the peripheral countries. The population of Germany and other core states have been understandably reluctant to contribute to these bailouts. Among those who recognise that it is the banks which are being rescued, such reluctance is even greater. This situation appears to have opened up divisions within the German elite on the wisdom of the Brussels strategy.

While most commentators focus on the problems caused by the absence of fiscal union, they ignore the larger issue which is that a single currency, instead of leading to economic convergence between regions, has increased the imbalances within Europe, a fissure that was concealed by the financial bubble. A single currency in Europe could only be socially advantageous to the majority of Europeans if it were closely linked to a project of reducing social inequality and disparities between regions. For this reason, the problems of uneven development in Europe will not be resolved by the creation of a fiscal union in the EU – they are more likely to be exacerbated. The effect of a fiscal union in a context where finance holds sway would be to transform the EU into a system of 'internal imperialism.' The peripheral states would be unable to compete with the economies of the core states. Monetary union exacerbates these problems because the peripheral states cannot adjust their currencies to become more competitive. The only way their economies could become more competitive is through lowering living standards, but lower living standards would further diminish their domestic economies. To add to this, fiscal union will almost certainly result in the abrogation of all serious decision-making by unelected officials in Brussels and Frankfurt. Both in its structure and in its strategic direction, the EU is being transformed from being an association for mutual protection into being something of a protection racket. If the EU continues this course, it seems reasonable to assume that twenty-first-century Europe will witness new battles for sovereignty and democracy, closely linked to struggles against impoverishment. A collapse of the single currency would not resolve the problems of the EU but it would have the merit of opening up serious debate about the future of Europe. It would also mean that decision-making bodies might be responsible to democratically elected assemblies and not just to financial institutions and corporations as is effectively the case at present.

Ireland and a World Order in Disarray

Irish state policy for over half a century has assumed a stable global order within which the US played a globally hegemonic role and Western Europe a closely subordinate one, somewhere between satellites and allies. While this broad pattern of power remains, it is no longer a stable one – indeed, all the evidence suggests that this is a global order in increasing disarray.

Aggregate growth rates in the North Atlantic economic bloc have been declining for four decades. So too have rates of investment. Recessions have become deeper and recoveries weaker. In the case of the 'Great Contraction' beginning with the financial crisis in 2008, it is questionable whether there has been any real recovery. Unemployment rates remained high, and wages were stagnant or fell. Investment is stagnant, leading some commentators to speak of an 'investment strike' by capital. Mountains of debt remain. Despite this, or because of it, the financial sphere retains its power and its central role in the North Atlantic economies and polities. Discussions about radical reform of the global financial architecture were abandoned once the immediate danger of an all-out financial crash receded. All the major political parties in North America and Europe – at least once in power – are committed to holding down wages and reducing social provision, while strengthening the position of Property. The combination of declining popular living standards and the further enrichment of the elites unavoidably stirs social tensions. The curtailing of democratic governance in Europe to facilitate elite enrichment creates an even more volatile mixture.

The financial crisis of 2007/8 revealed to the world the structural flaws in the global financial order, and the dangers of relying on the dollar as a hegemonic currency. While the US retains its vast sea and air power, it is (unlike Britain in the nineteenth century) a debtor not a creditor nation, and America's creditors are increasingly worried that they will be unable to pay their debts, or that these repayments will be massively devalued. The fact that there is no viable alternative world currency to the dollar is not a symptom of global stability, but of deepening disorder. The assumption that the North Atlantic bloc will continue to dominate the global economic and political order looks increasingly implausible.

The Irish intellectual and political elites defend their strategic orientation of subordinating the country to the requirements of North Atlantic capital on the grounds of realism; any other approach is considered naive and utopian. Yet events are demonstrating that it is the neoliberal dogmas which they espouse that are creating a dystopian world, and only a reorganisation of social priorities will enable Ireland and Europe to escape this fate. This will necessitate not only strengthening social provision and popular living standards, but ensuring – through one means or another – that the huge accumulations of wealth which exist in Ireland and across Europe are invested productively.

Asserting sovereignty need not involve withdrawing from 'Europe': the choice is not between autarky and market domination, between economic isolation and subservience to Washington or Brussels. On the contrary, small semi-peripheral countries like Ireland can and need to play an active political role by seeking to restructure Europe, establishing alliances with other states and popular movements, peripheral and core, inside and outside the EU, to create a more just and sustainable world order.

Further Reading

This is a short list of books and articles for anyone wanting to read more on the issues dealt with in the book. It is not intended as a comprehensive bibliography. More detailed referencing of the books and articles mentioned here can be found in the Bibliography section.

PREFACE

Ciaran Brady's *Interpreting Irish History: The Debate on Historical Revisionism* provides a useful collection of articles that debate the main trends in Irish historical studies. David Miller's essay in the collection he edited, *Re-thinking Northern Ireland* shows how academic historiography contributed to closing down critical debate on the Northern conflict.

ANGLO-FRENCH IRELAND

There is no general history of Anglo-French society that takes into account the more recent research. However the work of historians such as Bartlett, Canny, Down, Empey, Frame, O'Brien and others has hugely advanced our understanding of this period and permits us to see it in the context of the wider changes occurring in late medieval Europe. Bartlett's *The Making of Europe* explores the expansion of the feudal order in the high middle ages, in the process making many comparisons between the experiences of Ireland and eastern Europe. The articles by Alan Bliss explore the complex linguistic makeup of Anglo-French Ireland. Robin Frame's *Ireland and Britain, 1170–1450* examines the relationship between the Dublin administration and the Gaelic clans. Canon Empey's work on settlement patterns brings out the distinctive features of the Irish medieval colony, and contrasts it to the English situation. Nicholas Canny's 1976 pamphlet provides crucial social and cultural background to the Pale elite in the late medieval period while Kevin Down's and A.F. O'Brien's articles on socioeconomic developments in southern and eastern Ireland have made invaluable contributions to the study of the economic and social structures of the region.

LATE GAELIC IRELAND

Gaelic and Gaelicised Ireland in the Middle Ages by Kenneth Nicholls is indispensible for anyone wanting to understand the complexity of Gaelic society in that period. *From Kings to Warlords* by Katherine Simms examines the changing political and military structures of Gaelic society. Nearys Patterson (1989) has argued persuasively that Gaelic social practices and law continued to operate down to the era of the Elizabethan conquest. *Gaelic Ireland* edited by Duffy et al, and *Rulers and Regions* edited by Edwards et al, are collections of essays that provide more detailed studies of Ireland in this era.

REFORMATION AND STATE FORMATION

Colm Lennon's *Sixteenth Century Ireland: The Incomplete Conquest* is a good overview of the century. Brendan Bradshaw's work on the origins of the Reformation and Counter-Reformation is seminal, especially his magisterial essay comparing the progress of the Reformation in Ireland and Wales. While Bradshaw's focus is primarily on the forces within the Old English community resistant to the Reformation, *The Reformation in Ireland* by S. Meigs explores the sources of opposition within Gaelic Ireland, especially the resistance of literate strata. Alan Ford's *Protestant Reformation* is a close study of the reformed church and the difficulties they faced in getting their message across. His work stresses the importance of the cultural divide, especially the linguistic one, in paralysing the efforts of the reformers reaching the indigenous population. Diarmad MacCulloch's *Reformation: Europe's House Divided* is a wide ranging and highly readable overview of the European Reformation.

Nicholas Canny's *Making Ireland British* is a detailed study of the plantation process in Munster, and the resulting social tensions. William Smyth's *Map-making, Landscapes and Memory* uses geographical methods to analyse the impact of the Conquest on Irish society. Smyth's book is a groundbreaking study that is essential reading for anyone wanting to understand the social implications of the conquest.

AGRARIAN SOCIETY & CAPITALIST DEVELOPMENT IN SCOTLAND AND IRELAND

Louis Cullen's *Economic History* and Cormac O'Grada' *New Economic History* are the standard works in the field. Denis O'Hearn's *The Atlantic Economy* places Irish economic development in the wider context of the rise of Atlantic capitalism. Tom Devine's *Scottish Nation: 1700–2000* is an excellent and accessible overview of modern Scottish history. Niall Davidson's articles in the *Journal of Agrarian Society* provide a detailed analysis of changes in agrarian social relations in Scotland. Tom Devine's essay on agrarian society in Scotland and Ireland and Ian Whyte's essay on urbanisation are both pioneering works of historical comparison.

Toby Barnard's *A New Anatomy of Ireland* explores the social hierarchies within the Irish Protestant world in the eighteenth century, throwing light on middle and lower class communities which are often hidden from view. David Dickson and Raymond Gillespie have written extensively on the social and economic history of Ireland in the seventeenth and eighteenth centuries. Dowling's *Tenant Right and Agrarian Society in Ulster* looks at the distinctive features of agrarian social relations in Ulster while William Crawford's articles explore the social changes in Ulster in this period, contrasting these with developments in Scotland and other parts of Ireland. Louis Cullen's *Emergence of Modern Ireland* looks at the social and cultural changes in the early modern period, paying particular attention to Catholic farming communities in the south and east of Ireland, and is a useful corrective to work which focuses on the more marginalised peasantry. *Peasants and Power* by Michael Beames provides an excellent overview of the rise of peasant movements in the pre-Famine era.

PARADOX OF ANGLICISATION

Jim Smyth's *Men of No Property* and Kevin Whelan's *Tree of Liberty* explore the social and cultural background to the popular radicalisation of the late eighteenth century. A huge amount has been published in recent decades on the 1840's famine. Christine Kinealy's *The Great Irish Famine* and Cormac O'Grada's *Black Forty Seven and Beyond*, are two of the best studies. Samuel Clark's *Social Origins of the Irish Land War* looks at the changes in agrarian society in the nineteenth century while Paul Bew's *Land and the National Question* explores the relationship between the peasant revolt and the quest for national independence. Declan Kiberd's *Inventing Ireland* and Terry Eagleton's *Heathcliff and the Great Hunger* examine some of the cultural implications of the colonial relationship between Britain and Ireland. David Miller's *Queen's Rebels* looks at the historical origins of Ulster Loyalism.

IRELAND AND EMPIRE

Historians often present the Land War in the late 1870s and early 1880s as the end of the Irish agrarian conflict. Fergus Campbell's *Land and Revolution* makes it clear that it was only the beginning of the end. His later *Irish Establishment* is an invaluable study of the Irish upper classes in the first decades of the century. Desmond Greaves' biography, *Liam Mellows and the Irish Revolution* explores the social roots of Irish republicanism. Conor Kostick's *Revolution in Ireland* examines the role of labour struggles in the War of Independence and Civil War. John Regan's *The Irish Counter-Revolution 1921–36* looks at the politics of the Irish bourgeoisie during the civil war and the formation of the Irish Free State. C.S. Andrews was a republican fighter who later became a key figure in the Fianna Fáil administration. His autobiographies *Dublin Made Me* and *Man of no Property* give a valuable insight into the political culture of the Dublin lower middle classes and the first generation of Fianna Fáil. The political culture of the Protestant working class in the north of Ireland is the subject of Henry Patterson's *Class Conflict and Sectarianism*. Michael Farrell's *Arming the Protestants* looked at how the Northern Ireland state consolidated its power.

THE LIMITS OF INDEPENDENCE

Joseph Lee's *Ireland: Politics and Society* is uneven but it provides a lot of valuable material on the independent Irish state whose economic history is surveyed in Cormac Ó Gráda's *The Rocky Road*. Ronan Fanning's *The Irish Department of Finance, 1952–58* while very sympathetic to its subject, nonetheless provides valuable insights into the state's financial structures and the political culture of its officials. Eoin O'Malley's *Industry and Economic Development* is a significant and largely neglected study of Irish development policies and their limitations. Dennis O'Hearn's *Inside the Celtic Tiger* analyses the structural limitations of the Celtic Tiger growth while Peadar Kirby's *Celtic Tiger in Distress* and Kieran Allen's *The Celtic Tiger* focus on the social inequalities generated by this growth. Matt Cooper's book *Who Really Runs Ireland* is a detailed account of the sordid layers of corruption that permeate the Irish state. Daniel Finn's essay 'Ireland on the Turn' in *New Left Review* 67 is a good introduction to contemporary Irish politics.

Northern Ireland: The Political Economy of Conflict* by Bob Rowthorn and Naomi Wayne is probably the best study of the structures of the Northern Ireland state and the social background to the conflict. Eamon McCann's *War in an Irish Town* is a highly readable account of the early years of the troubles in Derry. Bowyer-Bell's *The Irish Troubles* is a highly detailed account of the first two decades of the conflict, while *Making Sense of the Troubles* by David McKittrick and David McVea is a good overview of the Northern Ireland war and the start of the peace process. Susan McKay's *Northern Protestants: An Unsettled People* provides a highly readable insight into the political culture of the Protestant community. *Rethinking Northern Ireland* edited by David Miller *Northern Ireland After the Troubles*, edited by Colin Coulter and M. Murray, are valuable collections of academic studies on Northern society after the peace process. *Sinn Féin and the Politics of Left Republicanism* by Eoin Ó Broin and *Provisional IRA: From Insurrection to Parliament* by Tommy McKearney are good introductions to the debates in left republicanism.

IRELAND IN A CHANGING WORLD ORDER

Europe and the People Without History by Eric Wolf is a wide-ranging study of how European invaders and settlers transformed the non-European world, in the process creating hugely distorted social formations. John Darwin's *After Tamerlane* shows how the European mercantile empires destroyed the manufacturing economies of Asia. *Late Victorian Holocausts* by Mike Davis rewrites the history of the Global South, showing how the great natural disasters of this period were brought about by social and political forces. *Planet of Slums* by the same author documents the enormous human misery created by the IMF's structural adjustment programmes.

David Harvey's *A Brief history of Neoliberalism* and Andrew Glynn's *Capitalism Unleashed* are two of the best and most accessible introductions to the rise of financialisation and its relation to the neoliberal project. The discussion papers produced by *Research on Money and Finance*, available online, are a major and ongoing contribution on our knowledge of the role played by finance and debt in the present world order. Good critical research on the EU is scant. *A Ruined Fortress?* edited by Alan Cafruny and Magnus Ryner is a good, but difficult read. Andy Storey's essay 'The European Project: Dismantling Social Democracy, Globalising Neoliberalism' is a lucid description of how the EU has been transformed by the rise of neo-liberalism.

Bibliography

Adams, J. R. R. (1987) *The Printed Word and the Common Man*. Belfast: Institute of Irish Studies, Queen's University of Belfast.

Aglietta, M. (1982) *A Theory of Capitalist Regulation: The US Experience*. London: Verso.

Ahmad, A. (1992) *In Theory: Classes, Nations, Literatures*. London, Verso.

Akenson, D. H. (1989) 'Pre-University Education, 1782-1870' in Vaughan (ed.) *A New History of Ireland, Vol. V*.

Allen, K. (2000) *The Celtic Tiger: The Myth of Social Partnership in Ireland*. Manchester: Manchester University Press.

Altvater, E. (1993) *The Future of the Market: An Essay on the Regulation of Money and Nature after the Collapse of 'Actually Existing Socialism'*. London: Verso.

Amin, S. (1976) *Unequal Development: An Essay on the Social Formations of Peripheral Capitalism*. New York: Monthly Review Press.

Anderson, B. (1983) *Imagined Communities: Reflections on the Origin and Spread of Nationalism*. London: Verso.

Anderson, K. (2010) *Marx at the Margins*. Chicago, IL: University of Chicago Press.

Anderson, P. (1974a) *Passages from Antiquity to Feudalism*. London: NLB.

Anderson, P. (1974b) *Lineages of the Absolutist State*. London: NLB.

Anderson, P. (1992) *English Questions*. London: Verso.

Anderson, P. (2007) 'Depicting Europe', *London Review of Books*, 20 Sept. 2007.

Andrews, C. S. (1979) *Dublin Made Me*. Dublin: Mercier Press.

Andrews, C. S. (1982) *Man of No Property*. Dublin: Mercier Press.

Anievas, A. (ed.) (2010) *Marxism and World Politics*. Abingdon: Routledge.

Annals of the Four Masters. Annals of the Kingdom of Ireland / by the Four Masters, from the Earliest Period to the Year 1616. Dublin: Hodges, Smith and Co. 1856.

Annals of Ulster: A Chronicle of Irish Affairs from A.D. 431 to A.D. 1540. Dublin: Printed for H. M. Stationery Office, 1887–1901.

Arensberg, C. & Kimball, S. (1968) *Family and Community in Ireland*. Cambridge, MA: Harvard University Press.

Arrighi, G. (1991) 'World Income Inequalities and the Future of Socialism', *New Left Review* 1/189.

Arrighi, G. (1994) *The Long Twentieth Century*. London: Verso.

Arrighi, G. (2005a) 'Hegemony Unraveling–I' in *New Left Review* 2/32 (March–April 2005).

Arrighi, G. (2005b) 'Hegemony Unraveling–II' in *New Left Review* 2/33 (May–June 2005).

Arrighi, G. (2008) *Adam Smith in Beijing: Lineages of the Twenty-First Century*. London: Verso.

Aston, T. H. & Philpin, C. H. E. (eds) (1985) *The Brenner Debate*. Cambridge: Cambridge University Press.

Austen, J. (1994) *Emma*. Harmondsworth: Penguin.

Bannerman, J. (1983) 'Literacy in the Highlands' in Cowan & Shaw (eds) *The Renaissance and Reformation in Scotland*.

Barnard, T. C. (1993) 'Protestants and the Irish Language' in *The Journal of Ecclesiastical History*, Vol. 44, No. 2, pp. 243–72.

Barnard, T. C. (2003) *A New Anatomy of Ireland: The Irish Protestants, 1649-1770*. New Haven, CT & London: Yale University Press.

Barrow, G. W. S. (1981) *Kingship and Unity: Scotland 1000-1306*. London: Edward Arnold.

Barrow, G. W. S. (1997) 'The Pattern of Non-Literary Manuscript Production and Survival in Scotland, 1200-1330' in Britnell (ed.) *Pragmatic Literacy, East and West, 1200-1330*.

Barrow, G. W. S. (ed.) (1974) *The Scottish Tradition*. Edinburgh: Scottish Academic Press.

Bartlett, R. (1993) *The Making of Europe: Conquest, Colonization and Cultural Change 950-1350*. London: Allen Lane.

Bartlett, R. & MacKay, A. (eds) (1989) *Medieval Frontier Societies*. Oxford: Clarendon.

Bartlett, T. & Hayton, D. W. (eds) (1979) *Penal Era and Golden Age: Essays in Irish History, 1690-1800*. Belfast: Ulster Historical Foundation.

Baugh, A. C. & Cable, T. (1993) *A History of the English Language*. London: Routledge.

Beames, M. (1983) *Peasants and Power*. Brighton: Harvestor.

Bellamy, Foster, J. (2010) 'The Financialisation of Accumulation', *Monthly Review*, Oct. 2010.

Bellofiore, et al (2011) 'The Global Crisis and the Crisis of European Neomercantilism', *Socialist Register*, Vol. 47, pp. 120–46.

Benjamin, W. (1977) *The Origins of German Tragic Drama*. London: NLB.

Bernstein, H. (1971) 'Modernization Theory and the Sociological Study of Development' in *Journal of Development Studies*, pp. 141–60.

Bew, P. (1978) *Land and the National Question in Ireland, 1858–82*. Dublin: Gill & Macmillan.

Bew, P. (1979) *The State in Northern Ireland, 1921–72: Political Forces and Social Class*. Manchester: Manchester University Press.

Binchy, D. A. (1975/1976) 'Irish History and Irish Law' (Part 1 & 2) in *Studia Hibernica*, No. 15, pp. 7–36 and No. 16 pp. 7–45.

Bliss, A. & Long, J. (1987) 'Literature in Norman French and English to 1534' in Cosgrove (ed.) *A New History of Ireland, Vol. II*.

Bliss, A. (1976) 'The English Language in Early Modern Ireland' in Moody, Martin & Byrne (eds) *A New History of Ireland, Vol. III*.

Bliss, A. (1984) 'Language and Literature' in Lydon (ed.) *The English in Medieval Ireland*.

Bloch, M. (1961) *Feudal Society Vol. 1 & 2*. London: Routledge & Kegan Paul.

Bossy, J. (1985) *Christianity in the West 1400–1700*. Oxford: Oxford University Press.

Bowyer Bell, J. (1993) *The Irish Troubles: A Generation of Violence 1967–1992*. Dublin: Gill and Macmillan.

Bowyer Bell, J. (1996) *In Dubious Battle: The Dublin and Monaghan Bombings 1972–1974*. Dublin: Poolbeg.

Boylan, C. (2007) 'Victorian Ideologies of Improvement: Sir Charles Trevelyan in India and Ireland' in Foley & O'Connor (eds) *Ireland and India: Colonies, Culture and Empire*.

Bradley, J. (ed.) (1988) *Settlement and Society in Medieval Ireland*. Kilkenny: Boethus.

Bradshaw, B. & Morrill, J. (eds) (1996) *The British Problem, c1534-1707: State Formation in the Atlantic Archipelago*. Basingstoke: Macmillan.

Bradshaw, B. & Roberts, P. (eds) (1998) *British Consciousness and Identity: The Making of Britain, 1533–1707*. Cambridge: Cambridge University Press.

Bradshaw, B. (1978) 'Sword, Word and Strategy in the Reformation in Ireland' in *The Historical Journal*, Vol. 21, No. 3, pp. 475–502.

Bradshaw, B. (1979) *The Irish Constitutional Revolution of the Sixteenth Century*. Cambridge: Cambridge University Press.

Bradshaw, B. (1996) 'The Tudor Reformation and Revolution in Wales and Ireland: The Origins of the British Problem' in Bradshaw & Morrill (eds) *The British Problem, c1534-1707*.

Bradshaw, B. (1998) 'The English Reformation and Identity Formation in Ireland and Wales' in Bradshaw & Roberts (eds) *British Consciousness and Identity: The Making of Britain, 1533–1707*.

Brady, C. (1986) 'Court, Castle and Country: The Framework of Government in Tudor Ireland' in Brady & Gillespie (eds) *Natives and Newcomers, 1534-1641*.

Brady, C. (1994) (ed.) *Interpreting Irish History: The Debate on Historical Revisionism*. Dublin: Irish Academic Press.

Brady, C. & Gillespie, R. (eds) (1986) *Natives and Newcomers: Essays on the Making of Irish Colonial Society, 1534–1641*. Dublin: Irish Academic Press.

Breatnach, P. A. (1990) 'An Appeal for a Guarantor', in *Celtica*, Vol. 21.

Brenner, R. (1985) 'Agrarian Class Structure and Economic Development in Pre-Industrial Europe' in Aston & Philpin (eds) *The Brenner Debate*.

Brenner, R. (1985) 'The Agrarian Origins of European Capitalism' in Aston & Philpin (eds) *The Brenner Debate*.

Brenner, R. (1996) 'The Rises and Declines of Serfdom in Medieval and Early Modern Europe' in Bush (ed.) *Serfdom and Slavery: Studies in Legal Bondage*.

Brenner, R. (2003) *Merchants & Revolution: Commercial Change, Political Conflict and London's Overseas Traders, 1550–1653*. London: Verso.

Britnell, R. (1996) *The Commercialisation of English Society, 1000–1500*. Manchester: Manchester University Press.

Britnell, R. (ed.) (1997) *Pragmatic Literacy, East and West, 1200–1330*. Woodbridge: Boydell Press.

Browne, H. (2011) 'What Do Governments Fear Most? They Fear Us. Dublin Wikileaks Cables Reveal Irish Govt. Grovelling to the US'. *Counterpunch*, 3 June 2011.

Browne, H. (2008) *Hammered by the Irish: How the Pitstop Ploughshares Disabled a US War-Plane – with Ireland's Blessing*. Petrolia: Counterpunch, and AK Press.

Brown, J. M. (ed.) (1977) *Scottish Society in the Fifteenth Century*. London: Edward Arnold.

Budge, I. & O'Leary, C. (1973) *Belfast Approach to Crisis: A Study of Belfast Politics, 1613–1970*. London: Macmillan.

Bush, M. L. (ed.) (1996) *Serfdom and Slavery: Studies in Legal Bondage*. Harlow: Longman.

Butler, W. F. T. (1925) *Gleanings from Irish History*. London: Longman.

Byres, T. J. (2006) 'Differentiation of the Peasantry Under Feudalism and the Transition to Capitalism: In Defence of Rodney Hilton' in *Journal of Agrarian Change*, Vol. 6 No. 1, January 2006, pp. 17–68.

Caball, M. (1998) *Poets and Politics: Continuity and Reaction in Irish Poetry, 1558–1625*. Cork: Cork University Press.

Caball, M. & Hollo, K. (2006) 'The Literature of Later Medieval Ireland, 1200–1600: From the Normans to the Tudors', in Kelleher & O'Leary (eds) *The Cambridge History of Irish Literature.*

Cafruny, A. W. & Ryner, M. (2003) *A Ruined Fortress? Neoliberal Hegemony and Transformation in Europe.* Lanham: Rowman and Littlefield.

Calendar of State Papers relating to Ireland (1860–1912). London: Longman.

Callinicos, A. (1999) *Social Theory: A Historical Introduction.* Oxford: Polity Press.

Cameron, E. (1991) *The European Reformation.* Oxford: Clarendon.

Campbell, F. (2005) *Land and Revolution.* Oxford: Oxford University Press.

Campbell, F. (2009) *The Irish Establishment 1879–1914.* Oxford: Oxford University Press.

Canny, N. P. (1975) *The Formation of the Old English Elite in Ireland.* Dublin: National University of Ireland.

Canny, N. P. (1976) *The Elizabethan Conquest of Ireland: A Pattern Established, 1565–76.* Hassocks: Harvester Press.

Canny, N. P. (2001) *Making Ireland British, 1580–1650.* Oxford: Oxford University Press.

Cebulla, A. & Smith, J. (1995) 'Industrial Collapse and Post-Fordist Overdetermination in Belfast', in Shirlow (ed.) *Development Ireland.*

Census of Ireland (1841) 'Report of the Commissioners Appointed to Take the Census of Ireland for the Year 1841', in *Parliamentary Papers* (1843), xxiv.

Census of Ireland (1881) 'General Report' in *Parliamentary Papers* (1882), lxxxvi.

Chang, H. J. (2003) *Kicking Away the Ladder.* London: Anthem Press.

Chenu, M. D. (1998) 'The Evangelical Awakening' in Little & Rosenwein (eds) *Debating the Middle Ages.*

Cipolla, C. M. (1969) *Literacy and Development in the West.* London: Penguin.

Clanchy, M. T. (1993) *From Memory to Written Record: England 1066–1307.* Oxford: Blackwell Publishers.

Clark, S. (1979) *Social Origins of the Irish Land War.* Princeton, NJ: Princeton University Press.

Clark, S. & Donnelly, J. S. (eds) (1983) *Irish Peasants: Violence and Political Unrest, 1780–1914.* Madison: University of Wisconsin Press.

Coleman, M. C. (2001) 'The Children Are Used Wretchedly: Pupil Responses to the Irish Charter Schools in the Early Nineteenth Century', in *History of Education,* Vol. 30, No. 4, pp. 339–57.

Colley, L. (1992) *Britons: Forging the Nation, 1707–1837.* London: Pimlico.

Comerford, R. V. (1985) *The Fenians in Context: Irish Politics and Society, 1848–82.* Dublin: Wolfhound.

Connolly, F. & Lynch, R. (2005) *The Great Corrib Gas Controversy.* Dublin: Centre for Public Inquiry.

Connolly, P. (1984) 'The Enactments of the 1297 Parliament' in Lydon (ed.) *The English in Medieval Ireland.*

Connolly, S. J. (1988) 'Albion's Fatal Twigs: Justice and Law in the Eighteenth Century' in Mitchison & Roebuck (eds) *Economy and Society in Scotland and Ireland 1500–1939.*

Connolly, S. J., Houston, R. A. & Morris, R. J. (eds) (1995) *Conflict, Identity & Economic Development: Ireland and Scotland, 1600–1939.* Preston: Carnegie Publishing.

Coolahan, J. (1981) *Irish Education: Its History and Structure.* Dublin: Institute of Public Administration.

Cooper, M. (2009) *Who Really Runs Ireland?* Dublin: Penguin Ireland.

Cosgrove, A. (1981) *Late Medieval Ireland, 1370–1541*. Dublin: Helicon.

Cosgrove, A. (ed.) (1987) *A New History of Ireland – Vol. 2: Medieval Ireland 1169–1534*. Oxford: Clarendon.

Coss, P. R. (1995) 'The Formation of the English Gentry' in *Past and Present*, No. 147, pp. 38–64.

Coulter, C. & Murray, M. (eds) (2008) *Northern Ireland after the Troubles: A Society in Transition*. Manchester: Manchester University Press.

Cowan, I. B. & Shaw, D. (eds) (1983) *The Renaissance and Reformation in Scotland*. Edinburgh: Scottish Academic Press.

Crawford, W. H. (1979) 'Change in Ulster in the Late Eighteenth Century' in Bartlett & Hayton (eds) *Penal Era and Golden Age*.

Crawford, W. H. (1983) 'Ulster as a Mirror of the Two Societies', in Devine & Dickson (eds) *Ireland and Scotland, 1600-1850*.

Cressy, D. (1980) *Literacy and the Social Order: Reading and Writing in Tudor and Stuart England*. Cambridge: Cambridge University Press.

Croker, T. C. (1824) *Researches in the South of Ireland*. London: John Murray.

Cronin, M. & Ó Cuilleanáin, C. (eds) (2003) *The Languages of Ireland*. Dublin: Four Courts Press.

Cullen, L. M. (ed.) (1969) *The Formation of the Irish Economy*. Cork: Mercier Press.

Cullen, L. M. (1972) *An Economic History of Ireland since 1660*. London: Batsford Academic.

Cullen, L. M. (1981) *The Emergence of Modern Ireland 1600–1900*. London: Batsford Academic.

Cullen, L. M. (1984) 'Establishing a Communications System: News, Post and Transport' in Farrell (ed.) *Communications and Community in Ireland*.

Cullen, L. M. (1990) 'Patrons, Teachers and Literacy in Irish: 1700–1850' in Daly & Dickson (eds) *The Origins of Popular Literacy in Ireland*.

Cullen, L. M., Smout, T. C. & Gibson, A. (1988) 'Wages and Comparative Development in Ireland and Scotland, 1565–1780' in Mitchison & Roebuck (eds) *Economy and Society in Scotland and Ireland 1500–1939*.

Curtis, C., Haase, T. & Tovey, H. (eds) (1996) *Poverty in Rural Ireland*. Dublin: Oak Tree Press.

Curtis, E. (ed.) (1932) *Calendar of Ormond Deeds 1172–1350*. Dublin: Stationery Office.

Curtis, E. & McDowell, R. B. (1968) *Irish Historical Documents, 1172–1922*. London: Methuen.

D'Art, D. & Turner, T. (2002) 'The Transformation of Irish Employment Relations' in D'Art & Turner (eds) *Irish Employment Relations in the New Economy*.

D'Art, D. & Turner, T. (eds) (2002) *Irish Employment Relations in the New Economy*. Dublin: Blackhall Press.

Daly, M. & Dickson, D. (eds) (1990) *The Origins of Popular Literacy in Ireland: Language Change and Educational Development 1700–1920*. Dublin: Department of Modern History, Trinity College Dublin.

Darwin, J. (2008) *After Tamerlane: The Rise and Fall of Global Empires, 1400–2000*. London: Penguin.

Darwin, J. (2011) *The Empire Project: The Rise and Fall of the British World-System 1830–1970*. Oxford: Oxford University Press.

Davidson, N. (2004a) 'The Scottish Path to Capitalist Agriculture 1: From the Crisis of Feudalism to the Origins of Agrarian Transformation (1688–1746)', in *Journal of Agrarian Change*, Vol. 4, No. 3, pp. 227–68.

Davidson, N. (2004b) 'The Scottish Path to Capitalist Agriculture 2: The Capitalist Offensive (1747–1815)' in *Journal of Agrarian Change*, Vol. 4, No. 4, pp. 411–60.

Davies, J. (1993) *A History of Wales*. London: Allen Lane.

Davies, J. (2000) 'Welsh' in Price (ed.) *Languages in Britain and Ireland*.

Davies, R. R. (1987) *The Age of Conquest, Wales 1063–1415*. Oxford: Oxford University Press.

Davies, R. R. (ed.) (1988) *The British Isles 1100–1500: Comparisons, Contrasts and Connections*. Edinburgh: John Donald.

Davies, R. (2001) 'Kinsmen, Neighbours and Communities in Wales and the Western British Isles, c1100–c1400' in Stafford, Nelson & Martindale (eds) *Law, Laity and Solidarities*.

Davis, M. (2001) *Late Victorian Holocausts: El Niño Famines and the Making of the Third World*. London: Verso.

Davis, M. (2004) 'Planet of Slums' in *New Left Review*, No. 26, pp. 5–34.

Davis, M (2007) *Planet of Slums*. London Verso.

Dawson, J. (1994) 'Calvinism and the Gaidhealtachd in Scotland' in Pettegree, Duke & Lewis (eds) *Calvinism in Europe, 1540–1620*.

Dawson, J. (1998) 'The Gaidhealtachd and the Emergence of the Scottish Highlands' in Bradshaw & Roberts (eds) *British Consciousness and Identity: The Making of Britain, 1533-1707*.

Derwin, D. (1995) 'The Dunnes Strike & Managing Change', in *Red & Black Revolution*, Issue 2, 9 November 1995.

Devine, T. M. (1988) 'Unrest and Stability in Rural Ireland and Scotland, 1760–1840' in Mitchison & Roebuck *Economy and Society in Scotland and Ireland 1500–1939*.

Devine, T. M. (1994) *Clanship to Crofter's War: The Social Transformation of the Scottish Highlands*. Manchester: Manchester University Press.

Devine, T. M. (2000) *The Scottish Nation: 1700–2000*. London: Penguin.

Devine, T. M. (2003) 'Irish and Scottish Development Revisited' in Dickson & Ó Gráda (eds) *Refiguring Ireland*.

Devine, T. M. (ed.) (1989) *Improvement and Enlightenment*. Edinburgh: John Donald.

Devine, T. M. & Dickson, D. (eds) (1983) *Ireland and Scotland, 1600–1850: Parallels and Contrasts in Economic and Social Development*. Edinburgh: John Donald.

Dickson, D. (1979) 'Middlemen' in Bartlett & Hayton (eds) *Penal Era and Golden Age: Essays in Irish History, 1690-1800*.

Dickson, D. (1987) *New Foundations: Ireland 1660-1800*. Dublin: Helicon.

Dickson, D. (1995) 'The Other Great Irish Famine' in Póirtéir (ed.) *The Great Irish Famine*.

Dickson, D. (2005) *Old World Colony: Cork and South Munster, 1630–1830*. Cork: Cork University Press.

Dickson, D. & Ó Gráda, C. (eds) (2003) *Refiguring Ireland*. Dublin: Lilliput Press.

Dillon, M. (1966) 'Ceart Ui Neill' in *Studia Celtica*, Vol. 1.

Dobb, M. (1963) *Studies in the Development of Capitalism*. New York: International Publishers.

Dolley, M. (1987) 'Coinage to 1534: The Sign of the Times' in Cosgrove (ed.) *A New History of Ireland – Vol. 2*.

Donaghey, J. & Teague, P. (2007) 'The Mixed Fortunes of Irish Unions: Living with the Paradoxes of Social Partnership' in *Journal Of Labor Research*, No. 28, pp. 19–41.

Donnelly, J. S. (1977–78) 'The Rightboy Movement, 1785–8' in *Studia Hibernica*, Nos. 17–18, pp. 120–202.

Donnelly, J. S. (1978) 'The Whiteboy Movement, 1761–5' in *Irish Historical Studies*, xxi, pp. 20–54.

Donnelly, J. S. (1995) 'Mass Eviction and the Great Famine' in Póirtéir (ed.) *The Great Irish Famine*.

Dowling, M. W. (1998) *Tenant Right and Agrarian Society in Ulster, 1600–1850*. Dublin: Irish Academic Press.

Down, K. (1987) 'Colonial Society and Economy in the High Middle Ages' in Cosgrove (ed.) *A New History of Ireland – Vol. 2*.

Duffy, P. (2001) 'Social and Spatial Order in the MacMahon Lordship of Airghialla in the Late Sixteenth Century' in Duffy, Edwards & FitzPatrick (eds) *Gaelic Ireland: c.1250–1650: Land, Lordship and Settlement*.

Duffy, P., Edwards, D. & FitzPatrick, E. (eds) (2001) *Gaelic Ireland: c.125–1650: Land, Lordship and Settlement*. Dublin: Four Courts Press.

Dumenil, G. & Levy, D. (2004) 'Neoliberal Income Trends' in *New Left Review*, Vol. 30, Nov.–Dec. 2004.

Dunne, T. J. (1980) 'The Gaelic Response to Conquest and Colonisation: The Evidence of the Poetry' in *Studia Hibernica*, No. 20, pp. 7–30.

Eagleton, T. (1995) *Heathcliff and the Great Hunger: Studies in Irish Culture*. London: Verso.

Edwards, D. (2001) 'Collaboration without Anglicisation: The MacGiollapadraig Lordship and Tudor Reform' in Duffy, Edwards & FitzPatrick (eds) *Gaelic Ireland: c.1250–1650: Land, Lordship and Settlement*.

Edwards, D. (ed.) (2004) *Regions and Rulers in Ireland 1100–1650*. Dublin: Four Courts Press.

Edwards, D. et al. (eds) (2007) *The Age of Atrocity*, Dublin: Four Courts Press

Ellis, S. (1985) *Tudor Ireland: Crown, Community and the Conflict of Cultures, 1470–1603*. London: Longman.

Ellis, S. G. & Barber, S. (1995) *Conquest and Union: Fashioning a British State, 1485–1725*. London: Longman.

Empey, C. A. (1986) 'Conquest and Settlement: Patterns of Anglo-Norman Settlement in North Munster and South Leinster' in *Irish Economic and Social History*, No. 13, pp. 5–31.

Enright, A. (2010) 'Sinking by inches: Ireland's Recession' in *London Review of Books*, 7 January 2010.

Fanning, R. (1978) *The Irish Department of Finance, 1952–58*. Dublin: Institute of Public Adminstration.

Farrell, B. (ed.) (1984) *Communications and Community in Ireland*. Cork: Mercier Press.

Farrell, M. (1976) *The Orange State*. London: Pluto.

Farrell, M. (1983) *Arming the Protestants*. London: Longwood.

Febvre, L. & Martin, H. J. (1976) *The Coming of the Book: The Impact of Printing, 1450–1800*. London: NLB.

Fentress, J. (1992) *Social Memory*. Oxford: Blackwell.

Ferritor, D. (2004) *The Transformation of Ireland, 1900–2000*. London: Profile.

Finn, D. (2011) Ireland on the Turn. *New Left Review*, No. 67, pp. 5–39.

Fisher, J. H. (1986) 'European Chancelleries and the Rise of Standard Written Languages' in *Essays in Medieval Studies Vol. 3*, University of Tennessee, www.illinoismedieval.org/ems/VOL3/fisher.html

Fitzpatrick, D. (1977) *Politics & Irish Life 1913–21*. Dublin: Gill & Macmillan.

Fitzpatrick, E. (2004) 'Parley Sites of O'Neill and O'Domhnaill in late Sixteenth-Century Ireland' in Edwards (ed.) *Regions and Rulers in Ireland 1100–1650*.

Fletcher, A. (2000) *Drama, Performance, and Polity in Pre-Cromwellian Ireland*. Cork: Cork University Press.

Flower, P. (1994) *The Irish Tradition*. Dublin: Lilliput Press.

Foley, T. & O'Connor, M. (eds) (2007) *Ireland and India: Colonies, Culture and Empire*. Dublin: Irish Academic Press.

Foner, E. (1978) 'Class, Ethnicity, and Radicalism in the Gilded Age: The Land League and Irish America' in *Marxist Perspectives*, Summer 1978, pp. 6–55.

Ford, A. (1985) *The Protestant Reformation in Ireland, 1590–1641*. Frankfurt am Main: Peter Lang Verlag.

Forsyth, K. (1998) 'Literacy in Pictland' in Pryce (ed.) *Literacy in Medieval Celtic Societies*.

Foster, R. F. (1988) *Modern Ireland 1600–1972*. London: Allen Lane.

Frame, R. (1998) *Ireland and Britain, 1170–1450*. London: Hambledon Press.

Garnham, N. (1997) 'How Violent was Eighteenth-Century Ireland?' in *Irish Historical Studies*, Vol. 30, No. 119, pp. 377–92.

Gellner, E. (1981) *Muslim Society*. Cambridge: Cambridge University Press.

Gerschenkron, A. (1962) *Economic Backwardness in Historical Perspective*. Cambridge, MA.: Harvard University Press.

Gillespie, R. (1991) *The Transformation of the Irish Economy, 1550–1700*. Dublin: Economic and Social History Society of Ireland.

Gillespie, R. (2002) 'Lay Spirituality and Worship, 1558–1750: Holy Books and Godly Readers' in Gillespie & Neely (eds) *The Laity and the Church of Ireland, 1000-2000*.

Gillespie, R. (2005) *Reading Ireland: Print, Reading and Social Change in Early Modern Ireland*. Manchester: Manchester University Press.

Gillespie, R. (2006) *Seventeenth Century Ireland: Making Ireland Modern*, Dublin: Gill and Macmillan.

Gillespie, R. & Neely, W. G. (eds) (2002) *The Laity and the Church of Ireland, 1000–2000*. Dublin: Four Courts Press.

Glynn, A. (2006) *Capitalism Unleashed: Finance Globalisation and Welfare*. Oxford: Oxford University Press.

Godelier, M. (1986) *The Mental and the Material: Thought Economy and Society*. London: Verso.

Goldthorpe, J. & Whelan, C. T. (eds) (1992) *The Development of Industrial Society in Ireland*. Oxford: Oxford University Press.

Goodcare, J. (1994) 'Scotland' in Scribner, Porter & Teich (eds) *The Reformation in National Context*.

Goody, J. (ed.) (1968) *Literacy in Traditional Societies*. Cambridge: Cambridge University Press.

Goody, J. (1977) *The Domestication of the Savage Mind*. Cambridge: Cambridge University Press.

Goody, J. (1983) *The Development of the Family and Marriage in Europe.* Cambridge: Cambridge University Press.

Goody, J. (1986) *The Logic of Writing and the Organisation of Society.* Cambridge: Cambridge University Press.

Goody J. (2004) *Capitalism and Modernity: the Great Debate.* Cambridge: Polity.

Goody, J. & Watt, I. P. (1968) 'The Consequences of Literacy' in Goody (ed.) *Literacy in Traditional Societies.*

Gowan, P. (1987) 'The Origins of the Administrative Elite' in *New Left Review* Vol. 1, No. 162., pp. 4–34.

Gowan, P. (1999) *The Global Gamble.* London: Verso.

Gowan, P. (2003) 'US Hegemony Today' in *Monthly Review* (July/August).

Gowan, P. (2010) 'Industrial Development and International Political Conflict in Contemporary Capitalism' in Anievas (ed.) *Marxism and World Politics.*

Graham, B. G. (1993) 'The High Middle Ages: c1100 to c1350' in Graham & Proudfoot (eds) *An Historical Geography of Ireland.*

Graham, B. G. & Proudfoot, L. J. (eds) (1993) *An Historical Geography of Ireland.* London: Academic Press.

Grahl, J. (2010) *The Subordination of European Finance.* Middlesex University Business School.

Gramsci, A. (1967) *The Modern Prince.* New York: International Publishers.

Gramsci, A. (1971) *Selections from the Prison Notebooks.* London: Lawrence and Wishart.

Grant, A. (1988) 'Scotland's "Celtic Fringe" in the late Middle Ages' in Davies (ed.) *The British Isles 1100–1500: Comparisons, Contrasts and Connections.*

Grant, A. (2000) 'Fourteenth Century Scotland' in Jones, M. (ed.) *The New Cambridge Medieval History, Vol. 6.*

Grant, A. & Stringer, K. (1995) 'Scottish Foundations' in Grant & Stringer (eds) *Uniting the Kingdom?*

Grant, A. & Stringer, K. (eds) (1995) *Uniting the Kingdom? The Making of British History.* London: Routledge.

Greaves, D. (1971) *Liam Mellows and the Irish Revolution.* London: Lawrence & Wishart.

Gurevich, A. (1985) *Categories of Medieval Culture.* London: Routledge, Kegan & Paul.

Haigh, C. (2001) 'Success and Failure of the English Reformation' in *Past and Present*, No. 173, pp. 24–49.

Hand, G. J. (1966a) 'The Status of the Native Irish in the Lordship of Ireland, 1272–1331' in *The Irish Jurist,* Vol. 1, No. 1, pp. 93–115.

Hand, G. J. (1966b) 'The Forgotten Statutes of Kilkenny: A Brief Survey' in *The Irish Jurist,* Vol. 1, No. 2, pp. 299–312.

Harman, C. (1998) *Marxism and History: Two essays.* London: Bookmarks.

Harvey, D. (2005) *A Brief History of Neoliberalism.* Oxford: Oxford University Press.

Hatcher, J. (1981) 'English Serfdom and Villeinage: Towards a Reassessment' in *Past and Present,* No. 90, pp. 3–39.

Hatcher, J. (1994) 'England in the Aftermath of the Black Death' in *Past and Present,* No. 144, pp. 3–35.

Hill, C. (1969) *Society and Puritanism in Pre-Revolutionary England.* London: Panther.

Hill, C. (1972) *The World Turned Upside Down: Radical Ideas during the English Revolution*. London: Temple Smith.

Hilton, R. (1985) *Class Conflict and the Crisis of Feudalism*. London: Hambledon Press.

Hobsbawm, E. J. (1968) *Industry and Empire: An Economic History of Britain since 1750*. London: Weidenfeld & Nicolson.

Hogan, D. & Osborough, W. N. (eds) (1990) *Brehons, Serjeants and Attorneys: Studies in the History of the Irish Legal Profession*. Dublin: Irish Academic Press.

Houston, R. A. (1988) *Literacy in Early Modern Europe: Culture and Education 1500–1800*. London: Longman.

Howe, S. (2000) *Ireland and Empire: Colonial Legacies in Irish History and Culture*. Oxford: Oxford University Press.

IMF (2006) 'Ireland: Financial System Stability Assessment Update', 7 July 2006, International Monetary Fund.

Inglis, T. (1998) *The Moral Majority: The Rise and Fall of the Catholic Church in Modern Ireland*. Dublin: UCD Press.

Ingram, G. (1984) *Capitalism Divided*. Basingstoke: Macmillan.

Irish Independent (2011) reported 1 June 2011.

Johnson, D. S. (1985) 'The Northern Ireland Economy 1914–1939' in Kennedy & Ollerenshaw (eds) *An Economic History of Ulster, 1820–1939*.

Jones, M. (ed.) (2000) *The New Cambridge Medieval History, Vol. 6*, Cambridge: Cambridge University Press.

Jones, T. (1971) *Whitehall Diary Vol. 3* (edited by Keith Middlemas). London: Oxford University Press.

Kalecki, M. (1943) 'Political Aspects of Full Employment' in *Political Quarterly*. Republished *Monthly Review*, Oct 2010.

Kelleher, M. & O'Leary, P. (eds) (2006) *The Cambridge History of Irish Literature*. Cambridge: Cambridge University Press.

Kelly, F. (1988) *A Guide to Early Irish Law*. Dublin: Dublin Institute for Advanced Studies.

Kelly, M. (2009) *The Irish Credit Bubble*. Dublin: UCD Centre for Economic Research.

Kelly, M. (2010a) *Whatever Happened to Ireland?* CEPR Discussion Paper 7811.

Kelly, M. (2010b) 'If You Thought the Bank Bailout was Bad, Wait Until the Mortgage Defaults Hit Home' in *Irish Times*, 11 Nov. 2010.

Kelly, M. (2011) 'Burden of Irish Debt could Yet Eclipse that of Greece' in *Irish Times*, 22 May 2011.

Kiely R. (2007) 'Poverty Reduction through Liberalisation? Neo-liberalism and the Myth of Global Convergence' in *Review of International Studies*, Vol. 33, No. 3, pp. 415–34.

Kemp, T. (1985) *Industrialisation in Nineteenth Century Europe*. London: Longman.

Kennedy, L. & Ollerenshaw, P. (eds) (1985) *An Economic History of Ulster, 1820–1939*. Manchester: Manchester University Press.

Kenny, C. (1987) 'The Exclusion of Catholics from the Legal Profession in Ireland, 1537–1829' in *Irish Historical Studies*, Vol. 25, No. 100, pp. 337–57.

Kenny, K. (ed.) (2004) *Ireland and the British Empire*. Oxford: Oxford University Press.

Kenny, K. (2004) 'The Irish in the Empire' in Kenny (ed.) *Ireland and the British Empire*.

Keogh, D. (1993) *The French Disease: The Catholic Church and Irish Radicalism, 1790–1800*. Dublin: Four Courts Press.
Kinealy, C. (1995) 'The Role of the Poor Law during the Famine' in Póirtéir (ed.) *The Great Irish Famine*.
Kinealy, C. (2002) *The Great Irish Famine*. Basingstoke: Palgrave.
Kirby, P. (2002) *The Celtic Tiger in Distress: Growth with Inequality in Ireland*. London: Palgrave Macmillan.
Kostick, C. (2009) *Revolution in Ireland: Popular Militancy 1917–1923*. Cork: Cork University Press.
Lanchester, J. (2011) Once Greece goes: ... Any hope for the Euro? *London Review of Books*, 14 June 2011.
Lapavitsas, C. (2009) 'Financialised Capitalism: Crisis and Financial Expropriation' in *Historical Materialism*, Vol. 17, No. 2, pp. 114–48.
Larkin, E. (1984) *The Historical Dimensions of Irish Catholicism*. Dublin: Four Courts Press.
Le Roy Ladurie, E. (1977) 'Occitania in Historical Perspective' in *Review: A Journal of the Fernand Braudel Center*, Vol. 1, No. 1, pp. 21–31.
Lee, J. (1969) 'The Railways in the Irish Economy' in Cullen (ed.) *The Formation of the Irish Economy*.
Lee, J. (1973) *The Modernisation of Irish Society, 1848–1918*. Dublin: Gill & Macmillan.
Lee, J. (1989) *Ireland: Politics and Society, 1912–1985*. Cambridge: Cambridge University Press.
Leerssen, J. (1996) *Mere Irish and Fíor-Ghael*. Cork: Cork University Press.
Lennon, C. (1994) *Sixteenth Century Ireland: The Incomplete Conquest*. Dublin: Gill & Macmillan.
Lewis, G. C. (1836) *On Local Disturbances in Ireland*. London: Fellowes.
Little, L. K. & Rosenwein, B. H. (eds) (1998) *Debating the Middle Ages*. Oxford: Blackwell Publishers.
Lyall, A. (1994) *Land Law in Ireland*. Dublin: Oak Tree Press.
Lydon, J. (ed.) (1984) *The English in Medieval Ireland*. Dublin: Royal Irish Academy.
Lydon, J. (1998) *The Making of Ireland: From Ancient Times to the Present*. London: Routledge.
Lyons, F. S. L. (1973) *Ireland since the Famine*. London: Fontana.
Lyons, M. C. (1984) *Manorial Administration and the Manorial Economy in Ireland, c.1200–c.1377*. Ph.D. Thesis, Trinity College Dublin.
MacCraith, M. (1995) 'The Gaelic Reaction to the Reformation' in Ellis & Barber (eds) *Conquest and Union: Fashioning a British State, 1485–1725*.
MacCulloch, D. (2003) *Reformation: Europe's House Divided*. London: Penguin.
Mackey, J. P. (ed.) (1989) *An Introduction to Celtic Christianity*. Edinburgh: T. & T. Clark.
MacQueen, H. L. (1995) *Common Law and Feudal Society in Medieval Scotland*. Edinburgh: Edinburgh University Press.
Mair, P. (2000) 'Partyless Democracy' in *New Left Review*, March-April 2000, pp. 21–35.
Mandel, E. (1978) *Late Capitalism*. London: Verso.
Marx, K. (1969) 'The British Rule in India' in *Selected Works Volume One* (Marx and Engels) Moscow: Progress Publishers.
Marx, K. (1976) *Capital Vol. 1*. Harmondsworth: Penguin.
Marx, K. & Engels, F. (1969) *Selected Works, Vol.1*, Moscow: Progress Publishers.

Marx, K. & Engels, F. (1985) *The Communist Manifesto*. Harmondsworth: Penguin.

Mayer, A. (1981) *The Persistence of the Old Regime*. London: Verso.

McBride, I. (1994) 'Presbyterians in the Penal Era' in *Bullán: An Irish Studies Journal*, Vol. 1, No. 2.

McCann, E. (1974) *War in an Irish Town*. London: Penguin.

McCarthy, C. (1971) *The Decade of Upheaval: Irish Trade Unions in the Nineteen Sixties*. Dublin: Institute of Public Administration.

McCarthy, J. F. (ed) (1990) *Planning Ireland's Future: The Legacy of T. K. Whitaker*. Dublin: Glendale Press.

McCaughey, T. (1989) 'Protestantism and Scottish Highland Culture' in Mackey (ed.) *An Introduction to Celtic Christianity*.

McCrum, R., MacNeil, R. & Cran, W. (1986) *The Story of English*. London: B.B.C. Publications.

McDonough, T. (ed.) (2005) *Was Ireland a Colony?* Dublin: Irish Academic Press.

McKay, S. (2000) *Northern Protestants: An Unsettled People*. Belfast: Blackstaff.

McKearney, P. (2011) *The Provisional IRA: From Insurrection to Parliament*. London: Pluto.

McKittrick, D. & McVea, D. (2000) *Making Sense of the Troubles*. Belfast: Blackstaff

McLeod, W. (2004) *Divided Gaels: Gaelic Cultural Identities in Scotland and Ireland c.1200–1650*. Oxford: Oxford University Press.

McMahon, D. (2004) 'Ireland, the Empire, and the Commonwealth' in Kenny (ed.) *Ireland and the British Empire*.

Medeiros, C. (2009) 'Asset-Stripping the State' in *New Left Review*, Vol. 55, No. 2, pp. 109–32.

Meenan, J. (1970) *The Irish Economy Since 1922*. Liverpool: Liverpool University Press.

Meigs, S. A. (1997) *The Reformation in Ireland: Tradition and Confessionalism, 1400–1690*. Dublin: Gill & Macmillan.

Miller, D. W. (1978) *Queen's Rebels: Ulster Loyalism in Historical Perspective*. Dublin: Gill & Macmillan.

Miller, D. W. (1983) 'The Armagh Troubles, 1784–95' in Clark & Donnelly (eds) *Irish Peasants: Violence and Political Unrest, 1780–1914*.

Miller D. W. (ed.) (1998) *Rethinking Northern Ireland*. London: Longman.

Mills, J. (1890/1891) 'Tenants and Agriculture near Dublin in the Fourteenth Century' in *Journal of the Royal Society of Antiquaries of Ireland*, Vol. 21.

Mitchell, A. (1974) *Labour in Irish Politics*. Dublin: Irish University Press.

Mitchison, R. (1983) 'Ireland and Scotland: The Seventeenth-Century Legacies Compared' in Devine & Dickson (eds) *Ireland and Scotland, 1600-1850*.

Mitchison, R. & Roebuck, P. (eds) (1988) *Economy and Society in Scotland and Ireland 1500–1939*. Edinburgh: John Donald.

Moody, T. W., Martin, F. X. & Byrne, F. J. (eds) (1976) *A New History of Ireland – Vol. 3: Early Modern Ireland 1534–1691*. Oxford: Clarendon.

Moody, T. W. & Vaughan, W. E. (eds) (1986) *A New History of Ireland – Vol. 4: Eighteenth Century Ireland 1691–1800*. Oxford: Clarendon.

Mooney, C. (1969) *The Church in Gaelic Ireland*. Dublin: Gill & Macmillan.

Morgan, H. (1993) *Tyrone's Rebellion: The Outbreak of the Nine Years War in Tudor Ireland*. Woodbridge: Boydell Press.

Muirson, D. (1974) 'Linguistic Relationships in Medieval Scotland' in Barrow (ed.) *The Scottish Tradition*.

Mulhern, F. (1998) *The Present Lasts a Long Time: Essays in Cultural Politics.* Cork: Cork University Press.

Murphy, B. (1967) 'The Status of the Native Irish after 1331' in *Irish Jurist*, Vol. 2, pp. 116–28.

Nauert, C. G. (1995) *Humanism and the Culture of Renaissance Europe.* Cambridge: Cambridge University Press.

Newman, J. (1964) *The Limerick Rural Survey.* Tipperary: Muintir na Tíre Rural Publications.

Newsinger, J. (1996) 'The Great Irish Famine: A Crime of Free Market Economics' in *Monthly Review – New York*, Vol. 47, No. 11, pp. 11–19.

Nicholls, K. W. (1972) *Gaelic and Gaelicised Ireland in the Middle Ages.* Dublin: Gill & Macmillan.

Nicholls, K. W. (1976) *Land, Law and Society in Sixteenth Century Ireland.* Dublin: National University of Ireland.

Nicholls, K. W. (1982) 'Anglo-French Ireland and after' in *Peritia*, No. 1, pp. 370–403.

Nicholls, K. W. (1987) 'Gaelic Society and Economy in the High Middle Ages' in Cosgrove (ed.) *A New History of Ireland – Vol. 2.*

Nowlan, K. B. (1984) 'The Origins of the Press in Ireland' in Farrell (ed.) *Communications and Community in Ireland.*

Ó Broin, E. (2009) *Sinn Féin and the Politics of Left Republicanism.* London: Pluto.

Ó Ciosáin, N. (1997) *Print and Popular Culture in Ireland.* Basingstoke: Macmillan.

Ó Cuív, B. (1961) *Seven Centuries of Irish Learning, 1000–1700.* Dublin: Stationery Office.

Ó Cuív, B. (1976) 'The Irish Language in the Early Modern Period' in Moody, Martin & Byrne (eds) *A New History of Ireland – Vol. 3.*

Ó Cuív, B. (1986) 'Irish Language and Literature: 1691–1845' in Moody & Vaughan (eds) *A New History of Ireland – Vol. 4.*

Ó Gráda, C. (1994) *Ireland: A New Economic History, 1780–1939.* Oxford: Clarendon Press.

Ó Gráda, C. (1997) *A Rocky Road: The Irish Economy since the 1920s.* Manchester: Manchester University Press.

Ó Tuathaigh, G. (1990) *Ireland before the Famine, 1798–1848.* Dublin: Gill & Macmillan.

O'Brien, A. F. (1993) 'Politics, Economy & Society: The Development of Cork and the Irish South-Coast Region c.1170–c1583' in O'Flanagan & Buttimer (eds) *Cork: History and Society.*

O'Connell, P. & Rottman, D. (1992) 'The Irish Welfare State in Comparative Perspective' in Goldthorpe & Whelan (eds) *The Development of Industrial Society in Ireland.*

O'Connor, E. (1992) *A Labour History of Ireland 1824–1960,* Dublin: Gill & Macmillan.

O'Donoghue, P. (1965) 'Causes of the Opposition to Tithes, 1830–38' in *Studia Hibernica*, No. 5, pp. 7–28.

O'Donovan, O. & Glavanis-Grantham, K. (eds) (2008) *Power, Politics and Pharmaceuticals.* Cork: Cork University Press.

O'Dowd, L., Rolston, B. & Tomlinson, M. (1980) *Northern Ireland: Between Civil Rights and Civil War.* London: CSE Books.

O'Dowd, M. (1986) 'Gaelic Economy and Society' in Brady & Gillespie (eds) *Natives and Newcomers.*

O'Flanagan, P. & Buttimer, C. (eds) (1993) *Cork: History and Society*. Dublin: Geography Publications.

O'Grada, C. (1999) *Black '47 and Beyond: the Great Irish Famine in History, Economy and Memory*. Princeton, NJ: Princeton University Press.

O'Hearn, D. (1998) *Inside the Celtic Tiger*. London: Pluto.

O'Hearn, D. (2001) *The Atlantic Economy: Britain, the US and Ireland*. Manchester: Manchester University Press.

O'Hearn, D. (2005) 'Ireland in the World Economy' in McDonough (ed.) *Was Ireland a Colony?*

O'Malley, E. (1989) *Industry and Economic Development: The Challenge of the Latecomer*. Dublin: Gill & Macmillan.

O'Riain, S. (2004) 'Falling over the Competitive Edge' in Peillon & Corcoran (eds) *Place and Non-Place: The Reconfiguration of Ireland*.

O'Toole, F. (2009) *Ship of Fools*. London: Faber.

Osborough, W. N. (1999) *Studies in Irish Legal History*. Dublin: Four Courts Press.

Otway-Ruthven, A. J. (1980) *A History of Medieval Ireland*. London: Benn.

Otway-Ruthven, J. (1951) 'The Organisation of Anglo-Irish Agriculture in the Middle Ages' in *Journal of the Royal Society of Antiquaries of Ireland*, Vol. 81, No. 1, pp. 1–13.

Pakenham, F. (1972) *Peace by Ordeal*. London: Sidgwick and Jackson.

Palmer, P. (2001) *Language and Conquest in Early Modern Ireland: English Renaissance Literature and Elizabethan Imperial Expansion*. Cambridge: Cambridge University Press.

Panitch, L. & Konings, M. (eds) (2009) *American Empire and the Political Economy of Global Finance*. London: Palgrave Macmillan.

Panofsky, E. (1960) *Renaissance and Renascences in Western Art*. Stockholm: Almqvist and Wiksell.

Pašeta, S. (1999) *Before the Revolution: Nationalism, Social Change and Ireland's Catholic Elite, 1879–1922*. Cork: Cork University Press.

Patterson, H. (1980) *Class Conflict and Sectarianism: The Protestant Working Class and the Belfast Labour Movement 1868–1920*. Belfast: Blackstaff Press.

Patterson, N. (1989) 'Brehon Law in the Late Middle Ages: "Antiquarian and Obsolete" or "Traditional and Functional"' in *Cambridge Medieval Celtic Studies*, No. 17, pp. 43–63.

Patterson, N. (1994) *Cattle-Lords and Clansmen: The Social Structure of Early Ireland*. Notre Dame & London: University of Notre Dame Press.

Pawlich, H. S. (1985) *Sir John Davies and the Conquest of Ireland: A Study in Legal Imperialism*. Cambridge: Cambridge University Press.

Peillon, M. & Corcoran, M. (eds) (2004) *Place and Non-Place: The Reconfiguration of Ireland*. Dublin: Institute of Public Administration.

Pettegree, A., Duke, A. & Lewis, G. (eds) (1994) *Calvinism in Europe, 1540–1620*. Cambridge: Cambridge University Press.

Picard, J. M. (2003) 'The French Language in Medieval Ireland' in Cronin & Ó Cuilleanáin (eds) *The Languages of Ireland*.

Póirtéir, C. (ed.) (1995) *The Great Irish Famine*. Cork: Mercier Press.

Polanyi, K. (1971) *Primitive, Archaic and Modern Economies*. Boston, MA: Beacon Press.

Pomeranz, K. (2000) *The Great Divergence: China, Europe and the Making of the Modern World Economy*. Princeton, NJ: Princeton University Press.

Poos, L. R. (1991) *A Rural Society after the Black Death: Essex 1350–1525*. Cambridge: Cambridge University Press.

Porter, R. & Teich, M. (eds) (1992) *The Renaissance in National Context*. Cambridge: Cambridge University Press.

Post, C. (1982) 'The American Road to Capitalism' in *New Left Review* 1/133.

Poulantzas, N. (1978) *Political Power and Social Class*. London: Verso.

Price, G. (ed.) (2000) *Languages in Britain and Ireland*. Oxford: Blackwell Publishers.

Price, G. (2000) 'Pictish' in Price (ed.) *Languages in Britain and Ireland*.

Proudfoot, L. J. (1993) 'Spatial Transformation and Social Agency: Property Society and Improvement c.1700–1900' in Graham & Proudfoot (eds) *An Historical Geography of Ireland*.

Pryce, H. (ed.) (1998) *Literacy in Medieval Celtic Societies*. Cambridge: Cambridge University Press.

Punch, M. (2009) *The Irish Housing System*. Dublin: Jesuit Centre for Faith and Justice.

Purcell, B. (1996) 'The Silence in Irish Broadcasting' in Rolston & Miller *War And Words: The Northern Ireland Media Reader*.

Quinn, D. B. (1966) *The Elizabethans and the Irish*. Itaca, NY: Cornell University Press.

Quinn, D. B. & Nicholls, K. W. (1976) 'Ireland in 1534' in Moody, Martin & Byrne (eds) *A New History of Ireland – Vol. 3*.

Regan, J. (1999) *The Irish Counter-Revolution 1921–36: Treatyite Politics and Settlement in Independent Ireland*. Dublin: Gill & Macmillan.

Robertson, J. (1977) 'The Development of the Law' in Brown (ed.) *Scottish Society in the Fifteenth Century*.

Rolston, B. & Miller, D. (eds) (1996) *War and Words: The Northern Ireland Media Reader*. Belfast: Beyond the Pale Publications.

Rosenwein, B. H. & Little, L. K. (1974) 'Social Meaning in the Monastic and Mendicant Spiritualities' in *Past and Present*, No. 63, pp. 4–32.

Rostow, W. W. (1962) *The Stages of Economic Growth: A Non-Communist Manifesto*. Cambridge, MA: Harvard University Press.

Rowthorn, B. & Wayne, N. (1988) *Northern Ireland: The Political Economy of Conflict*. Cambridge: Polity Press.

Rumpf, E. & Hepburn, A. C. (1977) *Nationalism and Socialism in Twentieth Century Ireland*. New York: Barnes and Noble.

Runciman, W. G. (1989) *A Treatise on Social Theory: Vol. 2, Substantive Social Theory*. Cambridge: Cambridge University Press.

Sablowski, T. (2009) 'Towards the Americanization of European Finance?' in Panitch & Konings *American Empire and the Political Economy of Global Finance*. London: Palgrave Macmillan.

Sanders, E. R. & Ferguson, M. W. (2002) 'Literacies in Early Modern England' in *Critical Survey*, Vol. 14, Part 1.

Scharpt, F. W. (2011) *Monetary Union, Fiscal Crisis, and the Pre-emption of Democracy*, Max Planck Institute for the Study of Societies, May 2011.

Scribner, B., Porter, R. & Teich, M. (eds) (1994) *The Reformation in National Context*. Cambridge: Cambridge University Press.

Sellar, W. D. H. (1988) 'The Common Law of Scotland and the Common Law of England' in Davies (ed.) *The British Isles 1100–1500: Comparisons, Contrasts and Connections*.

Sellar, W. D. H. (1989) 'Celtic Law and Scots Law: Survival and Integration' in *Scottish Studies*, No. 29.

Share, P. & Tovey, H. (2003) *A Sociology of Ireland*. Dublin: Gill & Macmillan.

Shirlow, P. (ed.) (1995) *Development Ireland, Contemporary Issues*. London: Pluto Press.

Shirlow, P. (2008) 'Belfast: A Segregated City' in Coulter & Murray (eds) *Northern Ireland after the Troubles: A Society in Transition*.

Siggins, L. (2010) *Once Upon a Time in the West*. London: Transworld Ireland.

Simms, K. (1978) 'Guesting and Feasting in Gaelic Ireland' in *Journal of the Royal Society of Antiquaries of Ireland*, Vol. 108, pp. 67–100.

Simms, K. (1986) 'Nomadry in Medieval Ireland: The Origins of the Creaght or Caoraigheacht' in *Peritia*, No. 5, pp. 379–91.

Simms, K. (1987) *From Kings to Warlords: The Changing Political Structures of Gaelic Ireland in the Later Middle Ages*. Woodbridge: Boydell Press.

Simms, K. (1989) 'Bards and Barons: The Anglo-Irish Aristocracy and the Native Culture' in Bartlett & MacKay (eds) *Medieval Frontier Societies*.

Simms, K. (1990) 'The Brehons of Later Medieval Ireland' in Hogan & Osborough (eds) *Brehons, Serjeants and Attorneys*.

Simms, K. (1998) 'Literacy and the Irish Bards' in Pryce (ed.) *Literacy in Medieval Celtic Societies*.

Slattery, L. (2012) 'Company Collapses Up by 20% to 160 a Month' in *Irish Times*, 3 January 2012.

Smith, L. B. (1998) 'Inkhorn and Spectacles: The Impact of Literacy in Late Medieval Wales' in Pryce (ed.) *Literacy in Medieval Celtic Societies*.

Smith, N. (2005) *Showcasing Globalisation? The Political Economy of the Irish Republic*. Manchester: Manchester University Press.

Smout, T. C. (1985) *A History of the Scottish People, 1560–1830*. London: Fontana Press.

Smout, T. C. (1989) 'Problems of Nationalism, Identity and Improvement in later Eighteenth-Century Scotland' in Devine (ed.) *Improvement and Enlightenment*.

Smyth, J. (1992) *The Men of No Property: Irish Radicals and Popular Politics in the Late Eighteenth Century*. Dublin: Gill & Macmillan.

Smyth, J. & Cebulla, A. (2008) 'The Glacier Moves? Economic Change and Class Structure' in Coulter & Murray (eds) *Northern Ireland after the Troubles: A Society in Transition*.

Smyth, W. J. (2006) *Map-making, Landscapes and Memory: A Geography of Colonial and Early Modern Ireland, c. 1530–1750* Cork: Cork University Press.

Southern, R. W. (1953) *The Making of the Middle Ages*. London: Hutchinson.

Spenser, E. (1970) *A View of the Present State of Ireland*. Oxford: Clarendon Press.

Stafford, P., Nelson, J. L. & Martindale, J. (eds) (2001) *Law, Laity and Solidarities*. Manchester: Manchester University Press.

Starkey, D. (1992) 'England' in Porter & Teich (eds) *The Renaissance in National Context*.

Stone, L. (1964) 'The Educational Revolution in England, 1560–1640' in *Past and Present*, No. 28, pp. 41–80.

Storey, A. (2006) 'The European Project: Dismantling the Social Model, Globalising Neoliberalism' in *Irish Review* 34, www.pana.ie/idn/european-project.04.pdf

Storey, A. (2008) *The Lisbon Treaty, the European Military Project and Europe's Role in the World*. Dublin: Afri.

Strauss, E. (1951) *Irish Nationalism and British Democracy.* London: Methuen.

Thompson, E. P. (1993) *Customs in Common.* Harmondsworth: Penguin.

Vaughan, W. E. (ed.) (1989) *A New History of Ireland, Vol. V.* Oxford: Clarendon Press.

Vilar P. (1971) 'The Age of Don Quixote' in *New Left Review,* 1/68.

Wakefield, E. (1812) *An Account of Ireland, Statistical and Political.* 2 Vols. London: Printed for Longman, Hurst, Rees, Orme, and Brown.

Walker, G. (1994) 'Empire, Religion and Nationality in Scotland and Ulster before the First World War' in Wood (ed.) *Scotland and Ulster.*

Wall, M. (1976) *The Penal Laws, 1691–1760: Church and State from the Treaty of Limerick to the Accession of George III.* Dundalk: Dundalgan Press.

Wallerstein, I. (1974) *The Modern World System – Vol. 1: Capitalist Agriculture and the Origins of the European World-Economy in the Sixteenth Century.* New York: Academic Press.

Walsh, K. (1988) 'The Clerical Estate in Later Medieval Ireland' in Bradley (ed.) *Settlement and Society in Medieval Ireland.*

Watt, J. (1987) 'Gaelic Polity and Cultural Identity' in Cosgrove (ed.) *A New History of Ireland – Vol. 2.*

Watt, J. (1998) *The Church in Medieval Ireland.* Dublin: University College Dublin Press.

Weber, E. (1979) *Peasants into Frenchmen: The Modernization of Rural France, 1870–1914.* London: Chatto and Windus.

Weber, M. (1958) *The Protestant Ethic and the Spirit of Capitalism.* New York: Charles Scribner's Sons.

Weber, M. (1991) *Essays in Sociology* (edited by H. H. Gerth & C. Wright Mills). London: Routledge.

Whelan, K. (1996) *The Tree of Liberty: Radicalism, Catholicism and Construction of Identity, 1760–1830.* Cork: Cork University Press.

Whyte, I. D. & Whyte, K. A. (1983) 'Some Aspects of the Structure of Rural Society in Seventeenth-Century Lowland Scotland' in Devine & Dixon (eds) *Ireland and Scotland, 1600–1850.*

Whyte, I. D. (1995a) *Scotland before the Industrial Revolution, c.1050–c.1750.* London: Longman.

Whyte, I. D. (1995b) 'Scottish and Irish Urbanisation in the Seventeenth and Eighteenth Centuries: A Comparative Perspective' in Connolly, Houston & Morris (eds) *Conflict, Identity & Economic Development: Ireland and Scotland, 1600–1939.*

Whyte, I. D. (1997) *Scotland's Society and Economy in Transition, c.1500–c.1760.* Basingstoke: Macmillan.

Wickham, C. (1992) 'Problems of Comparing Rural Societies in Early Medieval Western Europe' in *Transactions of the Royal Historical Society,* 2, pp. 221–46.

Wickham, J. (2004) 'Cows in Dublin: Public Spaces and Public Transport' in Peillon & Corcoran (eds) *Place and Non-Place: The Reconfiguration of Ireland.*

Wilde, W. R. (1979) *Irish Popular Superstitions.* Dublin: Irish Academic Press.

Williams, G. (1989) 'Medieval Wales and the Reformation' in Mackey (ed.) *An Introduction to Celtic Christianity.*

Wolf, E. R. (1982) *Europe and the People without History.* Berkley, CA: University of California Press.

Wolff, P. (1971) *Western Languages, A.D. 100–1500.* London: Weidenfeld & Nicolson.

Wood, E. M. (2003) *Empire of Capital.* London: Verso.

Wood, I. (ed.) (1994) *Scotland and Ulster.* Edinburgh: Mercat Press.

Wormald, J. (1980) 'Bloodfeud, Kindred and Government in Early Modern Scotland' in *Past and Present,* No. 87, pp. 54–97.

Wormald, J. (1985) *Lords and Men in Scotland: Bonds of Manrent, 1442–1603.* Edinburgh: John Donald.

Index

Act of Union (1801), 114, 138, 144
Africa, 166, 206
Agriculture and agrarian social
  relations
  agrarian resistance, 89–90, 119–20;
  capitalist transformation of, 85–9;
  decline of farming population,
  159; manorial economy, 7, 10,
  15, 18, 22, 68, 74–5, 68;
  'middlemen', 91–2; 107; pastoral
  economy, 1, 7, 10, 14, 18, 29–34,
  52, 57–8, 74–6, 85, 91, 141, 157,
  195; serfdom, 9–14, 36, 47, 55,
  60, 69–70, 74, 190, 192, 193
Ahmad, Aijaz, 137–8
Algeria, 127
America (*See also Latin America*), 80,
  118, 125–6, 196–8, 210–11
  United States, 126, 146, 167–8,
  173–5, 196–7, 205–7
Amin, Samir, 201
Anderson, Benedict, 135
Anderson, Perry, 203
Anglo-Irish Bank 172
Antrim, 105, 128, 180
Arensberg, Conrad & Kimball, Solon,
  154
Aristocracy, 17–20, 74–80, 142–4
  Anglo-French, 6–8, 18–21, 58;
  Anglo-Irish, 90–100, 119, 121–2,
  138, 143–4; English landowners,
  68–73, 79; Gaelic elite, 31, 43;
  Indian landed elite, 140–1; 'Old
  English' elite 45–50, Scottish
  59–65, 78, 85, 87, 89, 103; Welsh
  gentry 55–6, 79
Armagh, 94, 180
Arrighi, Giovanni, 5, 195
Austen, Jane, 102
Australia, 196–7
Austria (Habsburg empire), 114, 137

Banking and finance, 155–8, 170–8,
  205–10

Barry, Tom, 153
Belfast, 109, 128–30, 148, 150–2,
  180–1, 183–4
Belfast Agreement 184
Benjamin, Walter, 106
Berkeley, Bishop, 118
Breen, Dan, 153
Brenner, Robert, 5, 84, 192–4
British Empire, 132, 137–49, 155,
  196–7
Bureaucratic administration, 7, 28,
  34–5, 61, 68
Burke, Ray, 176

Calvin, John, 2, 44, 51, 64
Campbell, Fergus, 144
Campbell, Sir George, 146
Canada, 146, 197
Capitalist social organisation 2–5, 202
  agrarian, 85–90; industrial
  capitalism, 84, 87–8, 94, 97–8,
  103, 119, 140, 143, 191, 194,
  196–7; transition to capitalism,
  81–103, 192–7
Catholic Emancipation, 114
Catholics, 2–3, 91–3, 95–6, 98, 100,
  104–5, 108–9, 114–15, 125,
  128–9, 138, 144–5, 147–8, 152,
  159, 179–85, 202
Celtic Tiger, 168–78
Churchill, Winston, 145–6
City of London, 156, 157, 179, 205
Civil Rights movement, 181, 204
Clark, Samuel, 126
Class conflict, 79, 90, 124–7, 147–8,
  151
Colonialism, 115, 137–8, 155, 194,
  197, 198
Communalism, 94, 100, 133, 148,
  178–86
Connaught, 10, 109, 125, 147, 151
Connolly, James, 148